Early Praise for *Programming Flutter*

I'm excited to read this book: ten years ago, I learned Android development reading a PragProg book, and this has changed my life forever. Now this book could change it again.

➤ **Giordano Scalzo**
   iOS Senior Software Engineer, NatWest Markets

Carmine's book is a comprehensive journey into Flutter. He leads you through the basics like widgets, standard library, packages, and plugins, and helps you to understand the more advanced topics like network, I/O, navigation, testing, debugging, and firebase. His book is a reference for practical suggestions, useful tips, and solid advice, without sacrificing the details. What I liked the most is that each chapter starts with a premise, and ends with a conclusion and "where we're going next," building up a natural, logical, and consequential narrative.

➤ **Alessio Salvadorini**
   Creative Technologist, Nokia

Great book for anyone who wants to start grasping Flutter.

➤ **Erdem Orman**
   Software Development Engineer, Amazon

If you want or need to do cross-platform mobile app development, you should have this book at hand. *Programming Flutter*, by Carmine Zaccagnino, walks you systematically through this important Google platform for building full apps that work with Android, iOS, and Google Fuchsia.

➤ **John Barry**
   Independent Editorial Consultant, various

Carmine's hands-on tutorial will help you understand Flutter and why it is the best solution to target iPhones and Androids with a single codebase. Great book for a great framework!

➤ **Paul Freiberger**
   Coauthor, *Fire in the Valley: The Birth and Death of the Personal Computer*

Programming Flutter

Native, Cross-Platform Apps the Easy Way

Carmine Zaccagnino

The Pragmatic Bookshelf

Raleigh, North Carolina

Many of the designations used by manufacturers and sellers to distinguish their products are claimed as trademarks. Where those designations appear in this book, and The Pragmatic Programmers, LLC was aware of a trademark claim, the designations have been printed in initial capital letters or in all capitals. The Pragmatic Starter Kit, The Pragmatic Programmer, Pragmatic Programming, Pragmatic Bookshelf, PragProg and the linking *g* device are trademarks of The Pragmatic Programmers, LLC.

Every precaution was taken in the preparation of this book. However, the publisher assumes no responsibility for errors or omissions, or for damages that may result from the use of information (including program listings) contained herein.

Our Pragmatic books, screencasts, and audio books can help you and your team create better software and have more fun. Visit us at *https://pragprog.com*.

The team that produced this book includes:

Publisher: Andy Hunt
VP of Operations: Janet Furlow
Executive Editor: Dave Rankin
Development Editor: Michael Swaine
Copy Editor: Jasmine Kwityn
Indexing: Potomac Indexing, LLC
Layout: Gilson Graphics

For sales, volume licensing, and support, please contact *support@pragprog.com*.

For international rights, please contact *rights@pragprog.com*.

ISBN-13: 978-1-68050-695-2
Book version: P1.0—February 2020

Contents

Part II — Doing More with Flutter

Acknowledgments

This book exists because Flutter was released and such a revolutionary technology needed a way for people to know about it and learn it however they prefer. So, before even talking about the book, it's necessary to remember how good it is for the developer community that Google has released Flutter and they're continuing to invest in it to make it even more revolutionary and important every day that passes.

Talking about the book, it has to be said that working with the Pragmatic Bookshelf has been great. First of all, I want to thank Andy Hunt, who as a publisher has built a wonderful team: starting from my very first interactions with Brian MacDonald over my proposal to write this book everyone has been thorough, welcoming, and helpful.

In particular, I want to thank Michael Swaine who, as the editor of this book, has been encouraging, helpful, and understanding throughout the process, never making me feel pressured and always helping and encouraging me when any issues arose or when I had questions about anything related to the book.

When bigger and more technical issues arose, production manager Janet Furlow has fixed them, allowing me to keep working on the content of the book instead. The cover Gilson Graphics made for the book is very nice as a visual metaphor of Flutter's multi-platform nature. In addition to those I have mentioned, I want to thank everyone else at the Pragmatic Bookshelf who has been involved in making the book as good as it is.

I want to thank everybody who has looked at the book and given me feedback, which I have taken on and tried to use to the best of my ability to make the book better for everyone. In particular, the technical reviewers who have been thorough and thoughtful in their feedback and the beta book readers who have taken their time to submit errata: it's been very important and seeing how thorough they have been has encouraged me to do as much as I could for the book. Thank you Giordano Scalzo, Alessio Salvadorini, Erdem Orman, Paul Freiberger, and John Barry.

I want to thank everyone I know informally: my friends and family have all been very encouraging and supportive and have made this journey more pleasant than it could have ever been without their support. Knowing the people close to me were happy with the fact that I was doing this was invaluable. I would also like to mention the people who were less close to me, who knew me barely or not at all previously and who have reached out to ask about the book because they made the results of my work feel like something closer to me.

Preface

This book is about Flutter, Google's open source software development kit (SDK) that can be used to develop applications across a wide range of platforms. We'll begin by taking a brief look at its history, followed by an overview of its features and what we will see during the course of this book.

At the end of this Preface you'll find information about the installation and usage of the Flutter SDK and integrated development environment (IDE) plugins.

A Brief History of Flutter

In 2015 Google unveiled Flutter, a new SDK based on the Dart language, as the next platform for Android development, and in 2017 an alpha version of it (0.0.6) was released to the public for the first time.

At I/O 2017 Google showed off using Flutter and its multi-platform capabilities, and continued promoting it at I/O 2018. Since then, Google has been investing in Flutter and recommending it as the way everyone should be developing mobile apps.

In December 2018 Flutter 1.0 was released and made available so that developers could begin using the SDK to make app creation easier.

At Google I/O 2019, Flutter support for desktop and web platforms was publicly announced. Tools for developing Flutter apps for Windows, macOS, Linux, and the web were released.

In addition to being unstable and untested, desktop development is being held back further by the lack of plugin support, which is very limited mostly because, at the time of writing, plugin tooling is still in the process of being developed, meaning that binaries for the platform-specific code for each platform has to be manually built and linked by editing the Google-provided

Makefiles that can be found in Google's dedicated *flutter-desktop-embedding* GitHub repository.[1]

On the other hand, web support is progressing quickly and shouldn't take much more than a rebuild of a working Flutter mobile project that doesn't have any native plugins or platform-specific code.

Why Flutter Matters and What We'll See in This Book

Flutter's entry into the mobile app development framework space is recent and, because of that, Flutter needs to carry significant improvements over existing frameworks and SDKs to actually be useful—and it does.

For one thing, with Flutter you'll be able to develop apps that work with Android, iOS, and Google Fuchsia,[2] (which might replace Android and/or Chrome OS at some point in the future). Flutter is developed by Google, but it fully supports iOS, and this means you can now also run an iOS emulator and build for iOS in Android Studio. However, you won't be able to build iOS apps on Linux or Windows because iOS emulation and compilation is still done through Xcode.

Flutter makes developing apps incredibly easy by allowing you to define the app's UI declaratively but in the same place and language you define the app logic (no XML UI files required). You can instanly preview the changes you make to your app using stateful hot reload.

Additionally, its cross-platform nature doesn't skimp on having a native look and feel, as the framework supports all of the typical native features of each of the operating systems (different app bar, different list drag to update, Material Design and Apple icons, etc.). The advantages compared to other cross-platform frameworks don't end there: you'll be able to run any native Kotlin/Java and Swift/Objective-C method using platform channels, as we'll see in Integrating Native Code: Making Plugin Packages, on page 130.

Even though it's really new, Flutter is already used by some big and established companies (as well as many smaller ones) to build cross-platform mobile apps, as you can see in Google's Flutter Showcase Page.[3]

We'll be using Flutter packages and plugins (many of them developed by Google) to build ever more useful apps, also introducing more advanced standard Flutter features such as navigation and animations.

---

1. https://github.com/google/flutter-desktop-embedding
2. https://en.wikipedia.org/wiki/Google_Fuchsia
3. https://flutter.dev/showcase

Don't Know Dart? Don't Worry About It

You might want to read Appendix 1, Introduction to Dart, on page 285 if you don't have much programming experience or find even the first chapter difficult to follow because of Dart's syntax; many Dart-specific constructs will be explained during the course of the book, but you might want to consider going through that appendix first if you find yourself struggling to understand the code.

Installing the SDK and the IDE Plugins

To use Flutter, you need to install its SDK, and to be able to get on with your programming in a quick and uncomplicated manner, you'll probably want to install the IDE tools too.

If you prefer to use the command line (maybe because you want to use other, perhaps lighter, IDEs or text editors) there will be guidance on the usage of the flutter command throughout the book.

Installing Flutter

The installation process for the Flutter SDK differs slightly for each operating system, so I'll separate the instructions into three sections. Skip ahead to the instructions specific to your platform and, if you want to install them, the part that covers IDE plugin installation.

At the time of writing, the latest stable version is 1.9.1 and requires a 495MB download on Linux (tar.xz archive), a 655MB download on Windows (zip archive), or a 786MB download on macOS (zip archive).

Installing on Linux

On a Linux machine only Android development is supported, so we will install just the Android SDK and the Flutter SDK itself. You'll receive guidance for both CLI and graphical installation methods.

Installing the Android SDK on Linux

If you have never developed Android apps, you need to install the Android SDK, which includes the tools needed to build and debug Android apps.

In order to use Flutter, you need to install Android Studio and the Android SDK tools. Flutter requires Android Studio to be installed, but you don't have to use it for development.

Alternatives to the Official Zip File

 On Gentoo and Arch Linux you can use packages to install the Android SDK and/or Android Studio:

- On Gentoo, you can install the Android Studio package[4] by running emerge --ask dev-util/android-studio;

- For Arch Linux there is an actively maintained and popular package available on the AUR called *android-studio*[5].

Start by heading over to the downloads page on the Android Developers page:[6] there you'll find links for the .zip download of Android Studio (around 1GB in size).

Regardless of what you choose, you might need to install some 32-bit libraries to make the SDK work on a 64-bit operating system:

- On Debian/Ubuntu, run sudo apt install libc6:i386 libncurses5:i386 libstdc++6:i386 lib32z1 libbz2-1.0:i386

- On Fedora, run sudo dnf install zlib.i686 ncurses-libs.i686 bzip2-libs.i686.

After that, we're ready to actually install the Android SDK.

To do that using the full Android Studio installer, after extracting the zip file you downloaded from Google's website, run the studio.sh script contained in the bin subdirectory. This will start a setup wizard. After you complete the setup of the SDK you can launch Android Studio by running that same studio.sh script.

Installing the Flutter SDK on Linux

This part will provide guidance for Linux installation aimed at beginners; if you are comfortable with the command line the CLI steps will be more predictable. (For complete Linux newbies it might be easier to follow GUI-oriented guidance since that's usually more familiar.)

Alternatives to the Tarball

 There are alternatives to installing the official tarball:

- Arch Linux has an actively maintained package in the AUR to install Flutter.[7]

---

4. packages.gentoo.org/packages/dev-util/android-studio
5. aur.archlinux.org/packages/android-studio/
6. https://developer.android.com/studio#downloads
7. aur.archlinux.org/packages/flutter/

The Linux download is a source tarball that also contains the script needed to run the flutter command, which means you just need to extract it and add the bin subdirectory of the extracted tarball to the PATH environment variable.

Before we can do that, we need to browse to the SDK archive[8] page on Flutter's official website and download the latest stable version.

Alternatively, in a CLI-only environment, you can download the 1.2.1 tarball using curl https://storage.googleapis.com/flutter_infra/releases/stable/linux/flutter_linux_v1.2.1-stable.tar.xz -o flutter_linux_v1.2.1-stable.tar.xz.

Extract the tarball you just downloaded with any GUI tool of your liking or by running the following command:

```
$ tar -xf flutter_linux_v1.2.1-stable.tar.xz
```

Now we need to add the executable script to the PATH environment variable.

Before doing this, you need to take note of the directory where you extracted the tarball. It contains a flutter directory, inside which there is a bin directory; we need to know the path to reach that bin directory.

If you are using the GUI, in most distribution it is available by browsing the directory's properties. It will be something along the lines of /home/username/Downloads/flutter_linux_v1.9.1-stable/flutter/bin if you have gone with the default settings for each piece of software used in the steps we described earlier. I suggest moving this to a more permanent path; ideally one at which you'll remember you have installed Flutter.

If you worked in the CLI using the commands just outlined, browse to your Flutter installation directory and then change the working directory to the flutter/bin subdirectory by running:

```
$ cd flutter/bin
```

and get the working directory by running:

```
$ pwd
```

which will return something along the lines of /home/username/flutter/bin (here you'll see the path where you installed Flutter, so your mileage may vary significantly).

---

8. https://flutter.dev/docs/development/tools/sdk/archive?tab=linux

Know Your Shell

 This section supposes that your shell is Bash.[9] This is the case for most Linux distributions (and Unix-like operating systems in general—some exceptions are the BSDs, which have tcsh,[10] ksh,[11] or ash,[12] and Arch Linux's installer, which runs on Zsh[13] but installs Bash by default) and, since you would need to manually install and configure a different one, you probably would know how to add a directory to its PATH.

To add this to the PATH environment variable, we need to edit ~/.bash_profile.

To do that using the GUI, you first need your file manager to display hidden files. If you can't find a file named .bash_profile in your home directory, you need to toggle the option that makes the file manager show hidden files, and this depends on the file manager that you're using:

- In Nautilus (a.k.a. GNOME Files, default in most distributions using the GNOME desktop like Ubuntu, RHEL, Fedora, and default SLED and Debian) you need to press Ctrl+H. This shortcut also works in PCManFM (part of the LXDE, as found in Lubuntu), Caja (part of Mate), and Thunar (part of the XFCE desktop, as found in Xubuntu).

- If you are using the KDE desktop (for example when running Kubuntu or when choosing it when installing distributions like openSUSE or Debian) and its default Dolphin file manager, use Alt++.

Once you have located a file called .bash_profile, open it with any text editor and add the following line to the end of it, in a new line:

```
export PATH=$PATH:/home/username/etc
```

where you'll replace */home/username/etc* with the string you took note of earlier.

If you prefer using the command line or just want a copy-paste experience from this installation guide, you can instead open a terminal window or TTY and run the following command:

```
$ echo "export PATH=$PATH:/home/username/etc" >> ~/.bash_profile
```

---

9.   en.wikipedia.org/wiki/Bash_(Unix_shell)

10.   https://en.wikipedia.org/wiki/Tcsh

11.   https://en.wikipedia.org/wiki/KornShell

12.   https://en.wikipedia.org/wiki/Almquist_shell

13.   https://en.wikipedia.org/wiki/Z_shell

replacing /home/username/etc with the path you found earlier for the extracted tarball's flutter/bin directory.

To actually be able to run the flutter command, you need to refresh your terminal's configuration by running:

```
$ source ~/.bash_profile
```

Installing on Windows

Just like on Linux, Windows-only Android development is supported, so we will install just the Android SDK with Android Studio and the Flutter SDK itself.

Installing the Android SDK on Windows

All you need to do to install the Android SDK on Windows is to download and run the Android Studio installation file available on the official download page.[14] This will also install the feature-rich Android Studio IDE. After installing Android Studio, you will be guided through the installation of the Android SDK.

Installing the Flutter SDK on Windows

To install the Flutter SDK on Windows you need to install Git for Windows first. You can find the installation file for it on its official download page.[15] During installation, you need to choose the *Use Git from the Windows Command Prompt* option.

After you have installed Git, download the latest version of Flutter from its official installation page.[16] This, unlike what happens with most of the software available for Windows, will download a zip archive (a.k.a. a compressed folder) that contains a flutter folder: extract it wherever you want (this will be the SDK folder any IDE plugin will ask you to enter).

If you want to run a command on the Flutter Console, run the flutter.bat script contained in the bin subfolder.

Installing on macOS

The advantage macOS has is that it also supports iOS building and debugging. To take advantage of that, we also need to install Xcode and the iOS SDK.

---

14. https://developer.android.com/studio#downloads
15. https://git-scm.com/download/win
16. https://flutter.dev/docs/development/tools/sdk/archive

Installing Xcode and the iOS SDK

To be able to run Flutter and use it for iOS development you need to download Xcode[17] and the iOS SDK[18] from Apple's official website.

Installing the Android SDK on macOS

Installing the Android SDK on macOS is really simple: head over to the Android Studio downloads page[19] to download the .dmg file that also includes the feature-rich but resource intensive Android Studio IDE.

Installing the Flutter SDK on macOS

Installing Flutter on macOS is very similar to installing Flutter on Linux. The main differences are that macOS uses the zip archive format instead of the more efficient tar.xz format, and there are no OS or GUI differences among distributions to contend with.

Start by downloading the latest stable .zip from Flutter's official website.[20]

Unzip it to any directory, then open the flutter directory you just extracted. Press ⌘+I and take note of the path that appears to the right of *Where:*.

Now, open a Terminal window and run the command:

```
$ nano ~/.bash_profile
```

After doing that, paste the following in the terminal window:

```
export PATH=$PATH:/example/path/to/flutter/bin
```

replacing /example/path/to/flutter/bin with the path you took note of earlier.

All that's left to do is to close the file using Ctrl-X and confirming you want to save the file by pressing Y.

To actually be able to run the flutter command, you need to refresh your terminal's configuration by running:

```
$ source ~/.bash_profile
```

Installing the IDE Plugins

The Flutter IDE plugins for VSCode and Android Studio are installed using the canonical installation tools and techniques for each IDE. They also require the installation of the respective Dart plugin.

---

17. https://developer.apple.com/xcode/
18. https://developer.apple.com/ios/
19. https://developer.android.com/studio#downloads
20. https://flutter.dev/docs/development/tools/sdk/archive?tab=macos

If you're not familiar with that process, we'll now discuss how to install the Flutter plugin on each IDE.

VSCode

To install the Flutter plugin for Visual Studio Code you need to open Visual Studio Code itself, then use the keyboard shortcut Ctrl-Shift-P to open the command palette, then type "Install extensions" and press Enter.

On the panel that opens up on the left, type Flutter and press Enter.

Click the Install button in the Flutter entry in the list, this will install both the Flutter and the Dart plugins.

Unlike the Flutter plugin for Android Studio, the Flutter plugin for Visual Studio Code plugin will auto-detect the location where the Flutter SDK is installed.

Android Studio

To install the Flutter plugin for Android Studio you need to navigate to File > Settings > Plugins, click *Browse repositories...*, type Flutter and click Install.

To create a Flutter Project in Android Studio you need to restart Android Studio if you haven't since installing the Flutter plugin, navigate to File > New Flutter Project, choose *Flutter Application* and give the app a name and a path, set the package name and you're done.

Using the CLI and the Plugins

There are two ways of interacting with the Flutter SDK: using the flutter CLI command directly or through the IDE plugins. The plugins for Android Studio and VSCode are very different to use, as they adapt to the usual conventions of the respective IDE.

Create a Flutter App Project

To create a Flutter app project, run the flutter create appname command or follow the procedure corresponding to the IDE you want to use to develop your app:

- In Android Studio, click on *File > New > New Flutter Project...* and follow the instructions that will appear on screen;

- In Visual Studio Code, hit Ctrl+Shift+P to open the Command Menu and type New Project, *Flutter: New Project* should appear as an option in the menu, click on it and then type a name for your app project.

Building and Running

You can build a Flutter app using the flutter build command when the working directory is the project's root directory (where pubspec.yaml is located):

- To build an APK for your app (standard Android installation file), use flutter build apk.

- To build an iOS application bundle, use flutter build ios.

- To build an Android App Bundle (the new generation Android installation file that reduces file size), use flutter build appbundle.

If you want to run the app directly on an open emulator or a device connected by USB (with USB Debugging turned on in the device's settings), use flutter run.

If you're using an IDE, you can use the Flutter plugin to run apps directly from the IDE.

To run an app on an open emulator or connected USB device:

- Using VSCode, press F5 or click on *Debug > Start Debug*.
- Using Android Studio, press Shift-F10 and click the button that looks like the one highlighted in the following image:

Hot Reload

Flutter comes with a feature you might know from other frameworks: hot reload. If you're not familiar with it, the hot reload feature allows you to update the app's current view based on changes you've made to the code without rebuilding the entire app which, as anyone who has ever tried knows, is very painful when you are making many small changes and trying to see how they affect the app.

This feature is accessible in both Android Studio and Visual Studio Code and, actually, also in the command line when you run an app using flutter run: pressing R in the terminal when that command is running will reload the app.

In Android Studio you need to find an icon like this in the *Run* menu at the bottom:

In Visual Studio Code you need to find an icon like this in the menu that appears at the top of the screen when you start debugging:

The app will immediately reload, showing any changes you've made to the app's code immediately on the connected emulator or device.

If you're running a recent version of Android Studio and/or Visual Studio Code, you'll have IDE access to two different but similar features: stateful hot reload and hot restart. The difference between the two is that the stateful hot reload (as the name implies) preserves each of the State objects and is faster, but it won't work with bigger changes that require those to be reloaded too, and for that there's hot restart.

When running an app using flutter run from the CLI, stateful hot reload is associated to the lowercase r character, while hot restart is achieved with the uppercase R character.

In both IDEs you'll find, next to the button shown above, a lightning bolt icon like the one you can see in the following VSCode screenshot:

The lightning bolt performs the stateful hot reload, while the typical *restart* icon performs the hot restart.

Updating and Maintaining Your Flutter Installation

You'll know when you need to update your Flutter SDK installation because you'll get a notice whenever you build or run an app.

To update your Flutter installation you need to run the flutter upgrade command, which will check and download anything that's needed using Git, so you need to have Git installed.

Flutter includes a tool called Flutter Doctor, available using the flutter doctor command, which will list information about the installed Flutter version, the Android/iOS SDK, the IDE plugins, and connected devices.

Other Flutter-Related Commands in the VSCode Plugins

Once the VSCode Flutter plugin is installed, opening the command palette and typing flutter will show all available commands.

Among these you'll want to get familiar with:

Flutter: Run Flutter Doctor
> Check if there are dependencies that need to be installed.

Flutter: New Project
> Creates a new Flutter project.

Flutter: Select Device
> Select the device on which you want to debug your app.

Flutter: Get Packages and Flutter: Upgrade Packages
> Commands for interacting with Flutter Packages (we'll discuss packages in Chapter 4).

Where We're Going Next: Let's Start Building Apps

Now that you're set up with all you need to build Flutter apps, we can start building apps.

You can begin by creating a new Flutter project and familiarizing yourself with the files generated by the SDK as well as the IDE's UI for managing Flutter projects. Once you feel comfortable working with it, you can move on to the first chapter, in which we'll learn the structure of a Flutter app and how to implement it.

Part I

Getting Started with Flutter

Even though Flutter is very easy to pick up, we need to actually know what it can do for us and how it's done.

That's what the chapters in this part are about: you'll write your first app and in the process learn what Flutter widgets are and how they can be used to create user interfaces.

After that, you'll start combining more and more Flutter widgets together, and, at the end of Part I, you'll learn how to use Dart packages to get Google-developed and third-party libraries to build more apps that use features not present in Flutter's (or Dart's) standard library.

You'll also learn how to run methods written in native Swift/Objective-C and Kotlin/Java to interact with low-level features that would otherwise be inaccessible in Flutter.

CHAPTER 1

Making Your First Flutter App

Let's get started actually writing some code and making apps to learn what you can do with Flutter.

Get Familiar with Dart Syntax and Flutter Classes

In this first section of the chapter, we'll take a look at the Flutter CLI's example code, review how to work with Dart code, and learn the basics of Flutter app architecture and implementation.

To create a new Flutter app, create a directory to contain the app's source code and, inside it, another directory called lib. The lib directory is where we'll add our Dart files defining what our app looks like and what our app does.

For now we won't work in the CLI, but once we're ready to build the app we will use flutter create to generate the files that are necessary for the app to build (which you'll get to know and edit in the appendix about app configuration). In addition to the files and directories directly related to Flutter and your app, the root of your Flutter app must also contain an android and an ios directory containing the configuration for the build system for each platform.

Inside the lib directory, create a file called main.dart.

Outside lib, create a file called pubspec.yaml and paste this in it:

```
firstapp/pubspec.yaml
name: flutter_example_name
description: Example description of a flutter app that makes
             great things happen.

dependencies:
  flutter:
    sdk: flutter
```

```yaml
dev_dependencies:
  flutter_test:
    sdk: flutter

flutter:
  uses-material-design: true
```

The pubspec.yaml file contains information about your project and its dependencies, which Flutter will need to build your app. Actually this file is required for any Dart package, but it'll take a while and a few chapters before we start looking at Dart packages that aren't Flutter apps.

Inside main.dart, write the following:

firstapp_starting/lib/main.dart

```dart
import 'package:flutter/material.dart';

void main() => runApp(MyApp());

class MyApp extends StatelessWidget {
  @override
  Widget build(BuildContext context) {
    return MaterialApp(
      title: 'Flutter Demo',
      theme: ThemeData(
        primarySwatch: Colors.blue,
      ),
      home: MyHomePage(title: 'Flutter Demo Home Page'),
    );
  }
}
class MyHomePage extends StatefulWidget {
  MyHomePage({Key key, this.title}) : super(key: key);
  final String title;

  @override
  _MyHomePageState createState() => _MyHomePageState();
}
class _MyHomePageState extends State<MyHomePage> {
  int _counter = 0;

  void _incrementCounter() {
    setState(() {
      _counter++;
    });
  }
  @override
  Widget build(BuildContext context) {
    return Scaffold(
      appBar: AppBar(
        title: Text(widget.title),
      ),
```

```dart
      body: Center(
        child: Column(
          mainAxisAlignment: MainAxisAlignment.center,
          children: <Widget>[
            Text(
              'You have pushed the button this many times:',
            ),
            Text(
              '$_counter',
              style: Theme.of(context).textTheme.display1,
            ),
          ],
        ),
      ),
      floatingActionButton: FloatingActionButton(
        onPressed: _incrementCounter,
        tooltip: 'Increment',
        child: Icon(Icons.add),
      ),
    );
  }
}
```

You'll get a simple view with a counter and a floating action button which, when clicked, increments a counter that is shown at the center of the view, like in this screenshot:

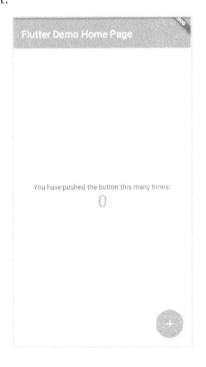

If the app doesn't work, try running:

```
$ flutter create .
```

As mentioned in the Preface, flutter create is the command used to create Flutter app projects, and executing it with a directory containing Flutter code will create the files and directories necessary for the app to compile for Android and iOS (and, as they become more stable, will also include the files needed for desktop development).

Keep in mind that you can fix most build problems not caused by errors in the code, especially after multiple builds, by running:

```
$ flutter clean
```

which will delete build files left by previous builds.

Analyze the Example Code

Let's break down this code so that you can understand this example.

The pubspec.yaml File

Before moving on to main.dart, which contains the main app code, we should take a brief look at the pubspec.yaml file, which we will discuss in greater detail in Chapter 4, Beyond the Standard Library: Plugins and Packages, on page 119 and, in even greater detail, in Appendix 2, Apple-Like Look and Additional App Configuration, on page 315.

It is important to understand that the pubspec.yaml file is not unique to Flutter apps: it is a feature of Dart packages and, as such, also contains all the information needed to make it a Flutter app.

In the first part we'll specify some metadata about the Flutter app. In this section, two attributes are set:

- The name, which is the Dart package name and it is the default app name that appears on the home screen or the app drawer. The one drawback with name is that it must be all lowercase and be a valid Dart identifier: it can't start with a digit, it can't contain any character other than letters and underscores (no spaces allowed) and it can't be a Dart keyword (like class, if, try, etc.). Thus, it is recommended to edit the app files in the android and ios directories, as explained in Platform-Specific Setup, on page 327, if you want an app name that doesn't fit within those restrictions and if you want to change the launcher icon.

- The description, which should be a brief, sentence or two explanation of the Flutter app.

In order to avoid build issues and as general good practice, the name of the directory that contains the root of the project (the lib directory and the pubspec.yaml file) should be the same as the Dart package name.

```
firstapp/pubspec.yaml
name: flutter_example_name
description: Example description of a flutter app that makes
            great things happen.
```

The rest of the file specifies the dependencies.

```
firstapp/pubspec.yaml
dependencies:
  flutter:
    sdk: flutter

dev_dependencies:
  flutter_test:
    sdk: flutter

flutter:
  uses-material-design: true
```

Since we are not using any third-party packages, we are just specifying the Flutter SDK itself as a dependency and, with the lines:

```
flutter:
  uses-material-design: true
```

we make sure that Material Design (Google/Android style) assets like icons are included.

The App Widget

```
import 'package:flutter/material.dart';
```

This brings in the Flutter classes we need to use. In this chapter you'll learn about the simplest ones and how to work with them (we'll look at many others as we continue in Chapter 2, Laying Out More Widgets, on page 27 as well).

```
void main() => runApp(new MyApp());
```

This line means that, when our code gets executed, we will start an app, and this app's behavior and appearance is specified inside a class called MyApp, which is defined as:

```
firstapp_starting/lib/main.dart
class MyApp extends StatelessWidget {
 @override
 Widget build(BuildContext context) {
   return MaterialApp(
     title: 'Flutter Demo',
     theme: ThemeData(
       primarySwatch: Colors.blue,
     ),
     home: MyHomePage(title: 'Flutter Demo Home Page'),
   );
 }
}
```

Let's break this down further.

Defining Widgets in Flutter

```
class MyApp extends StatelessWidget
```

In Flutter every UI element or collection of UI elements is a widget, which is an immutable object. This means we can't change a widget's member variables: if there are any, they have to be declared as final or constant. You can find more information on Dart variables in Variables and Conditions, on page 286.

There are two kinds of widgets:

- Stateless widgets (subclasses of StatelessWidget), which get rendered when the app starts and when a parent widget gets re-rendered, like MyApp.

- Stateful widgets (subclasses of StatefulWidget), which you can re-render at any time by calling the setState() function, like this app's MyHomePage, which is covered in The Home Page Widget, on page 9.

The app widget is the collection of every other widget, so it is a widget. In this case it is a StatelessWidget.

Working with Stateless Widgets

```
firstapp_starting/lib/main.dart
@override
Widget build(BuildContext context) {
  return MaterialApp(
    title: 'Flutter Demo',
    theme: ThemeData(
      primarySwatch: Colors.blue,
    ),
    home: MyHomePage(title: 'Flutter Demo Home Page'),
  );
}
```

This is the build method, which gets called when the widget needs to be rendered and returns a Widget object, which is every widget's superclass.

In this case it gets called just once: when the app starts, given that MyApp doesn't have a parent widget (it is every other widget's parent widget).

In MyApp's build method it is specified that the MyApp widget (the app itself) is a MaterialApp, which means that our app will use Material Design features that are part of the standard library.

The code sets, using the MaterialApp constructor, an app title, a theme with a primary swatch (a range of similar colors, as specified in Google's Material Design guidelines), and a home page, which will be of class MyHomePage and have the title "Flutter Demo Home Page".

The Home Page Widget

This defines the aforementioned MyHomePage class, which is a StatefulWidget (a widget that has a state, unlike MyApp) with a title member and a state, which is _MyHomePageState:

firstapp_starting/lib/main.dart
```
class MyHomePage extends StatefulWidget {
 MyHomePage({Key key, this.title}) : super(key: key);
 final String title;

 @override
 _MyHomePageState createState() => _MyHomePageState();
}
```

In Dart, the underscore (_) in _MyHomePageState has an effect akin to the one private has in languages like Java and is explained in The underscore, on page 292.

The Advantage of Stateful Widgets

Stateful widgets have the ability to be re-rendered programmatically, allowing the developer to build an app that reacts to changes in the data it is showing or representing.

Because of this, they are more complex than stateless widgets: a stateful widget has a state, which is represented by a State object, which contains the widget's logic and mutable data. As I mentioned in the previous section, widgets themselves are immutable, so they need a different object (the State) to hold the mutable data.

They get re-rendered when you call the setState() function, which notifies the framework that the state of the widget has changed and it needs to be re-rendered (by calling its build method again) to show the changes to the user.

The MyHomePage Widget

The line:

```
MyHomePage({Key key, this.title}) : super(key: key);
```

defines MyHomePage's arguments (as explained in Constructors, on page 307). Since they are wrapped in braces, they are named arguments, which is why, when calling MyHomePage's constructor, the syntax was:

```
MyHomePage(title: 'Flutter Demo Home Page')
```

The unused key parameter is used by the framework to identify which widgets to re-render. You can provide it and it can be useful, but it's optional, and we won't need it for this app.

We'll talk about keys in the next chapter in The Key, on page 74.

You can find more information on Dart class and constructor definitions in Classes, on page 306.

Inside _MyHomePageState is where the app's logic is defined:

```
firstapp_starting/lib/main.dart
class _MyHomePageState extends State<MyHomePage> {
 int _counter = 0;

 void _incrementCounter() {
   setState(() {
     _counter++;
   });
 }
 @override
 Widget build(BuildContext context) {
   return Scaffold(
     appBar: AppBar(
       title: Text(widget.title),
     ),
     body: Center(
       child: Column(
         mainAxisAlignment: MainAxisAlignment.center,
         children: <Widget>[
           Text(
             'You have pushed the button this many times:',
           ),
           Text(
             '$_counter',
             style: Theme.of(context).textTheme.display1,
           ),
         ],
       ),
     ),
```

```
    floatingActionButton: FloatingActionButton(
      onPressed: _incrementCounter,
      tooltip: 'Increment',
      child: Icon(Icons.add),
    ),
  );
}
}
```

```
class _MyHomePageState extends State<MyHomePage>
```

_MyHomePageState is defined as the state of the widget MyHomePage.

firstapp_starting/lib/main.dart
```
int _counter = 0;

void _incrementCounter() {
  setState(() {
    _counter++;
  });
}
```

This declares a counter and defines a function that increments the counter and triggers a re-render by changing the state of the widget (calling setState()).

The Main build Method for the Home Page

firstapp_starting/lib/main.dart
```
@override
Widget build(BuildContext context) {
  return Scaffold(
    appBar: AppBar(
      title: Text(widget.title),
    ),
    body: Center(
      child: Column(
        mainAxisAlignment: MainAxisAlignment.center,
        children: <Widget>[
          Text(
            'You have pushed the button this many times:',
          ),
          Text(
            '$_counter',
            style: Theme.of(context).textTheme.display1,
          ),
        ],
      ),
    ),
```

```
    floatingActionButton: FloatingActionButton(
      onPressed: _incrementCounter,
      tooltip: 'Increment',
      child: Icon(Icons.add),
    ),
  );
}
```

Use of a Widget to Provide the Basic App Structure: The Scaffold

This time the widget we return is a Scaffold, the basic Material Design visual layout structure; in other words, it is a generic container for all of our app content.

A Scaffold has an AppBar, which (using a Text widget) displays the title which was set earlier in MyHomePage's constructor.

Build the App's Body

The body of our Scaffold is wrapped inside a Center widget, which centers our content in the middle of the page.

The Center's child (the content which it centers) is a Column, which displays its children in a vertical stack.

The first Text widget simply displays a String, whereas the second displays the counter with a built-in theme called display1.

Add the Floating Action Button

Not centered (but inside the Scaffold, outside the body, in its own floatingAction-Button attribute) is the FloatingActionButton which, when pressed, calls the _incrementCounter function we saw previously.

Quite easy to understand are the tooltip code and the Icon widget (again, everything is a widget here) inside of it (its "child") which is a simple plus (or "add", as it is called) sign.

Every time we click the FAB the counter is incremented and the state changes, the setState() call triggers the build method again and the UI gets reloaded with the updated counter.

What We've Seen and Where We're Going

This is a very simple app: it's just a MaterialApp that contains a Scaffold, with a simple FAB in the lower right and, in the middle, a Column with two Text widgets showing the number of times the FAB has been clicked.

This is very simple, but the only way to really understand how something is done is by doing it, so the next section is going to focus on adding new features to the existing code.

Give the App Your Personal Touch

Now let's modify what we've seen. We'll change the app color to be green, add a red reset button to reset the counter to 0, make the app display the string "None" instead of the counter when the counter is at 0 and change the appBar's title text. In doing this, we'll get a feel for how to make simple changes, and also an introduction to more complex Flutter syntax.

The result will look like this:

Change the App's Primary Color

We'll start editing our app with the simplest change: changing the color to green. This is as simple as changing the following few lines in MyApp's build method:

firstapp_starting/lib/main.dart
```
theme: ThemeData(
  primarySwatch: Colors.blue,
),
```

Go ahead and change Colors.blue to Colors.green so that those lines instead read as follows:

firstapp/lib/main.dart
```
theme: ThemeData(
  primarySwatch: Colors.green,
),
```

Make the Counter Display "None" Instead of 0

Now, let's change the counter text in the middle so that it displays "None" instead of 0.

To do this, we'll add a _displayedString variable to _MyHomePageState, below the counter's declaration.

Locate the following line:

```
int _counter = 0;
```

and, below it, add:

```
String _displayedString;
```

After we've done that, we need to set this variable to "None" if the counter is 0 and to a string representation of the counter if that isn't the case. We're going to need a conditional.

Use Conditionals in Flutter

To do this every time the counter is increased (which we do using a call to setState that triggers a re-render that calls the build method), this needs to be part of _MyHomePageState's build method. So, just above:

```
return new Scaffold(
```

add:

firstapp/lib/main.dart
```
if(_counter == 0) {
  _displayedString = "None";
} else {
  _displayedString = _counter.toString();
}
```

This is a simple if-else construct and, like in many other languages, it could also be expressed in a braceless way as:

```
if(_counter == 0) _displayedString = "None";
else              _displayedString = _counter.toString();
```

or, with a conditional expression, as:

```
_displayedString = _counter == 0 ? "None" : '$_counter';
```

You can find more information about conditional constructs and expressions in Conditional Constructs and Expressions, on page 303.

Set the Counter Text

Now we need to replace the counter with the string we've just generated.

Use String Literals in Dart

At the moment, the code we're using to generate the Text widget for the counter looks like this:

```
firstapp_starting/lib/main.dart
Text(
  '$_counter',
  style: Theme.of(context).textTheme.display1,
),
```

You might have noticed the syntax currently used to display the counter to the user:

```
'$_counter'
```

The single quotes (unlike in C, C++, and Java, single and double quotes are the same in Dart) enclose a string literal, and inside this string literal is a variable name (_counter) preceded by a dollar sign.

Use String Interpolation

In this case, this is an alternative to the syntax we used earlier to convert an integer to a string (_counter.toString()).

This is how string literals work in Dart: they are enclosed in single or double quotes. And we can include variables in string literals by preceding the variable name with a dollar sign.

If we need to use string interpolation with an expression or dot notation (for example, to use member variables of objects or display results of expressions), we need to enclose the variable name in braces. We'll need to do this shortly for the app title.

You can find more information about string literals and string interpolation in Characters and Strings, on page 286.

Back to our example. Since we now want to display a string, we can replace:

```
'$_counter'
```

to be just:

```
displayedString
```

since we don't need to use string literals.

Change the App's Title

To change the appBar's title to "An app that can count to [0, 1, 2, 3...]" we need to use string interpolation.

We will use a fixed string defined in the app's constructor and a variable part, which will be created inside the build method.

The fixed part is the title we give to MyHomePage's constructor (and which then becomes widget.title), which will be "An app that can count to":

firstapp_starting/lib/main.dart
```
  home: MyHomePage(title: 'Flutter Demo Home Page'),
);
```

will have to become:

firstapp/lib/main.dart
```
  home: MyHomePage(title: 'An app that can count to'),
);
```

Now we need to edit _MyHomePageState's build method again, since that's what gets called every time the app's state changes, and that's where the variable part of the string will have to be generated.

To do what I just described, locate the following lines:

firstapp_starting/lib/main.dart
```
appBar: AppBar(
  title: Text(widget.title),
),
```

and change:

```
widget.title
```

to:

```
'${widget.title} $_counter'
```

so that those lines now instead read as follows:

firstapp/lib/main.dart
```
appBar: AppBar(
  title: Text('${widget.title} $_counter'),
),
```

As you can see, we've done the opposite of what we did to the counter, and we had to use braces for widget.title because dot notation was needed to access a member variable.

Add a Reset Button

The last thing we need to do to get to the app in the screenshots shown earlier is to add the reset button.

Before we add the button itself, let's define a simple method that changes the state and resets the counter to 0.

Use setState() to Reset the Counter

Inside _MyHomePageState's definition, below _incrementCounter()'s definition, add the following code:

firstapp/lib/main.dart
```
void _resetCounter() {
  setState(() {
    _counter = 0;
  });
}
```

This is very similar to _incrementCounter() but, instead of incrementing the counter, we set it to 0.

Make the Reset Button

Now that we've defined a method that resets the counter and triggers a re-render, we need to create a button to call that function. So before we do that, we need to know how we do that with Flutter.

Buttons in Flutter: The FlatButton and the IconButton

If we want to quickly create a button in Flutter we can choose between a FlatButton or an IconButton.

The FlatButton is ideal when you want a button that displays text: it has a child attribute that is usually a Text widget, but you have the option to set it to anything.

The reason why the FlatButton is used mostly for text buttons is that using an IconButton exists specifically for the creation of icon-based buttons, by allowing the developer to specify an Icon object as its icon attribute, with the button only consisting of the icon and a small amount of padding.

One of the attributes that show the difference in focus is that the FlatButton's color attribute controls the color of the button itself (the background to its content), whereas the IconButton's color attribute control's the icon's color.

A RaisedButton also exists, but it is just a slightly different looking FlatButton.

Implement the Reset Button

For this example we'll make a FlatButton.

To add the button, locate the following lines in _MyHomePageState's build method:

firstapp_starting/lib/main.dart
```
children: <Widget>[
  Text(
    'You have pushed the button this many times:',
  ),
  Text(
    '$_counter',
    style: Theme.of(context).textTheme.display1,
  ),
],
```

and add, inside the square brackets, the following to the list of widgets:

firstapp/lib/main.dart
```
FlatButton(
  onPressed: _resetCounter,
  color: Colors.red,
  child: Text(
    "Reset counter",
    style: Theme.of(context).textTheme.button,
  ),
),
```

First of all, the action we want to perform is to fire the _resetCounter function, so we set that as the onPressed attribute.

The FlatButton's color attribute should not be confused with the CSS attribute that goes by the same name: as I described earlier, it changes the button's background color, not the text color, which we'll leave black.

The child attribute is just a text string with the built-in button text theme.

The final code is:

firstapp_oldfab/lib/main.dart
```
import 'package:flutter/material.dart';

void main() => runApp(MyApp());

class MyApp extends StatelessWidget {
 @override
 Widget build(BuildContext context) {
   return MaterialApp(
     title: 'Flutter Demo',
     theme: ThemeData(
       primarySwatch: Colors.green,
     ),
```

```
      home: MyHomePage(title: 'An app that can count to'),
    );
  }
}
class MyHomePage extends StatefulWidget {
  MyHomePage({Key key, this.title}) : super(key: key);
  final String title;

  @override
  _MyHomePageState createState() => _MyHomePageState();
}

class _MyHomePageState extends State<MyHomePage> {
  int _counter = 0;
  String _displayedString;

  void _incrementCounter() {
    setState(() {
      _counter++;
    });
  }
  void _resetCounter() {
    setState(() {
      _counter = 0;
    });
  }
  @override
  Widget build(BuildContext context) {
    if(_counter == 0) {
      _displayedString = "None";
    } else {
      _displayedString = _counter.toString();
    }
    return Scaffold(
      appBar: AppBar(
        title: Text('${widget.title} $_counter'),
      ),
      body: Center(
        child: Column(
          mainAxisAlignment: MainAxisAlignment.center,
          children: <Widget>[
            Text(
              'You have pushed the button this many times:',
            ),
            Text(
              _displayedString,
              style: Theme.of(context).textTheme.display1,
            ),
            FlatButton(
              onPressed: _resetCounter,
              color: Colors.red,
```

```
                child: Text(
                  "Reset counter",
                  style: Theme.of(context).textTheme.button,
                ),
              ),
            ],
          ),
        ),
      ),
      floatingActionButton: FloatingActionButton(
        onPressed: _incrementCounter,
        tooltip: 'Increment',
        child: Icon(Icons.add),
      ),
    );
  }
}
```

Now, build and run or reload the app and the result will be the same as the screenshots we saw earlier.

Make a Custom Widget: Our Own Button

That FloatingActionButton is a default button class and it looks like a default button: it is the same as the one used in various other apps and you've probably seen it many times before.

What if, instead of using that default-looking button, we wanted to use a custom-made button to make it look exactly like we want?

The Button We'll Create

Let's say we want to make a text button with rounded corners and a nice ink splash effect when we tap it, like the one in these pictures:

Split Dart Code into Separate Files

First, let's create a new Dart file called OurButton.dart inside the lib directory and define our own StatelessWidget called OurButton, which will be a custom RawMaterialButton. In the new file, we'll import the basic Flutter API we need and define our class:

```
import 'package:flutter/material.dart';

class OurButton extends StatelessWidget {
}
```

Define a Custom Widget

Now, inside OurButton's curly braces, we'll define the constructor arguments and we'll set them as "required", since we need all of them and we will be setting all of them in our code:

firstapp/lib/OurButton.dart
```
OurButton({
  Key key,
  @required this.text,
  @required this.textColor,
  @required this.backgroundColor,
  @required this.splashColor,
  @required this.onPressed
}) : super(key: key);
```

For each of these arguments we need a variable to store them, like we do in the following lines:

firstapp/lib/OurButton.dart
```
final String text;
final Color textColor, backgroundColor, splashColor;
final VoidCallback onPressed;
```

Now, like for all widgets, we need a build method which, in this case, will be:

firstapp/lib/OurButton.dart
```
@override
Widget build(BuildContext context) {
  return RawMaterialButton(
    onPressed: onPressed,
    fillColor: backgroundColor,
    splashColor: splashColor,
    padding: ButtonTheme.of(context).padding,
    child: Text(
      text,
      style: TextStyle(color: textColor),
    ),
    shape: StadiumBorder(),
  );
}
```

The button we're making is a RawMaterialButton, which is a bare-bones button class that allows us to customize much more of its appearance than a simpler FlatButton.

More specifically, the arguments we're passing to its constructor are:

- onPressed, which is the same as the other onPressed attributes we've seen, and we assign OurButton's onPressed attribute to it.

- fillColor, which is the same as the color attribute we saw used for the FlatButton earlier in the chapter: it's the button's background color, which will be set to OurButton's backgroundColor attribute, to show how our custom button's attribute names can be different when compared to those of the widget we are basing it on.

- splashColor is the color used for the inksplash effect and we use the padding argument to give a normal (default) amount of padding to our button.

- child is simply a Text, using the color specified in OurButton's arguments as the text color.

- shape is the button's shape, and we're using a StadiumBorder() to give our button the rounded corners we wanted.

The entire OurButton.dart source code is:

firstapp/lib/OurButton.dart
```dart
import 'package:flutter/material.dart';

class OurButton extends StatelessWidget {
 OurButton({
   Key key,
   @required this.text,
   @required this.textColor,
   @required this.backgroundColor,
   @required this.splashColor,
   @required this.onPressed
 }) : super(key: key);
 final String text;
 final Color textColor, backgroundColor, splashColor;
 final VoidCallback onPressed;
 @override
 Widget build(BuildContext context) {
   return RawMaterialButton(
     onPressed: onPressed,
     fillColor: backgroundColor,
     splashColor: splashColor,
     padding: ButtonTheme.of(context).padding,
```

```
    child: Text(
      text,
      style: TextStyle(color: textColor),
    ),
    shape: StadiumBorder(),
  );
}
}
```

Use the Custom Button in Our App

To use our custom button in the main.dart file we need to import the file we just created by inserting, at the top of the file, the following:

import `'OurButton.dart'`;

and, in _MyHomePageState's build method, replace:

firstapp_starting/lib/main.dart
```
floatingActionButton: FloatingActionButton(
  onPressed: _incrementCounter,
  tooltip: 'Increment',
  child: Icon(Icons.add),
),
```

with:

firstapp/lib/main.dart
```
floatingActionButton: OurButton(
  text: 'Make the counter ${_counter+1}',
  textColor: Colors.white,
  backgroundColor: Theme.of(context).primaryColor,
  splashColor: Theme.of(context).primaryColorLight,
  onPressed: _incrementCounter,
),
```

Among the arguments we're passing there is a string with the expression _counter+1, which requires curly braces around it.

After that, we're done!

The full main.dart source code is:

firstapp/lib/main.dart
```
import 'package:flutter/material.dart';
import 'OurButton.dart';

void main() => runApp(MyApp());

class MyApp extends StatelessWidget {
  @override
```

```dart
  Widget build(BuildContext context) {
    return MaterialApp(
      title: 'Flutter Demo',
      theme: ThemeData(
        primarySwatch: Colors.green,
      ),
      home: MyHomePage(title: 'An app that can count to'),
    );
  }
}

class MyHomePage extends StatefulWidget {
  MyHomePage({Key key, this.title}) : super(key: key);
  final String title;

  @override
  _MyHomePageState createState() => _MyHomePageState();
}

class _MyHomePageState extends State<MyHomePage> {
  int _counter = 0;
  String _displayedString;

  void _incrementCounter() {
    setState(() {
      _counter++;
    });
  }
  void _resetCounter() {
    setState(() {
      _counter = 0;
    });
  }
  @override
  Widget build(BuildContext context) {
    if(_counter == 0) {
      _displayedString = "None";
    } else {
      _displayedString = _counter.toString();
    }
    return Scaffold(
      appBar: AppBar(
        title: Text('${widget.title} $_counter'),
      ),
      body: Center(
        child: Column(
          mainAxisAlignment: MainAxisAlignment.center,
          children: <Widget>[
            Text(
              'You have pushed the button this many times:',
            ),
```

```
      Text(
        _displayedString,
        style: Theme.of(context).textTheme.display1,
      ),
      FlatButton(
        onPressed: _resetCounter,
        color: Colors.red,
        child: Text(
          "Reset counter",
          style: Theme.of(context).textTheme.button,
        ),
      ),
    ],
  ),
),
floatingActionButton: OurButton(
  text: 'Make the counter ${_counter+1}',
  textColor: Colors.white,
  backgroundColor: Theme.of(context).primaryColor,
  splashColor: Theme.of(context).primaryColorLight,
  onPressed: _incrementCounter,
),
);
}
}
```

Where We're Going Next

Now that we know how a simple Flutter app is made, how widgets are defined, and some basic Dart syntax, we can try to combine widgets to form a more complex UI composition, and that's just we'll learn to do in the next chapter.

CHAPTER 2

Laying Out More Widgets

We have built a simple Flutter app starting from an example. Now it's time to start writing apps from scratch so that you'll be able to build any kind of app a client or employer might request of you. In this chapter you will learn about the different Flutter layout and content widgets, and how to add your own custom assets to Flutter apps.

After this chapter you should be able to create any Flutter layout and be able to apply the principles explained in the other feature-oriented chapters to the app you want to build.

We'll go through the different ways of laying out widgets with small examples to show them in action in a realistic context.

As an example of some of the different layout widgets that will be shown in this chapter, here are the widgets that we'll be using to build a calculator in the next chapter:

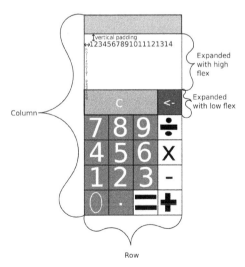

Introducing Layout Widgets

There are multiple widgets that you can use for layout purposes, and some of them might look very similar.

Starting from the widgets needed for the example shown above and explained in the next chapter, we will obviously be citing the simple vertical and horizontal visual layout structures:

- The Column, described in detail in The Column, on page 41, which allows you to stack widgets vertically, like we did in Chapter 1. It should not be confused with the Stack, which is actually used to display widgets on top of others.

- The ListView, described in detail in The ListView, on page 44, which allows you to create (potentially infinite) scrollable lists of widgets.

- The Row, described in detail in Horizontal Layout: The Row, on page 59, which allows you to display widgets side by side.

- The GridView, described in detail in The GridView, on page 64, which is used to create scrollable grids, a lot like ListView's are used to create scrollable mono-dimensional lists.

Additionally, this chapter will cover the Expanded widget (in Fill the Space Available in the View Using Expanded, on page 71), which is used to create Column or Row children of different sizes.

We'll also talk about Slivers (in Slivers, Custom Scrollables, and Collapsable App Bars, on page 73), which are used for advanced scrolling, and the Key (in The Key, on page 74), which I told you to ignore in the previous chapter.

In the next chapter, we'll combine together many of the widgets covered here (more on that in Chapter 3, Building a Calculator App, on page 77).

So let's begin.

We'll start with the simple and ubiquitous Padding and Container, as you'll use them together with many other widgets when building apps, and then we'll talk about how to Add Your Own Assets to the App, on page 33.

Contain and Add Padding to Widgets Using Invisible Layout Widgets

Some widgets are not meant to add visible content to your app but instead are simply used to move other widgets inside the available space or change the shape and size of a widget in order to make the app look exactly how you want it to look.

They all operate on a child widget, and you can use them to change the shape and size of that widget or to separate the widget from other widgets.

Add Padding to a Widget

There might be cases in which a widget in your app has to (or should) be a certain distance away from all or some other widgets—for example, if the widget has to be separated from other widgets in a list or grid, or if there are multiple small widgets used for interaction close to each other, or maybe just because it looks better with some empty space.

The space that gets left empty is called *padding*, and is usually defined in terms of the amount of pixels for each direction that are left empty.

You can add padding to the outside of a widget by wrapping it inside a Padding widget.

Padding takes a child and the padding option as named arguments, so you can create a Text with 20px padding the following way:

```
Padding(
  padding: EdgeInsets.all(20.0),
  child: Text("Example text"),
)
```

The padding option takes an object of type EdgeInsetsGeometry, which we'll learn about in the next section.

EdgeInsetsGeometry and EdgeInsets: Defining the Amount and Position of Padding

You can generate objects of type EdgeInsetsGeometry using the following constructors of the class EdgeInsets:

- EdgeInsets.all(paddingAmount), where paddingAmount is a double value specifying the amount of padding, which adds padding everywhere around the content.

- EdgeInsets.symmetric(vertical: paddingAmountVertical, horizontal: paddingAmountHorizontal), where both arguments are optional and specify the amount of padding for each side in the respective axis.

- EdgeInsets.only(top: paddingAmountTop, bottom: paddingAmountBottom, left: padding-AmountLeft, right: paddingAmountRight), where all four arguments are optional and specify the amount of padding for the respective side of the content.

There are other constructors for EdgeInsets (like EdgeInsets.fromWindowPadding() and EdgeInsets.fromLTRB()) but they are not really very useful with Padding.

EdgeInsetsDirectional.only() and EdgeInsetsDirectional.fromSTEB() also exist, and they are just like EdgeInsets.only() and EdgeInsets.fromLTRB(), but they use start, top, bottom, and end relative to the direction in which text is written and are useful when padding has to change whether the text goes from left to right (like when writing text in the Latin alphabet) or from right to left (like when writing text in the Arabic script or Hebrew alphabet).

The Container and the BoxDecoration

The Container is a generic containment widget, and it has multiple uses, depending on the options we decide to set:

- We can choose to constrain the child to a set width and height.

- We can choose to add a background color to a widget or set of widgets.

- We can add padding to a widget.

- We can make the Container of a shape other than square or rectangular using BoxDecoration.

- We can do all or some of these at the same time.

For example, we can create white text with a blue background and 20 pixel padding between the edges and the text, all limited to a 200x50 rectangle with the following code:

```
Container(
  color: Colors.blue,
  padding: EdgeInsets.all(20.0),
  width: 200.0,
  height: 50.0,
  child: Text("Prova", style: TextStyle(color: Colors.white)),
)
```

BoxDecoration

BoxDecoration, instead, is used to determine the Container's features.

You can assign it to the Container's decoration option and you might be interested in the following options:

- padding, which takes EdgeInsetsGeometry and is the same as Padding.padding.

- shape, which can be BoxShape.circle or BoxShape.rectangle.

- color, image, or gradient, which are used to specify the background, since the BoxDecoration isn't actually used just for the shape and, if you decide to use the Container.decoration, you need to move arguments such as color to the BoxDecoration's constructor.

- borderRadius which, when set for a rectangle-shaped box, creates rounded edges of the set BorderRadius, which can be set as the same for all edges using BorderRadius.circular(radius) (where radius is a double number).

Using the following Container and BoxDecoration:

```
Container(
  width: 300.0,
  height: 300.0,
  decoration: BoxDecoration(
    shape: BoxShape.circle,
    color: Colors.black,
  ),
  child:
    Center(
      child: Text(
        "Test Text",
        style:TextStyle(
          color: Colors.yellowAccent,
          fontSize: 30
        )
      ),
    ),
),
```

You can make a circle with yellow text in it like this:

And, just to show how they can work anywhere, you can have two in a Column (explained a bit further later in The Column, on page 41) in the following way (also see the figure on page 33):

```
Column(
  mainAxisAlignment: MainAxisAlignment.spaceEvenly,
  children: [
    Container(
      width: 300.0,
      height: 300.0,
      decoration: BoxDecoration(
        shape: BoxShape.circle,
        color: Colors.black,
      ),
      child: Center(
        child: Text(
          "The First Text",
          style:TextStyle(
            color: Colors.yellowAccent,
            fontSize: 30
          )
        ),
      ),
    ),
    Container(
      width: 300.0,
      height: 300.0,
      decoration: BoxDecoration(
        shape: BoxShape.circle,
        color: Colors.black,
      ),
      child: Center(
        child: Text(
          "The Second Text",
          style:TextStyle(
            color: Colors.lightBlueAccent,
            fontSize: 30
          ),
        ),
      ),
    ),
  ],
),
```

More detailed examples of the usage of a Container and BoxDecoration can be found in Make Round Widgets, on page 49.

Add Your Own Assets to the App

Flutter allows developers to ship files with apps to, for example, use custom icons instead of the ones provided by Flutter. You can use this feature with any kind of file.

Where to Put the Files

In the root of the app's source tree (where pubspec.yaml resides) you'll create one or more directories and inside those directories is where you should put the files you want to ship with your app.

Editing pubspec.yaml

Inside pubspec.yaml, locate a line that starts with flutter (if you don't have it yet, just add it at the end of the file) and, after that, indented inside it, add another called assets, in the following way:

```
...
flutter:
  assets:
...
```

Inside it, add the directories you want to load assets from, prefaced with - .

For example, if you wanted to add a directory called icons, that would look like:

```
flutter:
  assets:
    - icons/
```

For multiple directories called, for example, dir0, dir1, and dir2, you would write something like this:

```
flutter:
  assets:
    - dir0/
    - dir1/
    - dir2/
```

Using the Assets

Assets are used in different ways depending on what data you want to load from them.

Loading Various Data from the Assets

To load data from a text-based asset, it needs to be part of an AssetBundle, so that you can access the data using the following methods:

- AssetBundle.loadString(), which is used to load strings from text assets.
- AssetBundle.load(), which is used to load bytes from a file.
- AssetBundle.loadStructuredData(), which is used to load any Dart type of data from a file.

All of these return Futures, so you'll need to use the facilities described in Asynchronous Code in Dart: The dart:async Library, on page 297 to get the value of the string.

Where You Can Get an AssetBundle

The basic AssetBundle all Flutter apps get is the rootBundle, which contains all of the assets we added to pubspec.yaml.

This means you can load a text file off the rootBundle directly in the following way:

```
rootBundle.loadString("path/to/file.txt")
```

Alternatively, you can use the DefaultAssetBundle, which is actually inherited from the parent MaterialApp and can be changed at runtime because it isn't a final variable like the rootBundle. The DefaultAssetBundle is accessed using the:

```
DefaultAssetBundle.of(context)
```

we used for the Theme in the previous chapter. This syntax will be clarified when we discover the full power of the InheritedWidget in InheritedWidgets, on page 165.

We can load data from it by using the usual:

```
DefaultAssetBundle.of(context).loadString("path/to/file.txt")
```

syntax, but the characterizing feature of this kind of AssetBundle is that it doesn't necessarily have to be the rootBundle (by default the DefaultAssetBundle is just the rootBundle): you can create your own class that extends the CachingAssetBundle interface, for example, and cache some strings you think you might want to fetch multiple times during your app's execution or replace it with a NetworkAssetBundle that loads the assets over the network.

You can't take advantage of either of those classes, though, if you don't know how to use an InheritedWidget first so I recommend you stick to using either the rootBundle directly or the DefaultAssetBundle and only worry about replacing the asset bundle later, when perhaps you're sure replacing the asset bundle is the best way to do what you're trying to achieve. If you really need to know how to do that now, InheritedWidgets, on page 165 is another reference to the section on InheritedWidgets.

Images

To use an image in the assets you can simply use the Image.asset as described in Displaying Images from the Assets, on page 40.

Displaying Images

Images can have different usages and they can come from different places, so displaying images in Flutter varies depending on where you want to load the images and what you need to use them for.

There are two classes that are used for this purpose. One is the Image, which is a widget like a Text, an Icon, or any other widget you've seen until now. The other is the ImageProvider, which is needed when you need to specify an image and externally manipulate its size or shape.

An Image widget is a representation of the image and you can add it to an app's layout anywhere, whereas the ImageProvider class is a source for an image and it is used to form widgets with that image.

Displaying Images from the Network

If you have a URL containing an image, in the form http://example.com/image.png, you can get its corresponding Image widget by using the Image.network constructor like this:

```
Image.network("http://example.com/image.png")
```

You can use it anywhere any other widget (like a Text or an Icon) can be used.

Change the Image's Attributes

You can change the following options:

- The scale, which is a double value, and you use it to set the scale at which the image is displayed.

- The maximum width and height in pixels.

- repeat, which controls whether the image will be repeated within the width and height and is of type ImageRepeat. By default, ImageRepeat is set to ImageRepeat.noRepeat, which leaves the remaining width and height as empty or transparent. The other options are ImageRepeat.repeatX and ImageRepeat.repeatY (which control whether the image can only be repeated along one axis or the other) and ImageRepeat.repeat (which enables the image to be repeated in all directions to fit the width and height).

- The color of the background of the widget, which is shown where there is transparency. This is also used around the image if the width and height are incompatible with the image's and repetition is not allowed.

- headers sets the headers for the HTTP request using a Map<String, String>.

- A semanticLabel String for screen reading accessibility services and an excludeFromSemantics bool if it's explicitly not needed.

Use Width, Height, and Repetition Attributes to Display Images the Way You Want Them

To further clarify how width, height, and repeat are used, we'll look at a few screenshots showing different combinations of size and repetition settings.

If you don't set anything at all, and just give a URL, like this:

```
Image.network(
  url
)
```

the image will be fitted to the view, as you can see in the first screenshot on page 37.

If you set a width lower than the view's width, like this:

```
Image.network(
  url,
  width: 200.0
)
```

the image will scale down to fit within that width (see the second screenshot on page 37).

Setting a width higher than the view's width will have no effect: the result will be the same as on the first screenshot on page 37. Setting a height higher or lower than the height the image will end up being normally (given that the image is width-restricted in this case) will have the same effect as the that we've seen when setting the width to a value higher or lower than the width of the view.

Things change when we set repeat to anything other than the default ImageRepeat.noRepeat: allowing for repetition makes it possible to fill a width/height ratio that is different when compared to the aspect ratio of the image that we want to display.

If we set both a width and an height the image will be repeated on the side ending up longer than the original image's aspect ratio—for example, if you set the height to an high value and the width to a low value and you set repetition to either ImageRepeat.repeat or ImageRepeat.repeatY, this code:

```
Image.network(
  url,
  width: 412.0,
  height: 450.0,
  repeat: ImageRepeat.repeatY // or ImageRepeat.repeat
)
```

will yield the result as seen in the first screenshot on page 39, with the image vertically repeated to fit the higher height.

If, instead, you set the height and width so that the image has more horizontal space than it has content (by constraining the height more), like in this example:

```
Image.network(
  url,
  width: 380.0,
  height: 180.0,
  repeat: ImageRepeat.repeatX // or ImageRepeat.repeat
)
```

you will get the result as seen in the second screenshot on page 39.

If we had just limited the height the result would be very similar, but the image would fill the entire horizontal space available by showing a bigger portion of the image in the repeated portions.

ImageProvider for Images from the Network

When we want to use the image from the network for an ImageProvider like, for example, we will when we discuss how to make round widgets in Make Round Widgets, on page 49, we need to use the NetworkImage class. The NetworkImage is created by passing to its contructor the URL of the image:

```
var imageProv = NetworkImage("http://example.com/image.png")
```

The NetworkImage constructor also allows for setting the scale of the image and the image GET request's HTTP headers.

Displaying Images from the Assets

We learned how to add assets to your Flutter app in Add Your Own Assets to the App, on page 33, but now you'll see the classes that are used to take the images you add there and display them.

Given the name of the asset you display that image asset in the following way:

```
Image.asset(
  "imagename.png",
)
```

ImageProvider for Asset Images

You can use images as ImageProviders using the AssetImage class:

```
AssetImage(
  "imagename.png",
)
```

Displaying Images from Memory

This is used when images are stored in memory as bytes using Image.toByteData(), which stores them as a Uint8List (we'll discuss this further in Lists of Bytes and More: the dart:typed_data library, on page 294). For example, to store an image called image in a variable called bytes, you would use the following:

```
var bytes = image.toByteData();
```

After you have done that, you might write that to a file or just leave it in memory.

If you wanted to display those bytes as an image again, you would write the following:

```
Image.memory(
  bytes
)
```

ImageProvider for Memory Images

You can use an image stored in memory as an ImageProvider using the Memory-Image class, which is used in the following way, as you might have predicted by now:

```
MemoryImage(
  bytes
)
```

Using an ImageProvider Inside an Image Widget

As an example, we'll use the ImageProvider to create an Image widget by passing the ImageProvider as the named image argument. This adds unnecessary complexity in this case, but it is important to understand how to create Image-Providers to be able to understand other examples throughout the book:

```
Image(
  image: NetworkImage(
    "http://example.com/image.png"
  ),
)
```

along with any scale, width, height, repetition, or other modifications to the image.

The same is also true for AssetImages and MemoryImages, and might help to explain the difference in the data contained in an ImageProvider when compared to an Image widget.

Vertical Layout

There are two options available when the developer needs to lay out items vertically, depending on what is needed: the Column and the ListView.

The Column

The Column is used to create a vertical stack of widgets, and it is not scrollable. It is used to display items next to each other vertically and not to create a list of items.

How You Use It

You can make a simple Column this way:

```
Column(
  children: <Widget> [
    // Widgets separated by commas
  ],
)
```

Layout Widget Options

You just need to put the widgets inside the square brackets of the Widget collection literal (more on collection literals and lists in Lists and collection literals, on page 289) and the widgets will be shown in a vertical stack, but there are a lot of options to customize in the constructor's arguments, like the mainAxisAlignment, which sets how the children widgets should be aligned along the main axis (in the case of a Column it is the vertical axis), and can be one of:

- MainAxisAlignment.start, MainAxisAlignment.center, or MainAxisAlignment.end, which will place the widgets as close as possible, respectively, to the start, middle, or end of the main axis.

- MainAxisAlignment.spaceAround, which uses half of the available space to separate the children from each other and the other half of it to separate the first and last of them from the start and end of the Column.

- MainAxisAlignment.spaceBetween, which uses the space to make the children as far as possible to each other.

- MainAxisAlignment.spaceEvenly, which separates each child from the next as much as the start of the Column to the first and the last to the end of the 'Column.

Closely related is the mainAxisSize, which can be either MainAxisSize.max or MainAxisSize.min.

There is also crossAxisAlignment, which sets how the children widgets should be aligned along the cross axis (in the case of a Column it is the horizontal axis) and can be one of the following:

- The default CrossAxisAlignment.center, which aligns the widgets so that their center is aligned.

- CrossAxisAlignment.start and CrossAxisAlignment.end which, respectively, align the widgets to the start or the end of the cross axis.

- CrossAxisAlignment.stretch, which makes the widgets occupy as much space as possible in the cross axis.

- CrossAxisAlignment.baseline, especially useful with Row's, which aligns the children's baseline.

What You Use It For

You can use a Column simply, like in the previous chapter, to show two widgets one on top of the other, like this:

```
Scaffold(
  appBar: AppBar(...),
  body: Column(
    crossAxisAlignment: CrossAxisAlignment.start,
    mainAxisAlignment: MainAxisAlignment.spaceBetween,
    children: <Widget> [
      Icon(Icons.arrow_upward),
      Text("This will be in the middle"),
      Text("This will be at the bottom")
    ],
  ),
)
```

but you will probably want to use it more often to group together widgets, perhaps forming a new and more complex widget:

```
class TwoTexts extends StatelessWidget {

  TwoTexts({this.firstText, this.secondText});

  String firstText, secondText;

  @override
  Widget build(BuildContext context) {
    return Column(
      children: <Widget> [
```

```
        Text(firstText),
        Text(secondText)
      ],
    );
  }
}
```

This will be especially useful inside ListViews, which we'll see in action now.

The ListView

The ListView is used to create a scrollable list of widgets.

It is used when there is a need to create long lists of similar (or the same) items, and it can dynamically load other elements when they are many (or unlimited).

The list can be expressed in multiple ways, as we will now see.

How You Use It

There are multiple constructors that you can use to create a ListView.

The default constructor works just like the Column's constructor: you just need to provide a List of Widgets as the children:

```
ListView(
  children: <Widget> [
    Text("1"),
    Text("2"),
    Text("3"),
    ...
  ],
)
```

This example shows the advantage of using another constructor, the ListView.builder constructor, which is used the following way:

```
ListView.builder(
  itemCount: 499,
  itemBuilder: (BuildContext context, int i) =>
    Text("${i+1}"),
)
```

This does the same and creates a list of 499 Text widgets with the numbers from 1 to 500.

But this constructor can also be useful when each element has something different—for example, if each Text needs a different, unrelated string.

After defining something like:

```
const strings = [
  "The First Widget",
  "The Second Widget",
  "The Third Widget",
  "The Last Widget"
]
```

or generating a List list using what is described in Generating Lists, on page 290.

You can create a ListView like this:

```
ListView.builder(
  itemCount: strings.length,
  itemBuilder: (BuildContext context, int i) =>
    Text(strings[i]),
)
```

There is also ListView.separated, which allows you to add a separator widget, in this case yet another Text for simplicity:

```
ListView.separated(
  itemCount: 500,
  itemBuilder: (context, i) =>
    Text("$i", style: Theme.of(context).textTheme.display1,),
  separatorBuilder: (context, i) =>
    i%3 == 0 ? Divider() : Padding(padding: EdgeInsets.all(0.5),),
)
```

This adds a divider widget[1] once every three numbers, starting from the space between the first and second widget, like in the following screenshot:

---

1.   https://material.io/design/components/dividers.html

This is especially useful when you want do display lists of items separated into categories.

Other uses for ListView in general are explained in the Row's usage section in Where You'll Use the Row Together with Other Widgets, on page 59.

shrinkWrap, when set to false (default), will make the list take up as much space as is available on the main axis. If, instead, you set it to true the grid's size will adapt to the size that is needed to display its children.

Customizing the Divider

The Divider can be customized to fit your app's overall look, feel and needs:

- You can set the color option to another color.

- You can set its height option by providing a double number to make the space bigger or smaller.

- You can set its indent option by providing a double number to make the line start at a different position along the horizontal axis.

Horizontal Lists

You can use scrollDirection to make a horizontally scrolling list, which is very useful if you want to have a horizontal list inside a vertical list. This can be seen in several apps and you'll see exactly why it is useful.

In the following example, I'll explain how to show many products, grouped in categories, using a combination of ListView.builder to display the categories and horizontal ListView.builder to show the products. We'll use example data, defined in the following way:

```
const categories = [
  "Automotive",
  "Books",
  "Electronics",
  "Food"
];

const products = [
  [
    "Car", "Tyre", "Fuel", "Oil"
  ],
  [
    "Programming Book", "Novel", "Politics Book", "Business Book"
  ],
  [
    "Desktop Computer", "Laptop", "Computer keyboard"
  ],
```

```
  [
    "Pasta", "Pizza", "Bread" "Cheese", "Ham", "Sausage", "Beef"
  ]
];
```

and then render the product list using something like:

```
return Scaffold(
  backgroundColor: Colors.greenAccent,
  appBar: AppBar(title: Text("List inside List example")),
  body: ListView.builder(
    itemCount: categories.length,
    itemBuilder: (context, i) =>
      Column(
        children: <Widget> [
          Text(categories[i]),
          Container(
            height: 150.0,
            child: ListView.builder(
              padding: EdgeInsets.all(10.0),
              scrollDirection: Axis.horizontal,
              itemCount: products[i].length,
              itemBuilder: (context, j) =>
                Padding(
                  padding: EdgeInsets.all(20.0),
                  child: Card(
                    child:Padding(
                      padding: EdgeInsets.all(10.0),
                      child: Text(
                        products[i][j],
                        style: Theme.of(context)
                                      .textTheme.display1,
                      ).
                    ),
                  ),
                ),
            ),
          ),
        ],
      )
  )
);
```

which produces the result as seen in the screenshot on page 48.

The Container is needed to constrain the internal ListView since it is inside another scrollable widget and the app wouldn't work without it.

More on the Card in The Card, on page 67.

The ListTile

The ListTile is the typical widget that is used with ListViews and is very common in chat apps: the typical row made of a (usually round) preview picture, on the left, and on the right side a title and an optional subtitle.

Implement a ListTile

ListTile is very common and useful and very easy to implement in Flutter:

```
ListTile(
  leading: Image(leftImage), // OPTIONAL
  title: Text(title),
  subtitle: Text(subtitle), // OPTIONAL
  onTap: () => openTile(), // OPTIONAL
)
```

leading is the little preview widget shown *before* the title, and it is usually an image, title is the big text description of the element, the subtitle is smaller and shown below, and onTap is the funciton that will be fired when the user taps on the tile.

There is also a (less common) trailing argument available to add a widget placed *after* the title.

For example, the following code, using the list icon as the leading icon:

```
ListView.builder(
  itemBuilder: (context, i) =>
    ListTile(
      leading: Icon(Icons.list),
      title: Text("title number ${i+1}"),
      subtitle: Text("subtitle"),
  ),
)
```

will produce:

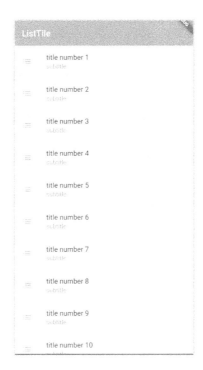

Make Round Widgets

You previously learned that the leading widget of a ListTile is usually round, but how can you make a round widget?

You build round widgets in two ways: using a CircleAvatar or using a BoxDecoration for a Container.

Use a Container to Make Widgets of Any Shape and Size

The most versatile and generic way is to contain the widget within a circular shape using a circle-shaped Container.

As an example of the usage of the container, the following code produces a normal square box with an icon and some text:

```
Container(
  height: 50.0,
  width: 50.0,
  color: Colors.blueAccent,
  child: Column(
    children: <Widget> [
      Icon(Icons.apps),
      Text(
        "Test",
        style: TextStyle(color: Colors.white),
      ),
    ],
  ),
)
```

just like in the following screenshot:

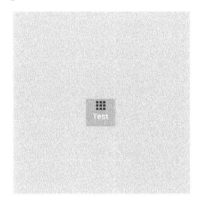

A Container can be made of any shape or size. Making it round is very simple, but you have to keep in mind that you need to move the color attribute to the BoxDecoration widget:

```
Container(
  height: 50.0,
  width: 50.0,
  child: Column(
    children: <Widget> [
      Icon(Icons.apps),
      Text(
        "Test",
        style: TextStyle(color: Colors.white),
      ),
    ],
  ),
  decoration: BoxDecoration(
    color: Colors.blueAccent,
    shape: BoxShape.circle,
  ),
)
```

and that produces:

Use a CircleAvatar to Round Widgets

The alternative is to use a CircleAvatar, which simplifies the process when it can be used.

A CircleAvatar is comparable to a pre-made circle container and it is optimized for rounding images, but it can also be used as a container.

For example, you could exactly replicate the Container example from before in a simpler way like this:

```
CircleAvatar(
  radius: 25.0,
  backgroundColor: Colors.blue,
  child: Center(
    child: Column(
      children: <Widget>[
        Icon(Icons.apps),
        Text("Test", style: TextStyle(color: Colors.white),)
      ],
    ),
  ),
),
```

Where the radius is the radius of the circle, the backgroundColor is the background color of the circle and the child is what will actually be displayed inside the circle.

The real advantage of using a CircleAvatar is that it allows you to cut an image into a round shape in a really easy way by simply passing an ImageProvider as the backgroundImage argument.

Using the pragprog.com website's PNG favicon[2] as an example, you would display it inside an app by using the Image.network contructor of the Image widget and passing the URL as the positional argument (as we'll do in the Chapter 5, Network and Storage I/O and Navigation, on page 141), like this:

```
Image.network("https://pragprog.com/favicon.png")
```

but that can't be used for the CircleAvatar's backgroundImage because it needs an ImageProvider, not an Image.

So you need to use the NetworkImage class, and pass that as the argument of the CircleAvatar, like in the following example:

```
CircleAvatar(
  backgroundImage: NetworkImage("https://pragprog.com/favicon.png"),
)
```

which produces the following round image:

Obviously you can change the radius to your liking by using the radius argument.

Use a CircleAvatar in a ListTile

Integrating it into a ListTile is as simple as using the CircleAvatar as the leading widget, like in the following example:

```
ListTile(
  leading: CircleAvatar(
    backgroundImage: NetworkImage("https://pragprog.com/favicon.png"),
  ),
  title: Text("Example"),
),
```

---

2. https://pragprog.com/favicon.png

which produces:

Use the Expandable ListTile: The ExpansionTile

The ExpansionTile is an expandable ListTile: it is just like a ListTile when it first gets rendered but you can, without leaving the current view, make an ExpansionTile taller and show more widgets, like more text or additional buttons and features.

You use the ExpansionTile like this:

```
ExpansionTile(
  leading: Image(leftImage), // OPTIONAL
  title: Text(title),

// ExpansionTile-specific arguments
  initiallyExpanded: true, // OPTIONAL default: false
  children: <Widget> [
    Row(
      children: [
        Text("Left on first row"),
        Text("Right on first row"),
      ],
    ),
    Text("Second row"),
  ],
  backgroundColor: Colors.green[100], // OPTIONAL
  // OPTIONAL, argument is a boolean, true if expanding, false if collapsing
  onExpansionChanged: (expanding) {return;},
)
```

Change the ExpansionTile's attributes

Most of the properties are the same as the ListTile's (except for onTap, which doesn't exist for ExpansionTiles), but trailing is different this time: if it is not specified it will be an arrow which, when clicked, rotates to show whether the widget is expanded or not.

There are four main ExpansionTile-specific arguments:

- initiallyExpanded, which can be set to true if you want the inital state of the widget to be the expanded state.

- children, which is the list of widgets to be displayed below the tile when it expands.

- backgroundColor, which is the background color of the list of children widgets.

- onExpansionChanged, with which you can set a function to be called when the tile is expanded.

For example, the following code:

```
ExpansionTile(
  leading: Icon(Icons.list),
  title: Text("title"),
  children: <Widget> [
    Row(
      mainAxisAlignment: MainAxisAlignment.spaceEvenly,
      children: [
        Text("Left on first row"),
        Text("Right on first row"),
      ],
    ),
    Text("Second row"),
  ],
)
```

produces:

which can be expanded to:

Dismissible ListTiles

A very common usage for ListTiles is as dismissible widgets, which means they can be deleted with a swipe gesture. A widget gains that ability by being wrapped in a Dismissible widget.

Dismissible requires a Key to be provided. It's not strictly necessary to understand Keys to use Dismissibles, but a more in-depth explanation will be provided in The Key, on page 74.

The Dismissible widget is used in the following way:

```
Dismissible(
  background: Container(color: Colors.green),
  key: Key(string),
  child: ListTile(
    title: Text(string),
  ),
)
```

where the background is what is shown behind the tile when it is swiped by the user. Setting it to a container makes it possible to choose the background color.

A complete implementation of Dismissible inside a ListView would be:

```
ListView.builder(
  itemCount: 20,
  itemBuilder: (context, i) => Dismissible(
    background: Container(
      color: Colors.red,
      child: Row(
        mainAxisAlignment: MainAxisAlignment.spaceBetween,
        children: [
          Icon(Icons.clear, color: Colors.white,),
          Icon(Icons.clear, color: Colors.white,),
        ],
      ),
    ),
    key: UniqueKey(),
    child: ListTile(
      leading: CircleAvatar(
        backgroundImage: NetworkImage("https://pragprog.com/favicon.png"),
      ),
      title: Text("Example ${i+1}"),
    ),
  ),
),
```

The UniqueKey is the most basic and uncomplicated Key, and it should be enough unless you need greater control over the widgets' state than is provided by Flutter by default. The Row with two spaced-out Icons.clear icons shows the Icon on both sides when the tile is swiped. That code generates the following list:

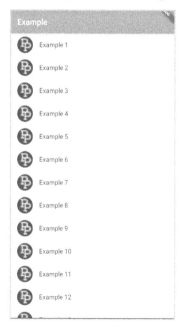

Partially swiping a tile shows the red background and an icon:

And completely swiping it removes the tile from the list with a nice animation, eventually leaving the list looking like this:

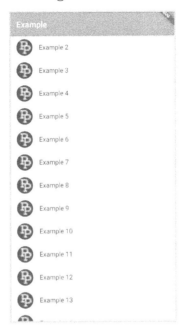

Displaying a SnackBar

In most apps, when a ListTile is dismissed, a SnackBar[3] is displayed at the bottom of the screen.

Displaying a SnackBar using Flutter is really simple:

```
Scaffold.of(context).showSnackBar(
  SnackBar(
    content: Text(
      "Tile #${i+1} was dismissed"
    ),
  ),
),
```

And it can be displayed automatically when a tile is dismissed by changing the code on page 56 to:

---

3.   https://material.io/design/components/snackbars.html#anatomy

```
ListView.builder(
  itemCount: 20,
  itemBuilder: (context, i) => Dismissible(
    background: Container(
      color: Colors.red,
      child: Row(
        mainAxisAlignment: MainAxisAlignment.spaceBetween,
        children: [
          Icon(Icons.clear, color: Colors.white,),
          Icon(Icons.clear, color: Colors.white,),
        ],
      ),
    ),
    key: UniqueKey(),
    child: ListTile(
      leading: CircleAvatar(
        backgroundImage: NetworkImage("https://pragprog.com/favicon.png"),
      ),
      title: Text("Example ${i+1}"),
    ),
    onDismissed: (direction) {
      Scaffold.of(context).showSnackBar(
          SnackBar(
            content: Text(
              "Tile #${i+1} was dismissed"
            ),
          ),
        );
      },
  ),
),
```

The SnackBar's constructor supports, in addition to the content, an action attribute, in the form of a SnackBarAction, which allows the developer to display a button that allows the user to take an action in response to the SnackBar's message:

```
SnackBar(
  content: Text("Something happened"),
  action: SnackBarAction(
    label: "DO SOMETHING ABOUT IT",
    onPressed: () {
      // do something about it
    },
  ),
),
```

A SnackBar built with that code looks like this:

Horizontal Layout: The Row

The Row lays out widgets side by side, and is very similar to a Column, with the difference being that the main axis and cross axis are the other way around.

How You Use It and What You Use It For

You can use a Row simply the following way:

```
Column(
  children: <Widget> [
    Text("This will be the left side"),
    Text("This will be the right side")
  ],
)
```

The options are the same as the Column's (with the cross axis becoming the vertical and the main axis becoming the horizontal) and you can find them in Layout Widget Options, on page 42.

Where You'll Use the Row Together with Other Widgets

Rows and Columns make for great bonding widgets: with them you can make your complex widgets made of simple elements.

For example, a simple social network post can be expressed with a Column with three elements: a Row showing the profile picture and the profile name, a big text in the middle, and at the bottom, a row showing the commands:

```
Column(
  children: <Widget> [
    Row(
      children: <Widget> [
        ProfilePicture(profileID),
        Text(profileName),
      ],
    ),
    Text(postText),
    Row(
      children: <Widget> [
        LikeButton(),
        CommentButton(),
        ShareButton()
      ],
    ),
  ],
)
```

This combination of widgets, but also just a Row of widgets, is easily inserted inside a ListView or GridView which, to keep with the running example of a social network, could be a social network feed.

This isn't hard to do—we'll start by making the respect the spaces and sizes needed for the different elements that compose it:

```
Column(
  children: <Widget> [
    Row(
      children: <Widget> [
        CircleAvatar(
          backgroundImage: ProfilePicture(profileID),
        ),
        Padding(
          padding: EdgeInsets.all(20),
          child: Text(profileName),
        ),
      ],
    ),
    Align(
      alignment: FractionalOffset.centerLeft,
      child: Padding(
        padding: EdgeInsets.all(5),
        child: Text(postText),
      ),
    ),
    Divider(),
    Row(
      children: <Widget> [
        LikeButton(),
        CommentButton(),
        ShareButton()
      ],
    ),
  ],
),
```

And all that's left to do to make this work is to replace the placeholder widgets with real widgets.

For the profile picture we'll use the same NetworkImage("https://pragprog.com/favi-con.png") we used previously, whereas the like, comment, and share buttons will be simple IconButtons:

```
Column(
  children: <Widget> [
    Row(
      children: <Widget> [
        CircleAvatar(
```

```
          backgroundImage: NetworkImage("https://pragprog.com/favicon.png"),
        ),
        Padding(
          padding: EdgeInsets.all(20),
          child: Text("Short poster"),
        ),
      ],
    ),
    Align(
      alignment: FractionalOffset.centerLeft,
      child: Padding(
        padding: EdgeInsets.all(5),
        child: Text("This is a short post, but that doesn't really matter"),
      ),
    ),
    Divider(),
    Row(
      children: <Widget> [
        IconButton(
          icon: Icon(Icons.thumb_up, color: Colors.redAccent),
          onPressed: () {},
        ),
        IconButton(
          icon: Icon(Icons.comment, color: Colors.greenAccent),
          onPressed: () {},
        ),
        IconButton(
          icon: Icon(Icons.share, color: Colors.blueAccent),
          onPressed: () {},
        ),
      ],
    ),
  ],
),
```

To create a complete view with a ListView of posts we should also store the post data separately in a List, since in a real app you're never going to hard-code such data.

To do that, we'll start by creating a class to contain the post data:

```
class Post {
  Post({this.profileName, this.profilePicture, this.postText});

  ImageProvider profilePicture;
  String profileName;
  String postText;
}
```

and a List of that class with some data:

```
List<Post> posts = [
  Post(
    postText: "This is a short post, but that doesn't really matter",
    profileName: "Short poster",
    profilePicture: NetworkImage("https://pragprog.com/favicon.png"),
  ),
  Post(
    postText: "This is a longer post, which really shows how the" +
    "widgets will naturally expand when there is more content to display.\n" +
    "At this, point, this line of text is just here because we need to" +
    "make this post so much bigger than the other one.",
    profileName: "Long poster",
    profilePicture: NetworkImage("https://pragprog.com/favicon.png"),
  ),
];
```

At this point, the resulting ListView is quite straightforward:

```
ListView.builder(
  itemCount: 2,
  itemBuilder: (context, i) => Card(
    child: Column(
      children: <Widget> [
        Row(
          children: <Widget> [
            CircleAvatar(
              backgroundImage: posts[i].profilePicture,
            ),

            Padding(
                padding: EdgeInsets.all(20),
                child: Text(posts[i].profileName,
                style: Theme.of(context).textTheme.subhead),
            ),
          ],
        ),
        Align(
          alignment: FractionalOffset.centerLeft,
          child: Padding(
                padding: EdgeInsets.all(5),
                child: Text(posts[i].postText,
                style: Theme.of(context).textTheme.body1),
          )
        ),
        Divider(),
        Row(
          children: <Widget> [
            IconButton(
              icon: Icon(Icons.thumb_up, color: Colors.redAccent),
              onPressed: () {},
            ),
```

```
        IconButton(
          icon: Icon(Icons.comment, color: Colors.greenAccent),
          onPressed: () {},
        ),
        IconButton(
          icon: Icon(Icons.share, color: Colors.blueAccent),
          onPressed: () {},
        ),
      ],
    ),
  ],
),
),
),
```

producing the following result:

Nested Rows and Columns can also be used to create grids, as described in Nested Rows and Columns, on page 67.

Making Grids

Depending on what you need to achieve with your app, a grid can be formed in two different ways: using the GridView or nested Rows and Columns.

The GridView

The GridView is to grids what the ListView is to vertical layout, and it is useful for grids similar to the ones seen in photo apps: long, scrollable grids of a variable number of fixed-size elements. A lot like a ListView, it can be created using multiple constructors. The default constructor will be discussed in the section Slivers, Custom Scrollables, and Collapsable App Bars, on page 73.

Grids with a Fixed Cross-Axis Count

The GridView.count() constructor takes a List of children Widgets and the crossAxisCount as the basic arguments to build the grid, like in the following example:

```
GridView.count(
  crossAxisCount: 3,
  crossAxisSpacing: 50.0,
  mainAxisSpacing: 100.0,
  padding: EdgeInsets.all(20.0),
  children: [1,2,3,4,5,6,7,8,9,10,11,12,13,14,15]
            .map(
              (n) =>
                Text(
                  "$n",
                  style: Theme.of(context).textTheme.display1,
                ),
            ).toList(),
)
```

which produces:

Grids with a Maximum Per-Widget Cross-Axis Extent

The GridView.extent constructor takes a List of children Widgets and the maxCrossAxisExtent, which is the maximum amount of pixels each child can take up on the cross-axis. The bigger the maxCrossAxisExtent is, the bigger each tile is going to be.

For example, the following:

```
GridView.extent(
  maxCrossAxisExtent: 50.0,
  crossAxisSpacing: 50.0,
  mainAxisSpacing: 100.0,
  padding: EdgeInsets.all(20.0),
  children: [1,2,3,4,5,6,7,8,9,10,11,12,13,14,15]
             .map(
               (n) =>
                 Text(
                   "$n",
                   style: Theme.of(context).textTheme.display1,
                 ),
             ).toList(),
)
```

produces, on a 2880x1440 560dpi screen with default Android scaling, the following grid:

Grids Built Using Builder Functions

The GridView.builder constructor which uses an itemBuilder to build the children and a gridDelegate for the size and position of the widgets, like the following example, which produces the same grid as the GridView.count example (on page 64):

```
GridView.builder(
  padding: EdgeInsets.all(20.0),

  itemCount: 15,

  gridDelegate: SliverGridDelegateWithFixedCrossAxisCount(
    crossAxisCount: 3,
    crossAxisSpacing: 50.0,
    mainAxisSpacing: 100.0,
  ),
  itemBuilder: (context, i) => Text("${i+1}"),
),
```

Grid delegates have (unusually long) names such as SliverGridDelegateWithFixedCrossAxisCount and SliverGridDelegateWithMaxCrossAxisExtent to get, respectively, the GridView.count and GridView.extent properties. They take grid layout-related properties as named arguments.

If you wanted to exactly replicate the behavior of the GridView.extent shown on page 65 you would write the following:

```
GridView.builder(
  padding: EdgeInsets.all(20.0),

  itemCount: 15,

  gridDelegate: SliverGridDelegateWithMaxCrossAxisExtent(
    maxCrossAxisExtent: 50.0,
    crossAxisSpacing: 50.0,
    mainAxisSpacing: 100.0,
  ),
  itemBuilder: (context, i) => Text("${i+1}"),

)
```

The GridView's Properties

Other grid properties are:

- childAspectRatio, which is the ratio between cross-axis and main axis size of each of the grid's children.

- shrinkWrap, which is the same as the ListView's (in How You Use It, on page 44).

- scrollDirection, which sets the direction along which the grid scrolls (which also serves as the main axis of the grid).

Nested Rows and Columns

If, instead, you need to create a (perhaps smaller) non-scrollable grid of a fixed number of widgets you would use a Column of Rows.

A simple 2x2 grid would be implemented in the following way:

```
Column(
  children: <Widget> [
    Row(
      children: <Widget> [
        Text(topLeftString),
        Text(topRightString),
      ],
    ),
    Row(
      children: <Widget> [
        Text(bottomLeftString),
        Text(bottomRightString),
      ],
    ),
  ],
)
```

The Card

The Card is a Material Design component[4] used to visually group together (or separate) widgets.

You can use it as part of the overall layout of an app or inside lists or grids.

For example, this code:

```
GridView.builder(
  padding: EdgeInsets.all(20.0),
  itemCount: 15,
  gridDelegate: SliverGridDelegateWithFixedCrossAxisCount(
    crossAxisCount: 3,
    crossAxisSpacing: 50.0,
    mainAxisSpacing: 100.0,
  ),
  itemBuilder: (context, i) => Card(
    child: Center(
      child: Text("${i+1}"),
    ),
  ),
),
```

---

4.   https://material.io/design/components/cards.html

nicely shows the space available for each GridView tile on those settings:

But a Card is used really often inside ListViews.

An example of the usage as a generic layout element will be given when we talk about making a calculator app in Chapter 3, Building a Calculator App, on page 77.

Using Buttons Specifically Designed for Cards

ButtonTheme.bar() is meant specifically for use inside Cards and ExpansionTiles.

It simply groups together buttons in a Row and gives them an adequate theme, like in the following example (we're generating pseudo-pseudo-random numbers around 3200 because it's not worth it to generate *real* pseudo-random numbers and would have yielded a less realistic result):

```
ListView.builder(
  itemBuilder: (context, i) {
    var n = 3231-i-i*23*(i%2)-1;
    Card(
      margin: EdgeInsets.all(10.0),
```

```
child: Column(
  children: <Widget>[
    Row(
      children: <Widget>[
        Padding(
          padding: EdgeInsets.all(10.0),
          child: CircleAvatar(
            backgroundImage: NetworkImage(
              "http://www.carminezacc.com/manstick.png",
            ),
          ),
        ),
        Text(
          "A Bot",
          style: Theme.of(context).textTheme.title,
        ),
        Text(
          "  @iamarealhuman$n",
          style: Theme.of(context).textTheme.overline,
        ),
      ],
    ),
    Padding(
      child: Text(
        "It might not be a human," +
        "but it acts almost like it would if it were a human.",
        style: Theme.of(context).textTheme.body1,
      ),
      padding: EdgeInsets.symmetric(vertical: 10.0, horizontal: 8.0),
    ),
    ButtonTheme.bar(
      // OPTIONAL:buttonColor: Colors.X,
      // OPTIONAL:colorScheme:
      //          ColorScheme.fromSwatch(primarySwatch: Colors.X)
      child: Row(
        children: <Widget>[
          FlatButton(
            child: Text("Follow"),
            onPressed: () => Scaffold.of(context).showSnackBar(
              SnackBar(
                content: Text(
                  "Now you follow @iamarealhuman$n"
                ),
              ),
            ),
          ),
          FlatButton(
            child: Text("Send Message"),
            onPressed: () => Scaffold.of(context).showSnackBar(
              SnackBar(
```

```
                        content: Text(
                          "You can't send messages to @iamarealhuman$n"
                        ),
                      ),
                    ),
                  ),
                ],
              ),
            ),
          ],
        ),
      );
    }
  ),
),
```

which produces the following list:

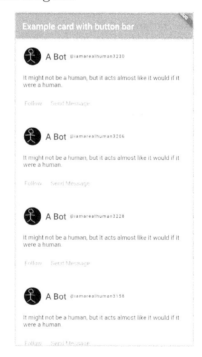

Another Material Design Element: The Chip

Since we're talking about Material Design components, another one that is integrated into Flutter and has similar uses to the Card is the Chip.[5]

They are used really often to display contact names inside some SMS or email apps, but also for filtering, making choices, and performing actions.

5.   https://material.io/design/components/chips.html

They are very small and are usually made of a round image or icon (called an avatar) and some text (called a label). It can optionally have a deleteIcon that calls the VoidCallback set as the onDelete option.

A Chip with a simple round CircleAvatar and a label can be built using the following code:

```
Chip(
  avatar: CircleAvatar(
    backgroundImage: NetworkImage("http://www.carminezacc.com/manstick.png"),
  ),
  label: Text("A Bot"),
),
```

and, when centered using Center, produces the following:

Fill the Space Available in the View Using Expanded

When using Rows and Columns you only use as much space as you need to and two of the same widget will always take up the same amount of space.

If you want to use all of the space in the view and split the space among the widgets in specific ways you need to use the Expanded widget.

How You Use It

An Expanded widget can only be used inside a Row or Column, and it takes a child argument for the widget to expand and an optional integer as the flex argument.

The child will be expanded to fill as much space as possible, and if there is more than one Expanded on the same Row or Column the space they will take up is directly proportional to their flex value.

For example, the following code:

```
Column(
  children: <Widget> [
    Expanded(
      flex: 5,
      child: (
        ...
      ),
    ),
    Expanded(
      flex: 2,
      child: (
        ...
      ),
    ),
  ],
)
```

Will space the widgets out like this:

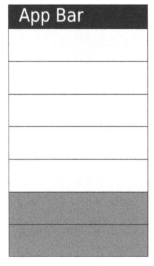

Excluding the app bar, every green or yellow rectangle represents 1/7 of the view, the yellow part (5/7 of the view) will be taken up by the first Expanded's child, whereas the green part (the remaining 2/7) will be where the second Expanded's child will reside.

We are going to make extensive use of Expanded in the next chapter when we build a calculator app.

Slivers, Custom Scrollables, and Collapsable App Bars

We've already covered most of what you need to know about scrollable widgets like ListViews and GridViews, but this section is going to be a deeper dive into the sea of Scrollable, ScrollViews, SliverLists, and other lower level, more customizable widgets. You'll also learn how to make the app bar collapsable when the user scrolls down.

How Flutter Determines How Far to Scroll

Flutter actually simulates scrolling using a Simulation widget, which simulates the movement of a point to which some forces are being applied in one-dimensional space, and the state of the simulation is used to determine scrolling position. These forces are changed depending on the desired scrolling behavior. This is set using the ScrollPhysics class, which you can use for the physics option.

primary in a ScrollView

primary is a boolean option that can be set for ScrollViews. If it is set to false, the view will only scroll if there are enough children to require scrolling.

Make a Collapsable App Bar

A common sight in scrollable apps is a collapsable app bar: it is especially visible in web browsers and, in another variant, in some profile pages of chat apps.

Usually it consists in the appbar disappearing when the user scrolls down and reappearing when the user scrolls up, usually even if the user doesn't scroll up to the top of the scrollable view.

It can be implemented using a CustomScrollView that contains a SliverAppBar and a SliverList (or, alternatively, a SliverGrid).

A SliverList is actually just a ListView that uses a SliverChildDelegate to generate its children like you would with ListView.builder(), but with an important twist: it is meant to be used as part of a CustomScrollView, which is a particular kind of widget that is used to create a custom scrollable widget using slivers like the SliverList and SliverAppBar.

To build an app with a collapsable app bar you need a normal MaterialApp with a Scaffold.

The difference is that you won't be adding an AppBar to the Scaffold but just using its body option and assigning it to a CustomScrollView:

```
@override
Widget build(BuildContext context) {
  return Scaffold(
    body: CustomScrollView(
      slivers: <Widget>[
        SliverAppBar(
          title: Text("A collapsable AppBar"),
        ),
        SliverList(
          delegate: SliverChildBuilderDelegate(
            (context, i) => ListTile(title: Text("$i"),),
          ),
        ),
      ],
    ),
  );
}
```

This doesn't actually do what we want, though: the app bar only reappears when the user scrolls to the top of the list, but that isn't the desired behavior, so we need to set the SliverAppBar's floating option to true so that it reappears when the user scrolls up from anywhere in the list:

```
SliverAppBar(
  title: Text("A collapsable AppBar"),
  floating: true,
),
```

But this isn't even completely the desired behavior: we want the SliverAppBar to appear even if we partially scroll up, so we also need to set snap to true (which only affects anything if floating is also set to true):

```
SliverAppBar(
  title: Text("A collapsable AppBar"),
  floating: true,
  snap: true,
),
```

The Key

The Key is used to uniquely identify a widget and it is used by the framework to update the elements that actually need to be updated.

You usually won't be using keys, since the framework will take care of them by itself, but you can use them to have greater control of widget state and updates.

In addition to that, there are widgets that explicitly ask for a key, like the Dismissibles we encountered in Dismissible ListTiles, on page 55.

Many Keys for the Same Keyhole

There are many kinds of Keys, and some are actually more useful than the plain Key constructor, which takes as a named argument a String that must be unique within the widget's parent.

```
ExampleWidget(
  key: Key("example")
)
```

GlobalKeys also exist and, because of their global scope, they have to be absolutely unique.

GlobalKeys allow for widgets to be moved to be a child of a completely different parent while preserving its state.

There also are LocalKeys, which have the same scope as the normal Keys, but have a few different constructors:

- The ValueKey, which takes a value of any type, not just a String.
- The UniqueKey, which takes no value at all and is always unique (what we used in Dismissible ListTiles, on page 55).

Using Keys

Most of the time, you don't need to use Keys; they only become necessary when widgets require you to set a Key, as happened when we talked about the Dismissible in Dismissible ListTiles, on page 55.

Where We're Going Next

In the next chapter we'll be using some of the layout widgets we've seen in this chapter together to build a calculator app.

CHAPTER 3

Building a Calculator App

Whew! You've learned a lot about the tools available to you in Flutter. Shall we put them to use? As promised, this chapter will focus on building a calculator app, using some of the structures and elements we saw throughout the previous chapter.

We'll start writing our app by showing you how to go from an empty file to a working Flutter app.

This time, create a Flutter project using the flutter create appname command or your IDE of choice, but this time delete everything inside the generated main.dart.

Importing Basic Dependencies

The first thing you should always do is import the dependencies.

In this case, we just need the same Flutter Material library that we used in the previous chapter:

layout/calculator/lib/main.dart
```
import "package:flutter/material.dart";
```

Writing main

Let's start from the simplest and least specific part of our app: the main function.

Using a Wrapper Class

In the previous chapter we defined a MyApp class and used main simply to run it, in the following way:

```
void main() =>
  runApp(MyApp());

class MyApp extends StatelessWidget {
  @override
  Widget build (BuildContext context) {
    return MaterialApp(
      // Actual app content and data
    );
  }
}
```

Skipping the Wrapper Class

The same effect would be achieved by simply writing:

```
void main() {
  runApp(MaterialApp(
    // other app content and data
  ));
}
```

This looks a lot shorter, but in a larger app it isn't really much by comparison.

If your app is entirely contained in one view it doesn't compromise app functionality, but if you need more views and need to have shared data you should consider writing a wrapper class for your app to keep things organized and clear.

And, in any case, you should only use the second form if you really need to keep your code compact or to save time to quickly write a small app.

So we will write the following:

layout/calculator/lib/main.dart
```
void main() => runApp(MyApp());

class MyApp extends StatelessWidget {
  @override
  Widget build(BuildContext context) {
    return MaterialApp(
      title: "Flutter Calculator",
      theme: ThemeData(
        primarySwatch: Colors.blue,
        backgroundColor: Colors.black26
      ),
      home: CalculatorHomePage(title: "Flutter Calculator", ),
    );
  }
}
```

The Calculator's Home Page

The home page will be stateful because it will have to reflect user interactions and input, so we'll define a simple StatefulWidget:

layout/calculator/lib/main.dart
```
class CalculatorHomePage extends StatefulWidget {
  CalculatorHomePage({Key key, this.title}) : super(key: key);
  final String title;

  @override
  _CalculatorHomePageState createState() => _CalculatorHomePageState();
}
```

and its state:

layout/calculator/lib/main.dart
```
class _CalculatorHomePageState extends State<CalculatorHomePage> {

}
```

How the App Will Be Structured

We will be using a separate file with a separate Calculation class to actually carry out calculations—implementing, adding, and deleting numbers and operators and computing expressions.

We will worry about that in Implement the Calculations, on page 98.

Layout

The base layout of the app will be the following:

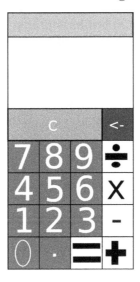

It is a simple calculator, and it can be implemented using the following Flutter layout structures:

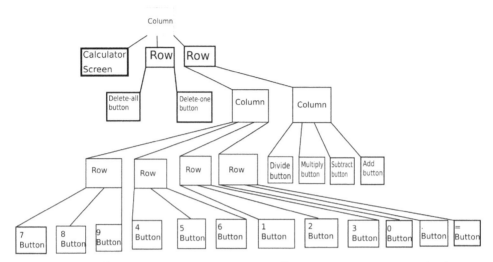

Representing Flutter apps as trees is a very effective way to visualize the layout of a Flutter app.

In this case, the app's main structure will be a Column with three children:

- The calculator's screen, which will a Card with some Text on it.

- A Row containing the button that deletes the entire expression and the button that deletes one character at a time, which will be a couple of FlatButtons.

- A Row for the rest of the calculator's buttons, which contains two Column widgets: one for the three columns containg the numbers (which is made up of four Rows of four buttons each), and one for the column containing the operator buttons.

To make the layout look and work better, we will be making expansive (no pun intended) use of the Expanded, but that will come later on in Make the App Look and Work Right with Expanded, on page 88.

Implement the Basic Layout

Inside _CalculatorHomePageState's curly braces, we'll define a build method with the usual Scaffold and AppBar:

layout/calculator_part1/lib/main.dart
```
@override
Widget build(BuildContext context) {
```

```
return Scaffold(
  appBar: AppBar(
    title: Text(widget.title),
  ),

  );
}
```

The Scaffold's body will be the following:

```
body: Column(
  crossAxisAlignment: CrossAxisAlignment.stretch,
  children: <Widget>[
    calculatorScreen,
    Row(
      crossAxisAlignment: CrossAxisAlignment.stretch,
      children: <Widget>[

      ],
    ),
    Row(
      crossAxisAlignment: CrossAxisAlignment.stretch,
      children: <Widget>[
        Column(
          crossAxisAlignment: CrossAxisAlignment.stretch,
          children: <Widget>[
            Row(
              crossAxisAlignment:  CrossAxisAlignment.stretch,
              children: <Widget>[

              ],
            ),
            Row(
              crossAxisAlignment:  CrossAxisAlignment.stretch,
              children:<Widget>[

              ],
            ),
            Row(
              crossAxisAlignment:  CrossAxisAlignment.stretch,
              children: <Widget>[

              ],
            ),
            Row(
              crossAxisAlignment:  CrossAxisAlignment.stretch,
              children: <Widget>[

              ],
            ),
          ],
        ),
```

```
    Column(
      crossAxisAlignment: CrossAxisAlignment.stretch,
      children: <Widget>[

      ],
    ),
  ],
),
],
),
```

The CrossAxisAlignment options are meant to stretch the widgets out wherever possible.

What that alone can't do will be done by Expanded (we'll talk about Expanded after we have defined the layout elements).

Let's Give the Calculator a Screen

Obviously the calculatorScreen at the top of the Column is just a placeholder; we need to replace it with a real, working screen that will be composed of the following: a wrapping and a Card and, inside it, a padded Text displaying a String, which represents the expression or result to be displayed.

But, before adding that, we need to declare that String inside the _CalculatorHome-PageState declaration, above the @override keyword preceding the build method declaration:

layout/calculator_part1/lib/main.dart
```
String _str = "0";
```

After you've done that, replace calculatorScreen (from the code on page 81) with:

layout/calculator_part1/lib/main.dart
```
Card(
  color: Colors.lightGreen[50],
  child: Padding(
    padding: EdgeInsets.all(15.0),
    child: Text(
      _str,
      textScaleFactor: 2.0,
    ),
  ),
),
```

Where Colors.lightGreen[50] is a very low intensity light green.

Color intensity (50, in this case) is specified on a scale where 500 is normal intensity (like using Colors.lightGreen) and higher numbers are higher intensity colors, usually used for accent color purposes.

Add the Deletion Row

The first Row widget is going to contain the button used to delete a single character and the button used to delete the entire expression.

All of the buttons in the app are going to call _CalculatorHomePageState methods, so we need to define them. So, directly below code on page 82, add the following empty method definitions, which we will fill up after we define the class to handle the calculations in Use the Calculation Inside the App, on page 107:

layout/calculator_part1/lib/main.dart
```
void add(String a) {
}

void deleteAll() {
}

void deleteOne() {
}

void getResult() {
}
```

Going back to app layout definition, the buttons will be FlatButtons, which you'll add to the first Row widget you can see in the code on page 81 by inserting, inside the square brackets of that Row's children attribute, the following code:

layout/calculator_part1/lib/main.dart
```
FlatButton(
  child: Text(
    'C',
    style: TextStyle(color: Colors.white),
  ),
  onPressed: (){deleteAll();},
  color: Colors.black54,
),
FlatButton(
  child: Text(
    '<-',
    style: TextStyle(color: Colors.white)
  ),
  onPressed: (){deleteOne();},
  color: Colors.black87,
),
```

Using this code will result in the button on the left (delete all) being gray and the one on the right (delete one character) being black.

That is because the number after the color name (which is used in this manner only with black and white) specifies how transparent they are; a low number means that they are very transparent and almost invisible and a high number is used to make something very opaque.

The Third Row

We have one more Row, which might sound strange until you look back at the structure of the app in the figure on page 80. That row will have two children:

- On the left, the numbers and the *dot* and *equals* buttons.
- On the right, the operator buttons.

Add the Number Buttons

The number buttons will be spread out across four rows:

- The first will contain the numbers 7, 8, and 9.
- The second will contain the numbers 4, 5, and 6.
- The third will contain the numbers 1, 2, and 3.
- The fourth will contain the number 0, the *dot*, and the button to calculate the result.

This means that, inside this Row we'll need another Column with four Rows as its children just to display the number buttons. The buttons will have white text on an intense blue background, except for the = button, which will have black text on a very light blue background. So, as the first child of the third Row of our app, we'll have the following:

layout/calculator_part1/lib/main.dart
```
Column(
  crossAxisAlignment: CrossAxisAlignment.stretch,
  children: <Widget>[
    Row(
      crossAxisAlignment:  CrossAxisAlignment.stretch,
      children: <Widget>[
        FlatButton(
          child: Text(
            '7',
            style: TextStyle(color: Colors.white),
          ),
          onPressed: () {add('7');},
          color: Colors.blueAccent,
        ),
        FlatButton(
          child: Text(
            '8',
            style: TextStyle(color: Colors.white),
          ),
          onPressed: () {add('8');},
```

```
            color: Colors.blueAccent,
          ),
        FlatButton(
          child: Text(
            '9',
            style: TextStyle(color: Colors.white),
          ),
          onPressed: () {add('9');},
          color: Colors.blueAccent,
        ),
      ],
    ),
  Row(
    crossAxisAlignment:  CrossAxisAlignment.stretch,
    children:<Widget>[
      FlatButton(
        child: Text(
          '4',
          style: TextStyle(color: Colors.white),
        ),
        onPressed: () {add('4');},
        color: Colors.blueAccent,
      ),
      FlatButton(
        child: Text(
          '5',
          style: TextStyle(color: Colors.white),
        ),
        onPressed: () {add('5');},
        color: Colors.blueAccent,
      ),
      FlatButton(
        child: Text(
          '6',
          style: TextStyle(color: Colors.white),
        ),
        onPressed: () {add('6');},
        color: Colors.blueAccent,
      ),
    ],
  ),
  Row(
    crossAxisAlignment:  CrossAxisAlignment.stretch,
    children: <Widget>[
      FlatButton(
        child: Text(
          '1',
          style: TextStyle(color: Colors.white),
        ),
        onPressed: () {add('1');},
```

```
            color: Colors.blueAccent,
          ),
          FlatButton(
            child: Text(
              '2',
              style: TextStyle(color: Colors.white),
            ),
            onPressed: () {add('2');},
            color: Colors.blueAccent,
          ),
          FlatButton(
            child: Text(
              '3',
              style: TextStyle(color: Colors.white)
            ),
            onPressed: () {add('3');},
            color: Colors.blueAccent,
          ),
        ],
      ),
      Row(
        crossAxisAlignment:  CrossAxisAlignment.stretch,
        children: <Widget>[
          FlatButton(
            child: Text(
              '0',
              style: TextStyle(color: Colors.white),
            ),
            onPressed: () {add('0');},
            color: Colors.blueAccent,
          ),
          FlatButton(
            child: Text(
              '.',
              style: TextStyle(color: Colors.white),
            ),
            onPressed: () {add('.');},
            color: Colors.blueAccent,
          ),
          FlatButton(
            child: Text('='),
            onPressed: () {
              getResult();
            },
            color: Colors.blue[50],
          ),
        ],
      ),
    ],
  ),
```

As you can see, = calls getResult() and the numbers call the add(number) method.

Add the Operators

To the right of the numbers, we'll add the operator buttons.

As an example, we'll implement the *divide* button as a FlatButton with an image from the assets on it.

To start, create a directory in the root of your project called icons.

Inside it, create or copy a file called divide.png, which will be the icon used for the divide button. You can find a divide.png icon suitable for this in the book's source code or on my website.[1]

After you've done that, edit pubspec.yaml and add the following at the bottom of it:

layout/calculator/pubspec.yaml
```
flutter:
  assets:
    - icons/
```

Now we can use that image in our code.

To use it, we need to use Image.asset as explained in Displaying Images from the Assets, on page 40.

More specifically for this example, the divide button will be implemented as follows:

layout/calculator_part1/lib/main.dart
```
FlatButton(
  child: Image.asset(
    "icons/divide.png",
    width: 10.0,
    height: 10.0,
  ),
  onPressed: () {add('÷');},
  color: Colors.blue[50],
),
```

The entire Column of operator buttons (with the other ones being normal Text-based buttons) will therefore be:

---

1. http://www.carminezacc.com/divide.png

layout/calculator_part1/lib/main.dart
```
Column(
  crossAxisAlignment: CrossAxisAlignment.stretch,
  children: <Widget>[
    FlatButton(
      child: Image.asset(
        "icons/divide.png",
        width: 10.0,
        height: 10.0,
      ),
      onPressed: () {add('÷');},
      color: Colors.blue[50],
    ),
    FlatButton(
      child: Text('x'),
      onPressed: () {add('x');},
      color: Colors.blue[50],
    ),
    FlatButton(
      child: Text('-'),
      onPressed: () {add('-');},
      color: Colors.blue[50],
    ),
    FlatButton(
      child: Text('+'),
      onPressed: () {add('+');},
      color: Colors.blue[50],
    ),
  ],
),
```

The buttons are of the same color as the = button (a very light blue).

Why a GridView Wouldn't Work

GridViews are meant for something completely different: building scrollable, probably variable grids that usually have more widgets than could be displayed comfortably in a non-scrollable grid.

What we are doing here is simply displaying a small, fixed amount of I/O widgets in both the vertical and horizontal axis, which you should do using nested Rows and Columns.

Make the App Look and Work Right with Expanded

Currently, the app wouldn't look right if you ran it on a device.

To make the buttons of the right shape and size, we need to wrap Rows, Columns, and the buttons themselves in Expanded.

Expand Elements to Divide the Space Inside the Main Column

We'll expand some elements to make them exactly as big as we want them to be.

In this case, the main Column will be divided in the following way:

- 2/7 of the space will be taken up by the calculator screen.
- 1/7 of the space will be taken up by the deletion row.
- The remaining 4/7 of the space (four times as much as the deletion row) will be taken up by the numbers and operators, so that every button (including the delete buttons) is of the same height.

As was explained in Fill the Space Available in the View Using Expanded, on page 71, the Expanded widget makes this really simple, requiring you to replace the calculator screen shown in the code on page 82 with this:

```
layout/calculator_part2/lib/main.dart
Expanded(
  flex: 2,
  child: Card(
    color: Colors.lightGreen[50],
    child: Padding(
      padding: EdgeInsets.all(15.0),
      child: Text(
        _str,
        textScaleFactor: 2.0,
      ),
    ),
  ),
),
```

Similarly, the first Row widget (the one containing the delete buttons, shown in the code on page 83) will have to be replaced with:

```
Expanded(
  flex: 1,
  child: Row(
    ...
  )
)
```

and the one containing the number buttons (shown in the code on page 84) will similarly have to be replaced with:

```
Expanded(
  flex: 4,
  child: Row(
    ...
  )
)
```

Expand Elements to Divide the Space Inside the Deletion Row

Three quarters of the space will be taken up by the *delete all* button and one quarter by the *delete one* button.

This means that those two FlatButtons will have to be expanded by replacing them with FlatButtons wrapped in two Expanded widgets with flex values of, respectively, 3 and 1:

```
layout/calculator_part2/lib/main.dart
Expanded(
  flex: 3,
  child: FlatButton(
    child: Text(
      'C',
      style: TextStyle(color: Colors.white),
    ),
    onPressed: (){deleteAll();},
    color: Colors.black54,
  ),
),
Expanded(
  flex: 1,
  child: FlatButton(
    child: Text(
      '<-',
      style: TextStyle(color: Colors.white)
    ),
    onPressed: (){deleteOne();},
    color: Colors.black87,
  ),
),
```

Expand Elements to Divide the Space Inside the Number and Operator Grid

Similarly, you will need to expand the numbers' Column with a flex of 3 and the operators' Column with a flex of 1 to make the buttons all of the same size.

Create ExpandedRow and ExpandedButton for the Rest of the Buttons

The number and operator buttons should all be of the same size, so they should all be wrapped in Expanded widgets with the same flex which, for simplicity, we'll set to the value 1.

The same is true for the Rows of number buttons: they all need to be expanded with the same flex.

To avoid repetition and to speed up replacement of many widgets, we'll build expanded FlatButton and Row classes, which will be called ExpandedButton and ExpandedRow.

They need to take all of the arguments and options we currently use, and build the corresponding widgets wrapped in Expanded.

They are defined, very simply, above main(), in the following way:

layout/calculator_part2/lib/main.dart

```
class ExpandedButton extends StatelessWidget {

  ExpandedButton({this.onPressed, this.child, this.color});

  final Widget child;
  final VoidCallback onPressed;
  final Color color;

  @override
  Widget build(BuildContext context) =>
    Expanded(
      flex:1,
      child: FlatButton(
        onPressed: onPressed,
        child: child,
        color: color,
      ),
    );
}

class ExpandedRow extends StatelessWidget {

  ExpandedRow({this.children, this.crossAxisAlignment});

  final List<Widget> children;
  final CrossAxisAlignment crossAxisAlignment;

  @override
  Widget build(BuildContext context) =>
    Expanded(
      flex:1,
      child: Row(
        children: children,
        crossAxisAlignment: crossAxisAlignment,
      ),
    );
}
```

After defining them, simply replace all of the operator button's Row widgets with ExpandedRow widgets and all of the operator and number FlatButtons and the calculator's layout should be complete.

The Finished Layout

If you have done everything correctly, you probably have ended up with the following code in main.dart:

layout/calculator_part2/lib/main.dart

```dart
import "package:flutter/material.dart";

class ExpandedButton extends StatelessWidget {

  ExpandedButton({this.onPressed, this.child, this.color});

  final Widget child;
  final VoidCallback onPressed;
  final Color color;

  @override
  Widget build(BuildContext context) =>
    Expanded(
      flex:1,
      child: FlatButton(
        onPressed: onPressed,
        child: child,
        color: color,
      ),
    );
}

class ExpandedRow extends StatelessWidget {

  ExpandedRow({this.children, this.crossAxisAlignment});

  final List<Widget> children;
  final CrossAxisAlignment crossAxisAlignment;

  @override
  Widget build(BuildContext context) =>
    Expanded(
      flex:1,
      child: Row(
        children: children,
        crossAxisAlignment: crossAxisAlignment,
      ),
    );
}

void main() => runApp(new MyApp());

class MyApp extends StatelessWidget {
  @override
  Widget build(BuildContext context) {
    return MaterialApp(
      title: "Flutter Calculator",
      theme: ThemeData(
```

```
          primarySwatch: Colors.blue,
          backgroundColor: Colors.black26
        ),
        home: CalculatorHomePage(title: "Flutter Calculator", ),
      );
    }
  }

  class CalculatorHomePage extends StatefulWidget {
    CalculatorHomePage({Key key, this.title}) : super(key: key);
    final String title;

    @override
    _CalculatorHomePageState createState() => _CalculatorHomePageState();
  }

  class _CalculatorHomePageState extends State<CalculatorHomePage> {
    String _str = "0";

    void add(String a) {
    }

    void deleteAll() {
    }

    void deleteOne() {
    }

    void getResult() {
    }

    @override
    Widget build(BuildContext context) {
      return Center(child: Scaffold(
        appBar: AppBar(
          title: Text(widget.title),
        ),
        body: Column(
          crossAxisAlignment: CrossAxisAlignment.stretch,
        // mainAxisAlignment: MainAxisAlignment.spaceAround,
        // mainAxisSize: MainAxisSize.max,
          children: <Widget>[
            Expanded(
              flex: 2,
              child: Card(
                color: Colors.lightGreen[50],
                child: Padding(
                  padding: EdgeInsets.all(15.0),
                  child: Text(
                    _str,
                    textScaleFactor: 2.0,
                  ),
                ),
              ),
```

```
          ),
        ),
      Expanded(
        flex: 1,
        child: Row(
          crossAxisAlignment: CrossAxisAlignment.stretch,
          children: <Widget>[
            Expanded(
              flex: 3,
              child: FlatButton(
                child: Text(
                  'C',
                  style: TextStyle(color: Colors.white),
                ),
                onPressed: (){deleteAll();},
                color: Colors.black54,
              ),
            ),
            Expanded(
              flex: 1,
              child: FlatButton(
                child: Text(
                  '<-',
                  style: TextStyle(color: Colors.white)
                ),
                onPressed: (){deleteOne();},
                color: Colors.black87,
              ),
            ),
          ],
        ),
      ),
      Expanded(
        flex: 4,
        child: Row(
          crossAxisAlignment: CrossAxisAlignment.stretch,
          children: <Widget>[
            Expanded(
              flex: 3,
              child: Column(
                crossAxisAlignment: CrossAxisAlignment.stretch,
                children: <Widget>[
                  ExpandedRow(
                    crossAxisAlignment:  CrossAxisAlignment.stretch,
                    children: <Widget>[
                      ExpandedButton(
                        child: Text(
                          '7',
                          style: TextStyle(color: Colors.white),
                        ),
```

```
        onPressed: () {add('7');},
        color: Colors.blueAccent,
      ),
      ExpandedButton(
        child: Text(
          '8',
          style: TextStyle(color: Colors.white),
        ),
        onPressed: () {add('8');},
        color: Colors.blueAccent,
      ),
      ExpandedButton(
        child: Text(
          '9',
          style: TextStyle(color: Colors.white),
        ),
        onPressed: () {add('9');},
        color: Colors.blueAccent,
      ),
    ],
  ),
  ExpandedRow(
    crossAxisAlignment:  CrossAxisAlignment.stretch,
    children:<Widget>[
      ExpandedButton(
        child: Text(
          '4',
          style: TextStyle(color: Colors.white),
        ),
        onPressed: () {add('4');},
        color: Colors.blueAccent,
      ),
      ExpandedButton(
        child: Text(
          '5',
          style: TextStyle(color: Colors.white),
        ),
        onPressed: () {add('5');},
        color: Colors.blueAccent,
      ),
      ExpandedButton(
        child: Text(
          '6',
          style: TextStyle(color: Colors.white),
        ),
        onPressed: () {add('6');},
        color: Colors.blueAccent,
      ),
    ],
  ),
```

```
ExpandedRow(
  crossAxisAlignment:  CrossAxisAlignment.stretch,
  children: <Widget>[
    ExpandedButton(
      child: Text(
        '1',
        style: TextStyle(color: Colors.white),
      ),
      onPressed: () {add('1');},
      color: Colors.blueAccent,
    ),
    ExpandedButton(
      child: Text(
        '2',
        style: TextStyle(color: Colors.white),
      ),
      onPressed: () {add('2');},
      color: Colors.blueAccent,
    ),
    ExpandedButton(
      child: Text(
        '3',
        style: TextStyle(color: Colors.white)
      ),
      onPressed: () {add('3');},
      color: Colors.blueAccent,
    ),
  ],
),
ExpandedRow(
  crossAxisAlignment:  CrossAxisAlignment.stretch,
  children: <Widget>[
    ExpandedButton(
      child: Text(
        '0',
        style: TextStyle(color: Colors.white),
      ),
      onPressed: () {add('0');},
      color: Colors.blueAccent,
    ),
    ExpandedButton(
      child: Text(
        '.',
        style: TextStyle(color: Colors.white),
      ),
      onPressed: () {add('.');},
      color: Colors.blueAccent,
    ),
    ExpandedButton(child: Text('=',), onPressed: () {
      getResult();
```

```
              },
              color: Colors.blue[50]),
          ],
        ),
      ],
    ),
  ),
Expanded(
  flex: 1,
  child: Column(
    crossAxisAlignment: CrossAxisAlignment.stretch,
    children: <Widget>[
      ExpandedButton(
        child: Image.asset(
          "icons/divide.png",
          width: 10.0,
          height: 10.0,
        ),
        onPressed: () {add('÷');},
        color: Colors.blue[50],
      ),
      ExpandedButton(
        child: Text('x'),
        onPressed: () {add('x');},
        color: Colors.blue[50],
      ),
      ExpandedButton(
        child: Text('-'),
        onPressed: () {add('-');},
        color: Colors.blue[50],
      ),
      ExpandedButton(
        child: Text('+'),
        onPressed: () {add('+');},
        color: Colors.blue[50],
      ),
    ],
  ),
),
              ],
            ),
          ),
        ],
      ),
    ));
  }
}
```

Running the app produces the following visual result:

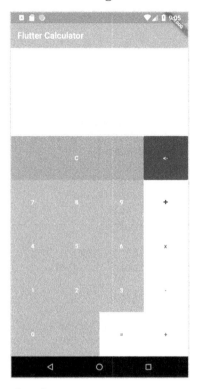

Implement the Calculations

Now it's time to make this really nice-looking calculator work. The way our calculator logic is going to work is not how expressions are usually parsed, but this way will show you how to parse and manipulate strings in Dart, and it will also show you how to do that using regular expressions. It's not the simplest solution and it's surely not the one with the lowest computational complexity, but it's a good example and it is supposed to make you more confident when writing Dart code that operates on strings.

The Calculation class needs to handle a few basic operations:

1. Add a digit or operator.

2. Display the current string containing all of the digits and operators that have been added.

3. Compute the result of the current expression.

4. Delete a digit or operator.

5. Delete the entire expression.

Being able to display the current string can also be used for debugging insertion and deletion as it displays the current state of the calculation.

The Calculation class needs to be able to take inputs one character at a time and to compute the result of an expression considering mathematical operator precedence rules.

To do that, we will implement the class in the following way: we will have a List of Strings, each of which will be either an operator or a number to make parsing and computing results simpler.

We will start implementing it by creating a file called calculator.dart inside the lib directory.

At this point we can start defining our Calculation and that data it needs inside calculator.dart:

```
layout/calculator/lib/calculator.dart
class Calculation {
  List<String> a = [];

}
```

The first behavior we'll define is adding a character to the current calculation.

We will implement a method called add(), which will take as an argument a String to be added to the calculation, after checking whether we add a new element to the List or not.

If the String we want to add is a digit and the previous String in the List is a number (it doesn't contain an operator), we will append it to the last String in the List, otherwise it will have to be added as a new element in the List.

Also, if the List is still empty, we will have to create a new element, unless the character we're trying to add is an operator, in which case we won't do anything at all because the expression wouldn't make sense with an operator as the first element.

To check whether a String contains operators we will use a regular expression to shorten the creation of complex conditions and avoid repeating them.

How to Use Regular Expressions in Dart

Regular expressions in Dart are achieved using the RegExp class.

Its constructor is used in the following way:

```
RegExp regExp = RegExp("REGULAREXPRESSION");
```

In our case, the regular expression to check if a string contains an operator is:

layout/calculator/lib/calculator.dart
```
final RegExp regExp = RegExp("[+\|-x÷]");
```

and we can check that a string (called string) matches that regular expression by using:

```
bool matches = regExp.hasMatch(string)
```

In the case of the regular expression we saw earlier, it will be true if the string contains an operator character, and false if it doesn't.

Implement add()

The first thing we will check is whether the List is empty and only adding the character if it's not an operator:

```
void add(String added) {
```

layout/calculator/lib/calculator.dart
```
if(a.isEmpty) {
  if(!regExp.hasMatch(added)) {
    a.add(added);
  }
}

}
```

If it's not empty, we need to check whether the previous element was an operator.

In that case, we need to do the same thing we did for the first element—we can't add another operator or a dot, but we can add a digit and it has to go into a separate List element:

layout/calculator/lib/calculator.dart
```
else if(regExp.hasMatch(a.last)) {
  if(!RegExp("[+\|-x÷.]").hasMatch(added)) {
    a.add(added);
  }
}
```

If the previous conditions haven't been met (and that means the previous element was a number) we can add anything, but we need to differentiate betweem operators and digits:

- An operator will have to go into its own separate List element;
- A digit will have to be appended to the current last List element.

That can be implemented very simply:

```
layout/calculator/lib/calculator.dart
else {
  if(regExp.hasMatch(added)) {
    if(!RegExp(".").hasMatch(a.last)) a.last+=".0";
    a.add(added);
  } else {
    a.last+=added;
  }
}
```

So the entire add() method, combining all of the possible conditions, is:

```
layout/calculator/lib/calculator.dart
void add(String added) {
  if(a.isEmpty) {
    if(!regExp.hasMatch(added)) {
      a.add(added);
    }
  }
  else if(regExp.hasMatch(a.last)) {
    if(!RegExp("[+\|-x÷.]").hasMatch(added)) {
      a.add(added);
    }
  }
  else {
    if(regExp.hasMatch(added)) {
      if(!RegExp(".").hasMatch(a.last)) a.last+=".0";
      a.add(added);
    } else {
      a.last+=added;
    }
  }
}
```

Implement getString()

This is going to be the simplest method—it's just going to display the concatenation of the strings in the List:

```
layout/calculator/lib/calculator.dart
String getString() {
  String str = "";
  a.forEach((String el) {str+=el;});
  return str;
}
```

Implement Deletion

To delete everything we just need to reset the List to its initial state:

```
layout/calculator/lib/calculator.dart
void deleteAll() => a = [];
```

But deleting one character at a time is more complicated, as we'll need to check multiple things:

1. Check if the List is empty, in that case we'll do nothing.

2. Check if the last element of the List is longer than one character, in that case we'll delete the last character of that string.

3. If the last element is just one character, we'll delete it completely.

Number 2 is a bit complicated: to delete the last character we actually need to assign to the last element a substring of itself with the last character deleted.

To create substrings, we are going to use the String.substring() method, which is used in the following way:

```
var substr = string.substring(startIndex, length);
```

where startIndex is an integer representing the index at which the substring starts (relative to the string from which the substring is created) and length is the length of the substring.

In this case, we need it to start from 0 and to have a length that is equal to the length of the original string with 1 subtracted to it.

Combining all of that, the code for the deleteOne method is as follows:

layout/calculator/lib/calculator.dart
```
void deleteOne() {
  if(a.length > 0) {
    if(a.last.length > 1) {
      a.last = a.last.substring(0, a.last.length-1);
    } else {
      a.removeLast();
    }
  }
}
```

Implement Result Calculation

At this point, all that's left to do is to calculate the result of the expression.

Before calculating the result, we'll need to consider the case in which a user accidentally ends the expression with an operator (starting it with an operator is prevented by add()).

We also need to check whether the string ends with a ., and that will require us to check whether a dot is left, a condition for which would be the following:

```
a.last.lastIndexOf(".") == a.last.length-1
```

If that condition is true, we need to take the substring with the last character removed.

Since it might end with both an operator and a dot, we need to check twice separately:

```
layout/calculator/lib/calculator.dart
if( regExp.hasMatch(a.last) )
  a.removeLast();
if(a.last.lastIndexOf(".") == a.last.length-1)
  a.last = a.last.substring(0, a.length-1);
```

Now we need to parse the calculation and compute its result.

The divisions we did in the rest of the methods are really useful: we just need to check each element in the String and, if it is an operator, we'll substitute the block composed by it and the adjacent elements with the result of the operation.

We will be implementing this using simple counter-based for loops because we need total control over which elements we're parsing.

Because of that, after we compute the result of each sub-calculation, we will decrease the counter by 1 so that the next iteration of the for loop will actually be the operator after the newly calculated result, as the following illustration shows:

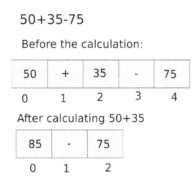

As this example shows, the newly calculated number takes the place that was occupied by the number to the left of the operator and the next operator takes the place of the operator we just considered.

Since the counter is currently at the index of the operator, we will have to decrement the loop's counter so that, when it is incremented again in the next iteration, it is the same value it was in the previous iteration.

Because of mathematical operator precedence rules, we will first check if the List contains multiplications or divisions:

```
layout/calculator/lib/calculator.dart
for(int i = 0; i < a.length; i++) {
  if(a[i] == "x") {
    a[i-1] = "${double.parse(a[i-1]) * double.parse(a[i+1])}";
    a.removeAt(i);
    a.removeAt(i);
    i--;
  } else if(a[i] == "÷") {
    a[i-1] = "${double.parse(a[i-1]) / double.parse(a[i+1])}";
    a.removeAt(i);
    a.removeAt(i);
    i--;
  }
}
```

and then check for additions or subtractions:

```
layout/calculator/lib/calculator.dart
for(int i = 0; i < a.length; i++) {
  if(a[i] == "+") {
    a[i-1] = "${double.parse(a[i-1]) + double.parse(a[i+1])}";
    a.removeAt(i);
    a.removeAt(i);
    i--;
  } else if(a[i] == "-") {
    a[i-1] = "${double.parse(a[i-1]) - double.parse(a[i+1])}";
    a.removeAt(i);
    a.removeAt(i);
    i--;
  }
}
```

At the end, the List should contain just one String containing the result of the whole expression.

We'll return that using:

```
layout/calculator/lib/calculator.dart
return double.parse(a[0]);
```

The getResult method, combining all of these pieces, is:

```
layout/calculator/lib/calculator.dart
double getResult() {
  if( regExp.hasMatch(a.last) )
    a.removeLast();
  if(a.last.lastIndexOf(".") == a.last.length-1)
    a.last = a.last.substring(0, a.length-1);

  for(int i = 0; i < a.length; i++) {
    if(a[i] == "x") {
      a[i-1] = "${double.parse(a[i-1]) * double.parse(a[i+1])}";
```

```
        a.removeAt(i);
        a.removeAt(i);
        i--;
      } else if(a[i] == "÷") {
        a[i-1] = "${double.parse(a[i-1]) / double.parse(a[i+1])}";
        a.removeAt(i);
        a.removeAt(i);
        i--;
      }
    }

    for(int i = 0; i < a.length; i++) {
      if(a[i] == "+") {
        a[i-1] = "${double.parse(a[i-1]) + double.parse(a[i+1])}";
        a.removeAt(i);
        a.removeAt(i);
        i--;
      } else if(a[i] == "-") {
        a[i-1] = "${double.parse(a[i-1]) - double.parse(a[i+1])}";
        a.removeAt(i);
        a.removeAt(i);
        i--;
      }
    }

    if(a.length != 1) throw Error();

    return double.parse(a[0]);
}
```

Wrapping Up the Calculation

The entire calculator.dart should be, at this point, the following:

layout/calculator/lib/calculator.dart
```
class Calculation {
  List<String> a = [];
  final RegExp regExp = RegExp("[+\\-x÷]");

  void add(String added) {
    if(a.isEmpty) {
      if(!regExp.hasMatch(added)) {
        a.add(added);
      }
    }
    else if(regExp.hasMatch(a.last)) {
      if(!RegExp("[+\\-x÷.]").hasMatch(added)) {
        a.add(added);
      }
    }
    else {
      if(regExp.hasMatch(added)) {
```

```
      if(!RegExp(".").hasMatch(a.last)) a.last+=".0";
      a.add(added);
    } else {
      a.last+=added;
    }
  }
}

String getString() {
  String str = "";
  a.forEach((String el) {str+=el;});
  return str;
}

double getResult() {
  if( regExp.hasMatch(a.last) )
    a.removeLast();
  if(a.last.lastIndexOf(".") == a.last.length-1)
    a.last = a.last.substring(0, a.length-1);

  for(int i = 0; i < a.length; i++) {
    if(a[i] == "x") {
      a[i-1] = "${double.parse(a[i-1]) * double.parse(a[i+1])}";
      a.removeAt(i);
      a.removeAt(i);
      i--;
    } else if(a[i] == "÷") {
      a[i-1] = "${double.parse(a[i-1]) / double.parse(a[i+1])}";
      a.removeAt(i);
      a.removeAt(i);
      i--;
    }
  }

  for(int i = 0; i < a.length; i++) {
    if(a[i] == "+") {
      a[i-1] = "${double.parse(a[i-1]) + double.parse(a[i+1])}";
      a.removeAt(i);
      a.removeAt(i);
      i--;
    } else if(a[i] == "-") {
      a[i-1] = "${double.parse(a[i-1]) - double.parse(a[i+1])}";
      a.removeAt(i);
      a.removeAt(i);
      i--;
    }
  }

  if(a.length != 1) throw Error();

  return double.parse(a[0]);
}
```

```
  void deleteOne() {
    if(a.length > 0) {
      if(a.last.length > 1) {
        a.last = a.last.substring(0, a.last.length-1);
      } else {
        a.removeLast();
      }
    }
  }

  void deleteAll() => a = [];
}
```

> ## Make Your Own Changes
>
> We have seen quite a lot of Dart code so far, but have you also been writing your own? If you haven't, here is a chance for you to make a very simple and slight improvement to our calculator app.
>
> The Calculation properly handles operator precedence, but it doesn't support parentheses. That's something you should be able to add on your own at this point by using additional regular expressions to find opening and closing parentheses and then evaluate expressions within the parentheses first.

Use the Calculation Inside the App

Import the Calculation into the main source code by adding, at the top of main.dart, the following:

```
import "calculator.dart";
```

You need to define a Calculation object for the _CalculatorHomePageState so, below:

layout/calculator/lib/main.dart
```
String _str = "0";
```

You need to add:

layout/calculator/lib/main.dart
```
var _calculation = Calculation();
```

You will also need to properly implement the _CalculatorHomePageState's add(), deleteOne(), and deleteAll() methods, which will have to be calls to setState() and the Calculation methods, like this:

layout/calculator/lib/main.dart
```dart
void add(String a) {
  setState((){
    _calculation.add(a);
    _str = _calculation.getString();
  });
}

void deleteAll() {
  setState(() {
    _calculation.deleteAll();
    _str = _calculation.getString();
  });
}

void deleteOne() {
  setState(() {
    _calculation.deleteOne();
    _str = _calculation.getString();
  });
}

void getResult() {
  setState(() {
    _str = _calculation.getResult().toString();
  });
  _calculation = new Calculation();
}
```

Wrapping Up the Calculator

If you followed everything and correctly put together all of the pieces of code related to the calculator, main.dart should be the following:

layout/calculator/lib/main.dart
```dart
import "package:flutter/material.dart";
import "calculator.dart";

class ExpandedButton extends StatelessWidget {

  ExpandedButton({this.onPressed, this.child, this.color, Key key}) :
    super(key: key);

  final Widget child;
  final VoidCallback onPressed;
  final Color color;

  @override
  Widget build(BuildContext context) =>
    Expanded(
      flex:1,
      child: FlatButton(
        onPressed: onPressed,
        child: child,
```

```dart
      color: color,
    ),
  );
}

class ExpandedRow extends StatelessWidget {

  ExpandedRow({this.children, this.crossAxisAlignment});

  final List<Widget> children;
  final CrossAxisAlignment crossAxisAlignment;

  @override
  Widget build(BuildContext context) =>
    Expanded(
      flex: 1,
      child: Row(
        children: children,
        crossAxisAlignment: crossAxisAlignment,
      ),
    );
}

void main() => runApp(MyApp());

class MyApp extends StatelessWidget {
  @override
  Widget build(BuildContext context) {
    return MaterialApp(
      title: "Flutter Calculator",
      theme: ThemeData(
        primarySwatch: Colors.blue,
        backgroundColor: Colors.black26
      ),
      home: CalculatorHomePage(title: "Flutter Calculator", ),
    );
  }
}

class CalculatorHomePage extends StatefulWidget {
  CalculatorHomePage({Key key, this.title}) : super(key: key);
  final String title;

  @override
  _CalculatorHomePageState createState() => _CalculatorHomePageState();
}

class _CalculatorHomePageState extends State<CalculatorHomePage> {

  String _str = "0";
  var _calculation = Calculation();

  void add(String a) {
    setState((){
      _calculation.add(a);
```

```
      _str = _calculation.getString();
    });
  }

  void deleteAll() {
    setState(() {
      _calculation.deleteAll();
      _str = _calculation.getString();
    });
  }

  void deleteOne() {
    setState(() {
      _calculation.deleteOne();
      _str = _calculation.getString();
    });
  }

  void getResult() {
    setState(() {
      _str = _calculation.getResult().toString();
    });
    _calculation = new Calculation();
  }

  @override
  Widget build(BuildContext context) {
    return Center(child: Scaffold(
      appBar: AppBar(
        title: Text(widget.title),
      ),
      body: Column(
        crossAxisAlignment: CrossAxisAlignment.stretch,
       // mainAxisAlignment: MainAxisAlignment.spaceAround,
       // mainAxisSize: MainAxisSize.max,
        children: <Widget>[
          Expanded(
            flex: 2,
            child: Card(
              color: Colors.lightGreen[50],
              child: Padding(
                padding: EdgeInsets.all(15.0),
                child: Text(
                  _str,
                  textScaleFactor: 2.0,
                ),
              ),
            ),
          ),
          Expanded(
            flex: 1,
            child: Row(
```

```
    crossAxisAlignment: CrossAxisAlignment.stretch,
    children: <Widget>[
      Expanded(
        flex: 3,
        child: FlatButton(
          child: Text(
            'C',
            style: TextStyle(color: Colors.white),
          ),
          onPressed: (){deleteAll();},
          color: Colors.black54,
        ),
      ),
      Expanded(
        flex: 1,
        child: FlatButton(
          child: Text(
            '<-',
            style: TextStyle(color: Colors.white)
          ),
          onPressed: (){deleteOne();},
          color: Colors.black87,
        ),
      ),
    ],
  ),
),
Expanded(
  flex: 4,
  child: Row(
    crossAxisAlignment: CrossAxisAlignment.stretch,
    children: <Widget>[
      Expanded(
        flex: 3,
        child: Column(
          crossAxisAlignment: CrossAxisAlignment.stretch,
          children: <Widget>[
            ExpandedRow(
              crossAxisAlignment:  CrossAxisAlignment.stretch,
              children: <Widget>[
                ExpandedButton(
                  child: Text(
                    '7',
                    style: TextStyle(color: Colors.white),
                  ),
                  onPressed: () {add('7');},
                  color: Colors.blueAccent,
                ),
                ExpandedButton(
                  child: Text(
```

```
            '8',
              style: TextStyle(color: Colors.white),
            ),
            onPressed: () {add('8');},
            color: Colors.blueAccent,
          ),
          ExpandedButton(
            child: Text(
              '9',
              style: TextStyle(color: Colors.white),
            ),
            onPressed: () {add('9');},
            color: Colors.blueAccent,
          ),
        ],
      ),
      ExpandedRow(
        crossAxisAlignment:  CrossAxisAlignment.stretch,
        children:<Widget>[
          ExpandedButton(
            child: Text(
              '4',
              style: TextStyle(color: Colors.white),
            ),
            onPressed: () {add('4');},
            color: Colors.blueAccent,
          ),
          ExpandedButton(
            child: Text(
              '5',
              style: TextStyle(color: Colors.white),
            ),
            onPressed: () {add('5');},
            color: Colors.blueAccent,
          ),
          ExpandedButton(
            child: Text(
              '6',
              style: TextStyle(color: Colors.white),
            ),
            onPressed: () {add('6');},
            color: Colors.blueAccent,
          ),
        ],
      ),
      ExpandedRow(
        crossAxisAlignment:  CrossAxisAlignment.stretch,
        children: <Widget>[
```

```
    ExpandedButton(
      child: Text(
        '1',
        style: TextStyle(color: Colors.white),
      ),
      onPressed: () {add('1');},
      color: Colors.blueAccent,
    ),
    ExpandedButton(
      child: Text(
        '2',
        style: TextStyle(color: Colors.white),
      ),
      onPressed: () {add('2');},
      color: Colors.blueAccent,
    ),
    ExpandedButton(
      child: Text(
        '3',
        style: TextStyle(color: Colors.white)
      ),
      onPressed: () {add('3');},
      color: Colors.blueAccent,
    ),
  ],
),
ExpandedRow(
  crossAxisAlignment:  CrossAxisAlignment.stretch,
  children: <Widget>[
    ExpandedButton(
      child: Text(
        '0',
        style: TextStyle(color: Colors.white),
      ),
      onPressed: () {add('0');},
      color: Colors.blueAccent,
    ),
    ExpandedButton(
      child: Text(
        '.',
        style: TextStyle(color: Colors.white),
      ),
      onPressed: () {add('.');},
      color: Colors.blueAccent,
    ),
    ExpandedButton(child: Text('=',), onPressed: () {
      getResult();
    },
```

```
                                color: Colors.blue[50])),
                      ],
                    ),
                  ],
                ),
              ),
            Expanded(
              flex: 1,
              child: Column(
                crossAxisAlignment: CrossAxisAlignment.stretch,
                children: <Widget>[
                  ExpandedButton(
                    child: Image.asset(
                      "icons/divide.png",
                      width: 10.0,
                      height: 10.0,
                    ),
                    onPressed: () {add('÷');},
                    color: Colors.blue[50],
                    key: Key("divide button")
                  ),
                  ExpandedButton(
                    child: Text('x'),
                    onPressed: () {add('x');},
                    color: Colors.blue[50],
                  ),
                  ExpandedButton(
                    child: Text('-'),
                    onPressed: () {add('-');},
                    color: Colors.blue[50],
                  ),
                  ExpandedButton(
                    child: Text('+'),
                    onPressed: () {add('+');},
                    color: Colors.blue[50],
                  ),
                ],
              ),
            ),
          ),
        ],
      ),
    ),
  ));
  }
}
```

and produce this working calculator as shown in the screenshots on page 115.

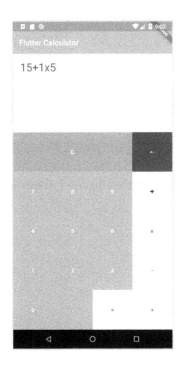 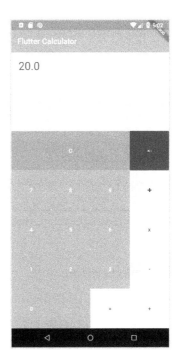

What If We Try to Divide by 0?

We worried about the expression being malformed (syntax errors), but we didn't worry about mathematical errors.

When writing a calculator in most programming languages (especially if using integer arithmetic, which isn't our case), making an app like ours (that doesn't compute square root or trigonometric functions) leaves us exposed to one thing that could make it crash: dividing by 0.

Dart, when using floating-point arithmetic like in our case, is smart enough to display the word *Infinity* instead of a result; this is nice because it doesn't cause the app to crash, but some could argue that it isn't really the correct answer in most cases: as the divisor approaches 0 the quotient approaches infinity, but division by zero in itself is impossible, so you might choose to display an error if you were making a calculator and were so inclined.

If that is the case, you would need to add a condition to each calculation in Calculation.getResult() to check whether there is an attempt at division by 0, throw an exception and catch it in the calling method.

> ## Throwing and Catching Exceptions
>
> This section can be considered an anticipation of Throwing and Catching Exceptions, on page 233, we are not going to cover the topic in detail and if you are not used to this kind of programming language feature, you should consider reading that first, and then reading this section.

Define the Exception

An exception in Dart is defined as a subclass of Exception, in the following way:

layout/calculator_error_if_divideby0/lib/calculator.dart
```
class DivideByZeroException implements Exception {

}
```

Throw the Exception

That exception can be thrown by using:

```
throw DivideByZeroException();
```

In this specific case, inside the definition of Calculation.getResult() in calculator.dart, at the point where we handle divisions (where you find else if(a[i] == "÷") {), we'll add:

layout/calculator_error_if_divideby0/lib/calculator.dart
```
if(double.parse(a[i+1]) == 0)
  throw DivideByZeroException();
```

so the part of getResult() that handles divisions and multiplications becomes:

layout/calculator_error_if_divideby0/lib/calculator.dart
```
for(int i = 0; i < a.length; i++) {
  if(a[i] == "x") {
    a[i-1] = "${double.parse(a[i-1]) * double.parse(a[i+1])}";
    a.removeAt(i);
    a.removeAt(i);
    i--;
  } else if(a[i] == "÷") {
    if(double.parse(a[i+1]) == 0)
      throw DivideByZeroException();
    a[i-1] = "${double.parse(a[i-1]) / double.parse(a[i+1])}";
    a.removeAt(i);
    a.removeAt(i);
    i--;
  }
}
```

Catch the Exception

Exceptions in Dart are caught using:

```
try {
  code_that_might_generate_exceptions();
} catch(exception) {
  print("$exception");
}
```

This code catches any kind of exception; if you wanted to catch only certain types of exceptions you would use:

```
try {
  code_that_might_generate_exceptions();
} on ExceptionClass catch(exception) {
  print("$exception");
}
```

And if you don't need to use the value of the exception you would leave out the catch(exception) part:

```
try {
  code_that_might_generate_exceptions();
} on ExceptionClass {
  print("you did something bad");
}
```

In the specific case, the code that might generate exceptions is the _str = _calculation.getResult().toString() function call and assignment and we want to set _str to something like *You mustn't divide by 0*.

The getResult() method will therefore become:

```
layout/calculator_error_if_divideby0/lib/main.dart
void getResult() {
  setState(() {
    try {
      _str = _calculation.getResult().toString();
    }
    on DivideByZeroException {
      _str = "You mustn't divide by 0";
    } finally {
      _calculation = new Calculation();
    }
  });
}
```

Adding a finally clause to reset the calculation regardless of whether or not the exception was thrown.

Where We're Going Next

In the next chapter we'll learn how to do things that go beyond the Flutter standard library using packages and plugins and how to make your own library and publish it on Dart Pub.

CHAPTER 4

Beyond the Standard Library: Plugins and Packages

Up until now we've seen how to build apps using just Flutter's standard library, but now we'll discover that we can go beyond it, and do things that we would have had a hard time doing before, or that we couldn't even do at all: let's talk about Flutter packages.

An Introduction to Packages

Like many languages, Dart allows developers to share modular code, which can be used by other developers to easily get commonly needed functionality that would otherwise require a complicated solution.

There are many generic Dart packages we can use to achieve functionality that is useful to both web applications and Flutter mobile apps, but there are also Flutter-specific packages, which use Flutter-specific features and only work with Flutter apps.

Generally, packages are written in Dart and are very similar to other languages' packages and libraries, but can communicate with device-specific Android/iOS code, which would make them *plugin packages*.

Finding Packages: Using Dart Pub

You can find packages by going to the *Dart Pub* homepage[1] and searching in the "Flutter" and "All" categories.

---

1. https://pub.dartlang.org/flutter

In the home page you will find the most commonly used packages, many of which are made by Google developers. Clicking on a package allows you to find usage information, how to install the package and a changelog.

Installing Packages

Once you've found a package you think you might want, you need to install it.

Dart packages get installed when they are specified as a dependency of an app, and you can do this by editing the pubspec.yaml file.

The Simple Way

Installing a package is very easy: you just need to edit the *dependencies* section of the pubspec.yaml file and add the string from the *Installing* section of the package in Pub. The strings you find there look like this:

```
packagename: ^version
```

And need to be added in pubspec.yaml, indented on the same level as the flutter: line, after the lines that look like the following:

```
dependencies:
  flutter:
    sdk: flutter
```

The IDE plugins download the packages automatically when you edit the file, but you can make Flutter download or update the dependencies by running the following command:

```
$ flutter packages get
```

All that's left to do is to import the package in your Dart file by adding, at the top of the file, the following line:

```
import 'package:packagename/filename.dart';
```

The file name is the same as the package name in most cases, but it's better to check on Pub, since it's usually specified in the *README.md*, *Example*, or *Installing* sections. If you're using the official IDE plugins the correct file name will also be suggested by the IDE.

import also has more features, which are explained in Mastering import, on page 312.

That's all you need to know if the package developers are using semantic versioning correctly and you just want to get all of the updates for the package that won't break your code, but there are cases in which simply copying and pasting from Pub to the dependencies isn't ideal or doesn't work at all.

Specifying the Package Version Manually

Understanding how to specify dependencies manually could be useful, for example, when you want to update to the next version, even if you need to change your code.

It could also be useful when you want a specific package version or always the latest package version, like would happen when you are the package developer.

Caret Syntax

The line we saw before declares that the project is dependent on the latest version of the package from Pub that is declared to be compatible with the version specified. For example, ^0.1.0 means any version in the 0.1 group, and ^1.2.3 means any version greater than or equal to 1.2.3 and less than 2.0.0. This is the most common way to specify the package version, and it is called *caret syntax*.

Other Ways to Specify the Package Version

The package versions can also be specified using mathematical comparison operators (for example, >=0.5.9 will use any version starting from 0.5.9).

These operators can also be combined (for example, you can use something like >=0.5.9 <2.5.3).

You can also use just:

`packagename:`

or:

`packagename:` *any*

if you want Flutter to download the latest version it can find, with no restrictions.

Fetching Packages from Locations Other Than Pub

The version isn't the only thing that you can specify in the dependencies list: if you don't want the package to be fetched from Pub, you can also specify where you want the package to be fetched from, which you might find useful, for example, when testing a new version that hasn't yet been published or when using a package that isn't on Pub at all.

Fetching from Git

For example, you can fetch the package from a Git repository:

```
packagename:
  git:
    url: git://github.com/username/packagename.git
```

If the package isn't in the root of the Git repository, you can specify a path within the repository where the package is located:

```
packagename:
  git:
    url: git://github.com/username/packagename.git
    path: path/to/pkg
```

Fetching from a Local Path

You can also fetch the package from a path in your local development environment:

```
packagename:
  path: ../packagename/
```

Package Usage Example

Now that you know how to install packages, you'll get to see packages in action.

Getting Started

We are going to build a simple app that displays the phone's battery and connectivity state using the *battery*[2] and *connectivity*[3] packages from Pub:

---

2. https://pub.dartlang.org/packages/battery
3. https://pub.dartlang.org/packages/connectivity

To use those packages, we'll start by adding the packages to our app's dependencies, and you can do that by adding the following to the dependencies in pubspec.yaml:

packages/battery_connectivity/pubspec.yaml
```
connectivity: ^0.3.1
battery: ^0.2.2
```

And import the packages in our code by adding to the top of the main Dart file the following:

packages/battery_connectivity/lib/main.dart
```
import 'dart:async';

import 'package:flutter/material.dart';
import 'package:battery/battery.dart';
import 'package:connectivity/connectivity.dart';
```

In addition to the packages we download from Pub, we also need Flutter's standard Material Design API and Dart's async library, which is needed to properly handle the asynchronous nature of the packages we are using.

The Main Function and Home Page Definition

The main function looks like any other main function that has been shown throughout this book:

packages/battery_connectivity/lib/main.dart
```
void main() => runApp(
  MaterialApp(
    title: "Battery and connectivity status",
    theme: ThemeData(primarySwatch: Colors.green),
    home: HomePage("Dashboard"),
  )
);
```

The home page will be a *Stateful* widget, since we want it to change when the battery or connectivity state changes:

packages/battery_connectivity/lib/main.dart
```
class HomePage extends StatefulWidget {
  HomePage(this.title);

  final String title;

  HomePageState createState() => HomePageState();
}
```

Defining the Home Page's State

Each battery and connectivity state is going to be shown in the form of a string (like Mobile Data or Full) and an icon, with each status being represented by a different color:

packages/battery_connectivity/lib/main.dart
```
class HomePageState extends State<HomePage> {
  String _connectionStatus = 'Unknown';
  IconData _connectionIcon;
  String _batteryStatus = 'Unknown';
  IconData _batteryIcon;
  Color _connectionColor = Colors.deepOrange;
  Color _batteryColor = Colors.deepOrange;
```

Getting the Battery and Connectivity Data: Asynchronous Programming Using Streams

Since the data we are going to be showing could change at any time, the packages allow the data to be used in the form of *Streams*, which allow your code to listen for changes in the data and define the actions that need to be taken using the new data when it changes.

In this case, we want to change the state of the widget by changing the strings and icons describing the connectivity and battery state.

We can do that using the following code:

packages/battery_connectivity/lib/main.dart
```
❶ StreamSubscription<ConnectivityResult> _connSub;
  StreamSubscription<BatteryState> _battSub;

  @override
  void initState() {
    super.initState();

❷   _connSub = Connectivity()
            .onConnectivityChanged
            .listen(( ConnectivityResult res) async {
      setState(() {
❸       switch(res) {
          case ConnectivityResult.mobile:
            _connectionStatus = 'Mobile Data';
            _connectionIcon = Icons.sim_card;
            _connectionColor = Colors.red;
            break;
          case ConnectivityResult.wifi:
            _connectionStatus = 'Wi-Fi';
            _connectionIcon = Icons.wifi;
            _connectionColor = Colors.blue;
            break;
```

```
        case ConnectivityResult.none:
          _connectionStatus = "No Connection";
          _connectionIcon = Icons.not_interested;
          _connectionColor = Colors.black;
      }
    });
  });
  _battSub = Battery()
              .onBatteryStateChanged
              .listen((BatteryState res) async {
    setState(() {
      switch(res) {
        case BatteryState.charging:
          _batteryStatus = 'Charging';
          _batteryIcon = Icons.battery_charging_full;
          _batteryColor = Colors.blueAccent;
          break;
        case BatteryState.full:
          _batteryStatus = 'Full';
          _batteryIcon = Icons.battery_full;
          _batteryColor = Colors.green;
          break;
        case BatteryState.discharging:
          _batteryStatus = 'In Use';
          _batteryIcon = Icons.battery_alert;
          _batteryColor = Colors.redAccent;
      }
    });
  });
}
```

❶ These two lines are used to define the StreamSubscriptions we'll be using in our app. *subscriptions* are used to run some code when the data returned by a Stream changes.

❷ We are calling the Connectivity constructor to get an object and listen on its member onConnectivityChanged Stream, which, like all Streams, has a listen member function, which takes as a positional argument the callback function to be called when the connectivity changes, which will usually be a call to setState(), since in most apps a change in a Stream means that the app's UI needs to be updated.

❸ In case you're not familiar with it, the usage of a switch statement is explained in Switch, on page 304. In this instance, we're using it to set different strings, icons, and colors for each connection and battery status.

❹ This is the same as what we've seen for the connectivity status, but for the battery status.

Since this code is doing a lot of different things, we'll break this down and explain each part.

Disposing of the StreamSubscriptions

For each subscription there needs to be an entry to the dispose() method to dispose of the subscription when it's not needed anymore. StreamSubscriptions have a cancel() method, which does exactly that. Since State classes need to override their superclass' dispose() method (which is the method that runs when that State isn't needed anymore, which is when the StatefulWidget isn't being rendered anymore), they need to call super.dispose():

packages/battery_connectivity/lib/main.dart
```
@override
dispose() {
  super.dispose();
  _connSub.cancel();
  _battSub.cancel();
}
```

You can find out more about Streams in Streams and StreamSubscriptions, on page 299.

Defining the App's UI

The build() method will be the following:

packages/battery_connectivity/lib/main.dart
```
@override
Widget build(BuildContext context) {
  return Scaffold(
    backgroundColor: Theme.of(context).backgroundColor,
    appBar: AppBar(
      title: Text(widget.title),
    ),
    body: Column(
      mainAxisAlignment: MainAxisAlignment.spaceAround,
      children: <Widget>[
        Row(
          children: <Widget>[
            Icon(_connectionIcon, color: _connectionColor, size: 50.0),
            Text(
              "Connection:\n$_connectionStatus",
              style: TextStyle(
                color: _connectionColor,
                fontSize: 40.0,
              ),
            ),
          ],
        ),
```

```
      Row(
        children: <Widget>[
          Icon(_batteryIcon, color: _batteryColor, size: 50.0),
          Text(
            "Battery:\n$_batteryStatus",
            style: TextStyle(
              color: _batteryColor,
              fontSize: 40.0,
            ),
          ),
        ]
      ),
    ],
  ),
);
}
```

The app's body is a Column, with the mainAxisAlignment set to MainAxisAlignment.spaceAround so the widgets occcupy the entire body, instead of being stacked closely on top:

packages/battery_connectivity/lib/main.dart
```
body: Column(
  mainAxisAlignment: MainAxisAlignment.spaceAround,
  children: <Widget>[
    Row(
      children: <Widget>[
        Icon(_connectionIcon, color: _connectionColor, size: 50.0),
        Text(
          "Connection:\n$_connectionStatus",
          style: TextStyle(
            color: _connectionColor,
            fontSize: 40.0,
          ),
        ),
      ],
    ),
    Row(
      children: <Widget>[
        Icon(_batteryIcon, color: _batteryColor, size: 50.0),
        Text(
          "Battery:\n$_batteryStatus",
          style: TextStyle(
            color: _batteryColor,
            fontSize: 40.0,
          ),
        ),
      ]
    ),
  ],
),
```

The Column contains two Rows, one showing the connection state, and one showing the battery state.

Showing the States

The connection state will be shown using a Row to show both the string and the icon of the color we set when the state changes:

packages/battery_connectivity/lib/main.dart
```
Row(
  children: <Widget>[
    Icon(_connectionIcon, color: _connectionColor, size: 50.0),
    Text(
      "Connection:\n$_connectionStatus",
      style: TextStyle(
        color: _connectionColor,
        fontSize: 40.0,
      ),
    ),
  ],
),
```

packages/battery_connectivity/lib/main.dart
```
Row(
  children: <Widget>[
    Icon(_batteryIcon, color: _batteryColor, size: 50.0),
    Text(
      "Battery:\n$_batteryStatus",
      style: TextStyle(
        color: _batteryColor,
        fontSize: 40.0,
      ),
    ),
  ]
),
```

The result is that each status is represented by a different Icon and string of a different color for each battery status:

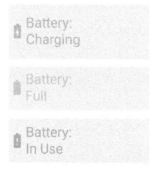

and for each connectivity status:

Making Your Own Packages

Now that you know how to use a package, you might want to know how to make your own package and how you can write platform-specific code to be used inside a Flutter app.

Creating the Package

Making a package is a lot like making an app.

If you're using Android Studio, you just need to use File -> New -> New Flutter Project.

If you only need to use multi-platform Dart code for your package, choose the Flutter Package option, if you also need to add iOS(Objective-C/Swift) or Android(Java/Kotlin) code, choose Flutter Plugin.

Interaction between Dart code and platform-specific code is described in Integrating Native Code: Making Plugin Packages, on page 130.

If you're using the command line, run this command:

```
flutter create --template=package packagename
```

If you want to create a plugin, replace the word *package* with *plugin*.

Package Development

Creating a normal Dart-only package is as simple as editing and creating Dart files in the lib folder, defining the functions and classes that you want your package to provide, and then publishing it, as explained in Publishing a Package to Pub, on page 137.

Integrating Native Code: Making Plugin Packages

The situation becomes more complicated when you want your package to communicate with platform-specific code, since you'll need to join together three different codebases written in three different languages.

Many native Android/iOS features are available using packages from Pub, but you might need to use a feature that isn't available in Flutter and that isn't supplied by any package, so you'll need to write your own platform-specific code to access that feature.

Although this chapter is about packages, the information in Connecting Flutter and Platform-Specific Code Together Using Platform Channels, on page 130 is also useful if you just want to connect Android and iOS code to just one app, without creating a package.

Creating a Plugin Package

You can create a plugin package using the following command:

```
flutter create --template=plugin packagename
```

This will let you use use Java for Android-specific code and Objective-C for iOS code but, especially in the iOS world, those languages are losing ground to Kotlin (for Android) and Swift (for iOS). Flutter actually also provides a template for those languages too, and if you want to use both Swift and Kotlin, you need to run this command instead:

```
flutter create --template=plugin -a kotlin -i swift packagename
```

As we've just seen, you can use flutter's -a option to specify the language to use for Android code and -i to specify the language for iOS code.

Connecting Flutter and Platform-Specific Code Together Using Platform Channels

We'll write the interface for our package in Dart, but we'll need to connect it to the platform-specific code, and you can do that using platform channels.

Platform channels aren't exclusive to packages: we can also use them with apps.

The Flutter code calls methods for the platform-specific code to execute through a platform channel, the platform-specific code listens on the channel, receives the method call, performs the actions it needs to perform, and returns a response.

How Platform Channels Work

To connect to our platform-specific code we'll use the MethodChannel class, which is Flutter's side of the interface between Flutter and platform-specific code.

We pass the channel name to its constructor, which is a unique String identi-fier for the channel in the entire app.

Since it has to be unique for the entire app, the channel name is usually prefixed by a domain name.

The channel works the following way: the Dart code invokes methods on the channel, the platform-specific code listens on the channel, waiting for a method call, which is dealt with by a method call handler, which sends the result back to the Dart code.

The response is received by the Dart code in the form of a Future.

Implementing the Flutter Interface in Dart

An example of a basic Flutter interface that can interact with platform-specific code is the following:

packages/making_plugins/lib/plugin_example.dart
```
import 'dart:async';
import 'package:flutter/services.dart';

class PluginExample {
  static const _platformChannel =
      MethodChannel('example.com/plugin_example');
  static Future<type> exampleMethod async {
    return await _platformChannel.invokeMethod('runExampleMethod');
  }
}
```

We can access platform channels using the *services* library, and we also need to use the async library to handle the Future, so the following lines need to be placed at the top of your Dart file:

packages/making_plugins/lib/plugin_example.dart
```
import 'dart:async';
import 'package:flutter/services.dart';
```

Then we define the class that will contain our code and we start by defining the channel we're going use, which will be example.com/plugin_example:

packages/making_plugins/lib/plugin_example.dart
```
static const _platformChannel =
    MethodChannel('example.com/plugin_example');
```

This string could be anything: you can prefix it with a real domain, a fake domain, or by no domain at all, but you should prefix it with a real domain if possible to make sure this doesn't clash with any other plugin's channel name. In this regard, it is very similar to Java package names, except the domain prefix is optional in this case.

After you've chosen the channel name, implement the actual interface for the package:

packages/making_plugins/lib/plugin_example.dart
```
static Future<type> exampleMethod async {
  return await _platformChannel.invokeMethod('runExampleMethod');
}
```

where in Future you would replace type with the type that you want the function to return.

For more information on what data types in Java and Swift correspond to the Dart data types, see the table Conversion Between Native Java/Apple and Dart Data Types, on page 313.

This is what will actually be called by the users of your package, and the only thing to bear in mind is that the way you call platform-specific code is by invoking methods using platformChannel.invokeMethod(METHOD_NAME).

Obviously for such a simple package you could skip defining the platformChannel variable and just use MethodChannel(CHANNEL_NAME).invokeMethod(METHOD_NAME), but that would not make the code much shorter and could be a really bad way to do things long term, so stick with declaring the channel beforehand like we showed in the example.

Implementing the Android Interface in Java

In the android directory there will be a source tree that looks just like an app's source tree, with the only difference being the actual content of the files.

An Android-specific Java plugin implementation looks like the following:

packages/making_plugins/android/src/main/java/com/example/pluginexample/PluginExamplePlugin.java
```java
package com.example.pluginexample;

import io.flutter.plugin.common.MethodChannel;
import io.flutter.plugin.common.MethodChannel.MethodCallHandler;
import io.flutter.plugin.common.MethodChannel.Result;
import io.flutter.plugin.common.MethodCall;
import io.flutter.plugin.common.PluginRegistry.Registrar;

public class PluginExample implements MethodCallHandler {
  public static void registerWith(Registrar registrar) {
    final MethodChannel channel =
      new MethodChannel(registrar.messenger(), "example.com/plugin_example");
    channel.setMethodCallHandler(new PluginExample());
  }
```

```
  @Override
  public void onMethodCall(MethodCall call, Result result) {
    if (call.method.equals("runExampleMethod")) {
      result.success(DATA_TO_RESPOND_WITH);
    } else {
      result.notImplemented();
    }
  }
}
```

Specifically, the Java file will be a class which implements the MethodCallHandler trait, and we'll need to define two methods for it: a registerWith() method, where we'll define what channel to listen on, and an onMethodCall() which gets called when a method is called on the channel:

packages/making_plugins/android/src/main/java/com/example/pluginexample/PluginExamplePlugin.java

```
public class PluginExample implements MethodCallHandler {
  public static void registerWith(Registrar registrar) {
    final MethodChannel channel =
      new MethodChannel(registrar.messenger(), "example.com/plugin_example");
    channel.setMethodCallHandler(new PluginExample());
  }

  @Override
  public void onMethodCall(MethodCall call, Result result) {
    if (call.method.equals("runExampleMethod")) {
      result.success(DATA_TO_RESPOND_WITH);
    } else {
      result.notImplemented();
    }
  }
}
```

Let's start dissecting the code by looking at registerWith():

packages/making_plugins/android/src/main/java/com/example/pluginexample/PluginExamplePlugin.java

```
public static void registerWith(Registrar registrar) {
  final MethodChannel channel =
    new MethodChannel(registrar.messenger(), "example.com/plugin_example");
  channel.setMethodCallHandler(new PluginExample());
}
```

This method is comparable to initState() in Flutter widgets: here you would add any action that has to be performed once and is necessary for the functionality of the package, including setting the class as the method call handler for the channel the plugin operates on.

More specifically, when a method is invoked, onMethodCall() gets called, with two arguments: one describing the call and another providing an interface to return a result.

onMethodCall() could be defined in the following way:

packages/making_plugins/android/src/main/java/com/example/pluginexample/PluginExamplePlugin.java
```
@Override
public void onMethodCall(MethodCall call, Result result) {
  if (call.method.equals("runExampleMethod")) {
    result.success(DATA_TO_RESPOND_WITH);
  } else {
    result.notImplemented();
  }
}
```

Since a plugin might call different methods on the same channel, the call argument provides information about the method call, more specifically:

- call.method, which is the name of the method that is being called, in this case this would be "runExampleMethod".

- call.arguments, which contains the arguments supplied by the caller code (if there are any), this topic is explained in greater detail in Adding arguments to Method Calls, on page 135.

The result is returned using the result argument: running result.success(DATA) will return DATA to the calling code, whereas running result.notImplemented() will tell the calling code that there the method that was called has not been implemented in the platform-specific code.

Implementing the iOS Interface in Swift

When you create a Swift plugin project, in the ios/Classes folder, you will find a Swift file where you will write the iOS-specific code:

packages/making_plugins/ios/Classes/SwiftPluginExamplePlugin.swift
```
import Flutter
import UIKit

public class PluginExample: NSObject, FlutterPlugin {
  public static func register(with registrar: FlutterPluginRegistrar) {
    let channel =
        FlutterMethodChannel(
                name: "example.com/plugin_swift",
                binaryMessenger: registrar.messenger()
        )
    let handler = PluginExample()
    registrar.addMethodCallDelegate(handler, channel: channel)
  }
```

```
    public func handle(call: FlutterMethodCall, result: @escaping FlutterResult) {
      if(call.method == "runExampleMethod") {
          result(DATA)
      }
    }
}
```

Instead of having a MethodChannel and a MethodCall, you'll use a FlutterMethodChannel and a FlutterMethodCall, but most of the same principles apply.

Registering is slightly different:

packages/making_plugins/ios/Classes/SwiftPluginExamplePlugin.swift
```
public static func register(with registrar: FlutterPluginRegistrar) {
  let channel =
      FlutterMethodChannel(
              name: "example.com/plugin_swift",
              binaryMessenger: registrar.messenger()
      )
  let handler = PluginExample()
  registrar.addMethodCallDelegate(handler, channel: channel)
}
```

The FlutterMethodChannel constructor arguments are named and not positional and you can set the method handler by using the FlutterPluginRegistrar's addMethodCallDelegate() method, passing the handler class as a positional argument and the channel as a named argument:

packages/making_plugins/ios/Classes/SwiftPluginExamplePlugin.swift
```
registrar.addMethodCallDelegate(handler, channel: channel)
```

onMethodCall becomes handle() and instead of using result.success() to return data it is just result(), with the rest of the differences being down to variations in syntax between Java and Swift:

packages/making_plugins/ios/Classes/SwiftPluginExamplePlugin.swift
```
public func handle(call: FlutterMethodCall, result: @escaping FlutterResult) {
  if(call.method == "runExampleMethod") {
      result(DATA)
  }
}
```

Adding arguments to Method Calls

Getting a value from a platform-specific API is useful, but sometimes you need to pass arguments to the called code, and you can do that by passing another argument to invokeMethod().

The arguments will then be available in Android's MethodCall and iOS's FlutterMethodCall in call.arguments.

Its type is dynamic in Dart, Object in Java, and id in Objective-C, meaning it could be anything.

For example, let's pass an integer number and multiply it by 10 to see how it's done.

The Dart interface is fairly simple:

```
static Future<int> multiplyBy10(int n) async {
    return await platformChannel.invokeMethod('multiplyBy10', n);
}
```

In the Android code, after casting the type of the arguments to int, it's as simple as returning the number multiplied by 10:

```
if(call.method.equals("multiplyBy10")) {
    result.success(((int) call.arguments)*10);
}
```

For the iOS code, in call.arguments you'll get an NSNumber NumberWithInt, so it takes a few extra steps to achieve this:

```
if(call.method == "multiplyBy10") {
        let arg = call.arguments as! NSNumber NumberWithInt
    result(NSNumber(value: arg.integerValue * 10))
}
```

Given that the NSNumber contains the actual number in the integerValue member, that's what we need to multiply by 10. After we've done that, we convert it back to an NSNumber and send it back to the calling code. For more information about the type conversions between Dart and platform-specific code, the section Conversion Between Native Java/Apple and Dart Data Types, on page 313 lists the most important ones.

Using the Package in an App Without Publishing to Pub

Let's suppose you have a directory structure that looks like the following:

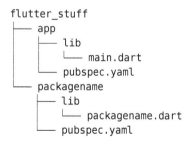

```
flutter_stuff
├── app
│   ├── lib
│   │   └── main.dart
│   └── pubspec.yaml
└── packagename
    ├── lib
    │   └── packagename.dart
    └── pubspec.yaml
```

and you want the app in the app directory to use the package in the packagename directory.

As we explained in Fetching Packages from Locations Other Than Pub, on page 121, you can just add:

```
packagename:
  path: ../packagename/
```

to the dependencies in pubspec.yaml and add:

```
import 'package:packagename/packagename.dart';
```

to app/libmain.dart and you will be able to access the package just like you would if you had used Pub.

Publishing a Package to Pub

Before you publish a package, you need to make sure you've filled in the package name, version, description, and any other information that you want to specify in pubspec.yaml, using Appendix 2, Apple-Like Look and Additional App Configuration, on page 315 as a reference.

A LICENSE file is also required.

If you don't know what license to use, the Dart developers recommend the two-clause BSD license,[4] but there are many resources online to compare licenses, like choosealicense.com[5] by GitHub.

You should also create a README.md file, as this will be used as a home page for your package in Pub.

At this point, simply run:

```
pub publish
```

in the command line and, if you have done everything correctly, your package will be publicly available on Pub.

Packages for Windows, macOS, and Linux

Flutter supports desktop platforms at an experimental stage. This means you could also develop Flutter plugins for desktop platforms.

---

4. https://en.wikipedia.org/wiki/BSD_licenses
5. https://choosealicense.com/licenses/

For up-to-date information on the state of this feature, you should consult Google's dedicated *flutter-desktop-embedding* GitHub repository.[6]

Where We're Going Next

Now that we know how packages work, we'll be able to use one of the most important features packages provide: HTTP networking, as we'll see in the next chapter.

---

6. https://github.com/google/flutter-desktop-embedding

Part II

Doing More with Flutter

Flutter is expandable and flexible. We've already seen how it works, so now we'll look at how Flutter's many features can be used to actually build useful apps.

In the chapters in this part you'll learn how to make HTTP requests, how to test and handle exceptions in Flutter apps, and then how to use Firebase to create a chat app.

The appendices will be about Dart syntax, Cupertino (iOS-like) widgets, pubspec.yaml, and how to change app name and launcher icon.

CHAPTER 5

Network and Storage I/O and Navigation

Writing apps that are isolated to the user's own phone is fine for some applications, but a great majority of apps need to interact with a web API or back end, which is what we'll be doing in this chapter.

Flutter's standard library doesn't include a standard networking component: even though you can actually use the network to fetch images, you can't make standard HTTP requests using just the Flutter/Dart standard library.

This is the reason why we are going to talk about it now: Flutter has a Google-developed package on Pub called *http*, which allows us to make HTTP requests and connect our app to a Web API.

The API

Since talking about actually creating a back end for your app would deviate significantly from the scope of this book, we'll be using a simple HTTP API that requires no authentication: the popular comic site XKCD's API.

Why XKCD?

You are probably already familiar with the XKCD website: its comics are often shared in engineering and computer-related communities (especially software development ones), and the XKCD API is very simple to use and requires no authentication, which means you will be able to use the code examples in this chapter without having to update placeholder API keys with ones you get by signing up for the usage of the API like you would if the example was about an API that requires authentication.

How the XKCD API Works

The XKCD API, like is the case for most HTTP end-points, sends JSON responses to simple GET requests.

Getting Data About XKCD Comics

For example, sending a standard GET request to https://xkcd.com/info.0.json returns something like this:

```
{
  "month": "1",
  "num": 2097,
  "link": "",
  "year": "2019",
  "news": "",
  "safe_title": "Thor Tools",
  "transcript": "",
  "alt": "CORRECTION: After careful evaluation," +
    "we have determined that the" +
    "axis label on this chart was printed backward.",
  "img": "https://imgs.xkcd.com/comics/thor_tools.png",
  "title": "Thor Tools",
  "day": "11"
}
```

which describes the latest comic XKCD has published, and you can see the current result yourself by navigating to that page in the browser.

The JSON Data

If you have never worked with JSON, it is just a way to describe an object from any object-oriented programming language (or, even more closely, a C-like struct) with a string: it is a single entity containing multiple fields, each one describing something different about the entity it's describing.

In this case, it's the latest comic XKCD has published and the following information about it:

- Which month it was released on (1 for January).
- The numerical ID for the comic (progressive, starting from 1 for the first ever XKCD comic).
- The link clicking the comic image on the websites points to[1] (usually empty).
- The year the comic was published.
- A usually empty *news* field.
- The text-only title of the comic (the normal *title* might contain HTML tags).
- A textual transcript (a description) of what's happening in the comic image, which hasn't been added to comics since number 1674.
- *alt* is an explanation of the joke or additional text meant to be viewed after seeing the comic image itself. It has been included in the official website

---

1. https://xkcd.com/2050/

in two ways: the desktop version displays it when the mouse hovers over the image, and the mobile version displays it when a button below the image is tapped.

- The comic image itself.
- The comic title, potentially containing HTML tags.
- The day of the month on which the comic was published.

In Dart code, we can parse and decode the JSON data and store it in a Dart Map using the dart:convert built-in Dart library, which provides the necessary json.decode(JSON) method to convert a JSON String to a Dart object, as well as a json.decode(var) method (which we won't use) that converts compatible Dart objects to JSON-formatted Strings.

How the Convert Library Works

The *dart:convert* library provides the json constant,[a] which is of type JsonCodec,[b] which has two methods: json.decode(), which takes a String as an argument and can return any Dart object, as its return type is dynamic, meaning it could be anything.

The other method is json.encode(), which does the exact opposite: it takes any Dart Object (again, it could be anything) and returns a String that can be used—for example, as part of a POST request if that's what we needed to do, and as we'll do later in the book.

———————

a. api.dartlang.org/stable/2.1.0/dart-convert/json-constant.html
b. api.dartlang.org/stable/2.1.0/dart-convert/JsonCodec-class.html

Getting Previous Comics

You can get the comics published prior to the current (and latest) one by sending a get request to https://xkcd.com/num/info.0.json where num is the comic number in chronological order (starting from 1); for example, you can get the first one by sending a GET request to https://xkcd.com/1/info.0.json.

There is no way to get a list of the comics from the API, but we can make a list of comics in reverse chronological order (from the latest to the earliest) by simply fetching the latest comic, then using its ID number (let's call it latestNum) to fetch the comics with numbers that go from latestNum-1 to 1.

The http Package

To make GET requests we need to use the *http* package. You can find the http package on Dart Pub.[2]

———————

2. https://pub.dartlang.org/packages/http

Let's start by creating a new Flutter app project using:

```
$ flutter create xkcd_app
```

and installing the HTTP package by adding the following to pubspec.yaml:

```
networking/xkcd_app/pubspec.yaml
dependencies:
  http: "^0.12.0+1"
```

Run flutter packages get to download and install the package if you aren't using the IDE plugins (which will do it automatically for you after you make changes to pubspec.yaml).

Using the http Package

The HTTP package can be used to make HTTP requests of all kinds.[3]

All of them are asynchronous, which means that, by default, they are ran in a separate thread without affecting the rest of the app's execution. You can choose to make them behave exactly like synchronous functions if their return value is vital to the prosecution of the app's execution.

Asynchronous Code in Dart

There are many ways to run asynchronous code in Dart, outlined in Asynchronous Code in Dart: The dart:async Library, on page 297, but the basic concept has already been explained in the previous chapter: calls to functions that return a Future (or Stream, which we won't be using in this chapter) and run in a separate thread are called asynchronous.

We can get the data returned by an asynchronous function by using an await expression:

```
var returnedData = await asyncFunction();
```

This can only be done in async functions and async functions have to return Futures, so asynchrony tends to propagate to all of the calling methods.

Making GET Requests

An HTTP request is made using http.get(), which is an async method that returns a Response inside a Future.

We can unwrap the inner Response using await:

```
var latestComicResponse = await http.get("https://xkcd.com/info.0.json");
```

---

3.   https://pub.dartlang.org/documentation/http/latest/http/http-library.html

and we can get the body of the response as a String by querying its body attribute, like we will need to do when we build our XKCD app:

```
var latestComicString = latestComicResponse.body;
```

We could also do everything in one line, enclosing the await expression in parentheses:

```
var latestComicString = (await http.get("https://xkcd.com/info.0.json")).body;
```

HTTP headers can be set by setting the headers named arguments to a Map<String, String>, like in the following example:

```
http.get(
  "http://example.com/exampleGet?testAttr=$val1&testAttr2=$val2",
  headers: {
    "Accept": "application/json",
    "Accept-Charset": "utf-8"
  }
)
```

Wikipedia has a comprehensive list of standard HTTP headers.[4]

The http package also provides http.read() and http.readBytes(), which are, respectively, just like http.get()()'s body and bodyBytes attributes.

For example, you could go from calling:

```
String res = (await http.get("http://example.com")).body;
```

to just:

```
String res = await http.read("http://example.com");
```

or go from:

```
String res = (await http.get("http://example.com")).bodyBytes;
```

to just:

```
String res = await http.readBytes("http://example.com");
```

Be careful, though, as you lose other attributes of the Response object (the type of data http.get() returns), such as:

- headers, which is needed when you need to read the response's headers;
- contentLength, which is the size (in bytes) of the response.

---

4. https://en.wikipedia.org/wiki/List_of_HTTP_header_fields

Making Other Requests

Other kinds of HTTP requests are also supported, and all of them support setting headers in the way we've just seen and all of them return Future<Response> objects:

- A POST request is made using http.post(), the request URL is provided as a positional argument and you can set the request body by setting the body named argument to whatever you want.

- A PUT request is made using http.put(), the request URL is provided as a positional argument and you can set the request body by setting the body named argument to whatever you want.

- A DELETE request is made using http.delete(), the request URL is provided as a positional argument.

- A PATCH request is made using http.patch(), the request URL is provided as a positional argument and you can set the request body by setting the body named argument to whatever you want.

- A HEAD request is made using http.head(), the request URL is provided as a positional argument.

Whenever it's possible to add a body attribute it's also possible to add an encoding attribute, which is of type Econding and is used to define the body's encoding. Some Encoding subclasses are AsciiCodec and Utf8Codec.

Parsing the JSON Response Body

The HTTP response body is just a string, so it is not useful unless it is parsed.

Manually parsing it would be incredibly time-consuming and pointless, since the dart:convert built-in library already provides a constant called json, which is of type JsonCodec, meaning it exposes two methods:

- json.encode(obj), which converts the obj object to a JSON string.
- json.decode(str), which converts the str JSON string to a Dart object.

In our specific case, we want to convert a JSON string to a Map<String, dynamic>, which allows us to access each of the comic's attributes by name as we'll see in the next section.

Using dart:convert, if we had previously stored the response body of a call to XKCD's API to a variable called latestComicString, we would be able to convert it to a Map by using:

```
Map<String, dynamic> latestComic = json.decode(latestComicString);
```

So the code we would add to our app if we needed to store the latest comic in a `Map` variable is:

```
Map<String, dynamic> latestComic = json.decode(
  await http.read("https://xkcd.com/info.0.json")
);
```

Writing Methods to Fetch Comics

A consideration has to be done before continuing with the implementation: the optimal data type to store comics is `Map<String, dynamic>`, which handles JSON objects perfectly.

Given that we know how to fetch comics, let's start writing some code to use that knowledge to write methods to fetch comics that we can use in our app!

Fetching the Latest Comic

Wrapping the code we discussed earlier into an arrow function isn't hard at all:

```
Future<Map<String, dynamic>> fetchLatestComic() async =>
  json.decode(
    await http.read("https://xkcd.com/info.0.json")
  );
```

We can access a `Map`'s field a lot like we would access `List` elements by using `varName["attrName"]` where `varName` is the name of the `Map` variable and `attrName` is the name of the attributes. This is exactly the same syntax used in Python to access dictionary elements. This is how you access every attribute:

```
var comic = fetchLatestComic();
int num = comic["num"];
String link = comic["link"];
String news = comic["news"];
String safe_title = comic["safe_title"];
String transcript = comic["transcript"];
String alt = comic["alt"];
ImageProvider img = NetworkImage(comic["img"]);
String title = comic["title"];
String MDYDate = "${comic["month"]}/${comic["day"]}/${comic["year"]}";
String DMYDate = "${comic["day"]}/${comic["month"]}/${comic["year"]}";
```

Fetching Previous Comics

Fetching by comic number is easy since the API is designed to do just that:

```
Future<Map<String, dynamic>> fetchComic(int n) async =>
  json.decode(
    await http.read("https://xkcd.com/info.0.json")
  );
```

But sorting reverse chronological is a lot harder, as we need to know the latest comic number to get the previous, and so on:

```
Future<Map<String, dynamic>> fetchComic(int n) async {
  int latestComicNum = ...;
  return json.decode(
    await http.read("https://xkcd.com/info.0.json")
  );
}
```

The obvious way to do that would be to just call fetchLatestComic and get the num attribute, like this:

```
int latestComicNum = fetchLatestComic()["num"];
```

But doing it that way would require two different GET requests to fetch each comic, and many of them are going to be redundant and useless.

Fetching the Latest Comic Number Just Once

Since we are going to use these methods inside an app, which will have a wrapper class around it (at least for the home screen), we can just pass it to that class when we run the app and then the fetchComic() method inside that class will be able to access it directly.

The New fetchComic

Fetching a comic is really simple this way, since we don't need to worry about the latest comic number, which will be provided by the class in which we'll define the method:

```
Future<Map<String, dynamic>> fetchComic(int n) async =>
  json.decode(
    await http.read(
      "https://xkcd.com/${latestComicNum-n}/info.0.json"
    )
  );
```

A Function to Get the Latest Comic Number

We need to get the latest comic number when we run the app though, and to do that we need to define a function that will fetch that when we need it:

```
Future<int> getLatestComicNumber() async =>
json.decode(
    await http.read('https://xkcd.com/info.0.json')
  )
  ["num"];
```

What If There's No Internet Connection?

If there is no Internet connection, the app will not work. This is a problem but, since we are downloading all of the comics anyway, we should be able to fix it just by saving them to permanent local storage so that we can load them when there is no Internet connection.

This has the added advantage of giving us the chance to optimize our app in a significant way: if we have the previous comics on local storage we don't need to fetch them from the Internet, so we finally eliminate all the redundant GET requests and we can just focus on getting new data when we need it.

What You Need to Build the UI: Navigation and the InheritedWidget

Before we actually build the UI for this app, we're going to discuss two important things: how to navigate between multiple views in Flutter and how to use InheritedWidgets. This will be a general introduction to the options Flutter offers for navigation; we'll only use some of these in the app. If you'd prefer to jump ahead to more advanced navigation, take a look at Build the App's Basic UI, on page 167 and then come back here when you want to learn about how to implement navigation in Flutter apps.

Navigation in Flutter

Flutter offers multiple options for navigating between views:

- push/pop navigation, useful when there is a home page and many pages accessible from it, potentially using a Drawer menu.

- Page-by-page navigation using the PageView and PageController, useful when there are a limited number of pages that can be considered on the same level.

Push/Pop Navigation Using the Navigator

Making an app that takes advantage of the Navigator for push/pop navigation is really simple.

Define the Pages

The first thing to do is to define the pages, which will be really simple:

```
class NewPage extends StatelessWidget {

  @override
  Widget build(BuildContext context) {
```

```
    return Scaffold(
      appBar: AppBar(title: Text("New Page"),),
      body: Center(
        child: FlatButton(
          color: Colors.black12,
          onPressed: () {},
          child: Text("Go back to the home page"),
        )
      ),
    );
  }
}

class HomePage extends StatelessWidget {
  @override
  Widget build(BuildContext context) {
    return Scaffold(
      appBar: AppBar(title: Text("Home Page"),),
      body: Center(
        child: Container(
          height: 100,
          child: Card(
            child: Column(
              children: <Widget>[
                Padding(
                  padding: EdgeInsets.all(10.0),
                  child: Text(
                    "Click the button to go to a new page",
                    style: Theme.of(context).textTheme.title,
                  ),
                ),
                ButtonTheme.bar(
                  child: FlatButton(
                    child: Text("Go to new page"),
                    onPressed: () {}
                  ),
                )
              ],
            )
          ),
        ),
      ),
    );
  }
}
```

which generates the following app in its initial state as shown in the screenshot on page 151.

I made the home page a bit more complex than it needed to be to differentiate the two pages visually.

Now comes the important part: that onPressed option for both pages, inside which we are going to add the navigation code.

I called this type of navigation &lquot;push&rquot;/&lquot;pop&rquot; because it uses two methods called Navigator.push() and Navigator.pop().

Push

You can navigate to a new page (contained in a Widget called NewPage) using the Navigator.push() in the following way:

```
Navigator.push(
  context,
  MaterialPageRoute(
    builder: (context) => NewPage(),
  ),
);
```

Navigator.push() takes two arguments: the BuildContext and a Route to the new page.

You can create a route using the MaterialPageRoute() constructor, which uses a builder callback function (which can be a call to the widget's constructor, as is the case in the example) to build the new view.

You can put that code inside the curly braces of the onPressed option for the FlatButton inside MyHomePage and the following view will be displayed when the user taps the button:

Pop

Even though the framework by itself has added a (working, by the way) *back* button in the top left, it is useful to know how to make a custom button to go back.

It is also incredibly simple:

```
Navigator.pop(context);
```

Adding that code to the curly braces of the onPressed attribute of NewPage's Flat-Button, tapping that button in the middle of the screen will make the app go back to the home page.

Using a Drawer Side Navigation Menu

A commonly seen navigation element is the Drawer,[5] which is the menu, seen in many apps, that opens by swiping right starting from the left edge of the

---

screen or by tapping the commonly seen button with three vertically stacked horizontal lines.

Like many items that are commonly used and placed outside the app body, a drawer is added to the app by using the drawer option of the Scaffold and setting it to a Drawer object:

```
Scaffold(
  appBar: AppBar(title: ...),
  drawer: Drawer(
    child: ...
  ),
  body: ...,
)
```

The Drawer class takes just three arguments (excluding the Key), which makes it one of the simplest widgets in the entire Flutter standard library in this respect.

Since one of them is the semanticLabel (which is a string used by accessibility tools such as screen readers to describe what they're seeing) and the other is the elevation (which is a double, also present in the Card, which is used to customize the shadow behind it), the only one that we're currently interested in is the child, which is usually a Column or a ListView (if you're worried about items not having enough vertical space).

For this example, we'll use a ListView.

Very often, the first element in the list is a DrawerHeader, which is a lot like a Container and usually includes either account information and facilities to switch accounts (if present), the name of the app and/or information about its creators, or a short description of what the menu is for.

Below it, a number of ListTiles are used to display navigation options.

If you decide to use a ListView, you should set its padding option to EdgeInsets.zero to avoid having gaps at the top and bottom of the screen.

Since we're talking about navigation so much, a Drawer for a public transportation or travel app could be the following:

```
Drawer(
  child: ListView(
    padding: EdgeInsets.zero,
    children: [
      DrawerHeader(
        decoration: BoxDecoration(
          color: Colors.red,
        ),
```

```
        child: Column(
          crossAxisAlignment: CrossAxisAlignment.start,
          mainAxisAlignment: MainAxisAlignment.end,
          children: [
            Text(
              "Profile Name",
              style: TextStyle(
                color: Colors.white,
                fontSize: 18,
              ),
            ),
            Text(
              "email@example.com",
              style: TextStyle(
                color: Colors.white,
                fontSize: 11,
                fontWeight: FontWeight.w300
              ),
            ),
          ]
        ),
      ),
      ListTile(
        leading: Icon(Icons.train),
        title: Text(
          "Tickets",
          style: Theme.of(context).textTheme.title,
        ),
      ),
      ListTile(title: Text("Buy Tickets"), onTap: () {}),
      ListTile(title: Text("My Tickets"), onTap: () {}),
      Divider(),
      ListTile(
        leading: Icon(Icons.person),
        title: Text(
          "Profile",
          style: Theme.of(context).textTheme.title,
        ),
      ),
      ListTile(title: Text("Profile information"), onTap: () {}),
      ListTile(title: Text("Past trips"), onTap: () {}),
      ListTile(title: Text("Loyalty program points"), onTap: () {}),
    ],
  )
),
```

First of all, it's important to clarify that just adding a drawer to a Scaffold causes the framework to automatically add a button to the app bar to expand it, as you can see with an empty Scaffold body as shown in the screenshot on page 155.

The Drawer itself looks like this:

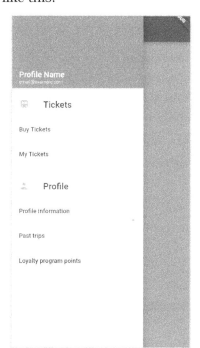

At this point, you might not be sure about how to actually use the drawer for navigation purposes, and that is because it's not done using Navigator.push(), but by changing the state of the home page and some data that can be used by build() to build the page and, after doing that, calling Navigator.pop() to go back to the home page.

This means the home page has to be a stateful widget (don't forget that, especially if you get a *setState isn't defined for HomePage* error) and it is a great chance to introduce Dart enums.

Enumerated Types

You can create an enumerated type of data by code like the following:

```
enum PageType {
  buyTickets,
  myTickets,
  profileInfo,
  pastTrips,
  myPoints
}
```

which creates a new type called PageType which can only be one of PageType.buyTickets, PageType.myTickets, PageType.profileInfo, PageType.pastTrips, or PageInfo.myPoints.

Even if you are not used to this kind of data type, you'll surely be able to understand it with the continuation of the travel app example.

Finishing Our Travel App's Navigation

To finish the travel app's navigation, add the code on page 156 to your app outside any class definition and a complete, working example of a State that implements the functionality I described is the following:

```
class HomePageState extends State<HomePage> {
  PageType _pageType = PageType.buyTickets;
  String _str;
  String _sub;

  @override
  Widget build(BuildContext context) {
    switch(_pageType) {
      case PageType.buyTickets:
        _str = "Buy Tickets";
        _sub = "You can buy your tickets here";
        break;
      case PageType.myPoints:
        _str = "My Points";
        _sub = "You can buy check your loyalty program points here";
        break;
```

```
    case PageType.myTickets:
      _str = "My Tickets";
      _sub = "You can see the tickets you've bought here";
      break;
    case PageType.pastTrips:
      _str = "My Past Trips";
      _sub = "You can check the trips you have made previously here";
      break;
    case PageType.profileInfo:
      _str = "My Profile Information";
      _sub = "You can see your profile information here";
  }
  return Scaffold(
    appBar: AppBar(
      title: Text("Programming Travels"),
      backgroundColor: Colors.red,
    ),
    drawer: Drawer(
      child: ListView(
        padding: EdgeInsets.zero,
        children: [
          DrawerHeader(
            decoration: BoxDecoration(
              color: Colors.red,
            ),
            child: Column(
              crossAxisAlignment: CrossAxisAlignment.start,
              mainAxisAlignment: MainAxisAlignment.end,
              children: [
                Text(
                  "Profile Name",
                  style: TextStyle(
                    color: Colors.white,
                    fontSize: 18,
                  ),
                ),
                Text(
                  "email@example.com",
                  style: TextStyle(
                    color: Colors.white,
                    fontSize: 11,
                    fontWeight: FontWeight.w300,
                  ),
                ),
              ]
            ),
          ),
          ListTile(
            leading: Icon(Icons.train),
```

```
      title: Text(
        "Tickets",
        style: Theme.of(context).textTheme.title,
      ),
    ),
    ListTile(
      title: Text("Buy Tickets"),
      onTap: () {
        setState(
          () => _pageType = PageType.buyTickets,
        );
        Navigator.pop(context);
      }
    ),
    ListTile(
      title: Text("My Tickets"),
      onTap: () {
        setState(
          () => _pageType = PageType.myTickets,
        );
        Navigator.pop(context);
      }
    ),
    Divider(),
    ListTile(
      leading: Icon(Icons.person),
      title: Text(
        "Profile",
        style: Theme.of(context).textTheme.title,
      ),
    ),
    ListTile(
      title: Text("Profile Information"),
      onTap: () {
        setState(
          () => _pageType = PageType.profileInfo,
        );
        Navigator.pop(context);
      }
    ),
    ListTile(
      title: Text("Past Trips"),
      onTap: () {
        setState(
          () => _pageType = PageType.pastTrips,
        );
        Navigator.pop(context);
      }
    ),
```

```
            ListTile(
              title: Text("Loyalty Program Points"),
              onTap: () {
                setState(
                  () => _pageType = PageType.myPoints,
                );
                Navigator.pop(context);
              }
            ),
          ],
        )
      ),
      Center(
        child: Padding(
          padding: EdgeInsets.all(10.0),
          child: Column(
            children: [
              Text(_str, style: Theme.of(context).textTheme.title),
              Text(_sub, style: Theme.of(context).textTheme.subtitle)
            ],
          ),
        ),
      ),
    );
  }
}
```

As you can see, each of the Drawer's ListTile sets the _pageType variable (which, by default, is PageType.buyTickets), reloads the home page using setState() and then calls Navigator.pop() to close the drawer.

build() checks which of them is the current _pageType and sets two strings (a title and a subtitle) accordingly. Those two strings are then displayed in a centered and padded Column as shown in the screenshot on page 160.

The result is working navigation using a Drawer menu.

Page-by-Page Navigation

Swipeable page-by-page navigation can be achieved using two kinds of view: the PageView and the TabBarView, the difference is that the first only allows navigation by swiping, whereas the second is used together with a TabBar below the AppBar.

If, instead, you just want something like the YouTube app: being able to switch between pages using a menu at the bottom of the screen, the way to go is with a BottomNavigationBar.

BottomNavigationBar

A BottomNavigationBar works a lot like a Drawer, but it's always visible at the bottom, so you don't need to use Navigator.pop().

More specifically, you add it to the Scaffold's bottomNavigationBar option, and you use it like this:

```
return Scaffold(
  // app body, appbar, etc.
  bottomNavigationBar: BottomNavigationBar(
    currentIndex: index,
    items: [
      BottomNavigationBarItem(
        icon: Icon( ... ),
        title: Text( ... ),
      ),
      BottomNavigationBarItem(
        icon: Icon( ... ),
        title: Text( ... ),
      ),
      // potentially more navigation items...
    ],
    onTap: (page) {
      setState(() {
        switch(page) {
```

```
        case 0:
          // Things to do if the user selects the first item
          index = 0;
          break;
        case 1:
          // Things to do if the user selects the second item
          index = 1;
        // Potentially other cases for more navigation items
      }
    });
  },
  ),
)
```

It has three main options:

- The items, which are the navigation options to be given to the user.

- The currentIndex, the value to which you assign will have to be changed manually when the user taps on a navigation item.

- The onTap callback, which takes an integer indicating which option has been tapped by the user.

A practical example of a full app home page class could be the following:

```
String _str;
int index = 0;

@override
Widget build(BuildContext context) {
  switch(index) {
    case 0:
      _str = "Home";
      break;
    case 1:
      _str = "Page 2";
      break;
    case 2:
      _str = "Page 3";
  }
  return Scaffold(
    appBar: AppBar(
      title: Text("Bottom Navigation Bar Example"),
      backgroundColor: Colors.red,
    ),
    body: Center(
      child: Text(
        "$_str",
        style: Theme.of(context).textTheme.display1
      ),
    ),
```

```
  bottomNavigationBar: BottomNavigationBar(
    currentIndex: index,
    items: [
      BottomNavigationBarItem(
        icon: Icon(Icons.home),
        title: Text("Home"),
      ),
      BottomNavigationBarItem(
        icon: Icon(Icons.looks_two),
        title: Text("Page 2"),
      ),
      BottomNavigationBarItem(
        icon: Icon(Icons.format_list_numbered_rtl),
        title: Text("Page 3"),
      ),
    ],
    onTap: (page) {
      setState(() {
        switch(page) {
          case 0:
            index = 0;
            break;
          case 1:
            index = 1;
            break;
          case 2:
            index = 2;
        }
      });
    },
  ),
);
}
```

which looks like the screenshot on page 163 and produces the desired behavior when the user taps on a navigation option.

PageView

The PageView is comparable to a horizontal ListView, but that only scrolls page by page.

You can use it as a part of the overall layout, but also as the entire body of the app's Scaffold, like in the following example:

```
Scaffold(
  appBar: AppBar(
    title: Text("PageView Example"),
    backgroundColor: Colors.teal,
  ),
  body: PageView(
    children: <Widget>[
      Center(
        child: Text(
          "Swipe left",
          style: Theme.of(context).textTheme.display1
        ),
      ),
      Center(
        child: Padding(
          padding: EdgeInsets.all(10.0),
          child: Text(
            "Swipe left again, or swipe right",
            style: Theme.of(context).textTheme.display1
          ),
        ),
      ),
```

```
    Center(
      child: Text(
        "Swipe right",
        style: Theme.of(context).textTheme.display1
      ),
    ),
  ],
 ),
)
```

which produces a simple view with an AppBar and, in the middle of the screen, a Text widget.

There is no other on-screen indication that the view has other pages, but swiping left moves the view to the next page and swiping right moves the view to the previous page.

In addition to the children, the PageView has a controller attribute, which can be set to a PageController.

The PageController has a useful option: the initialPage, which is an integer specifying the page (starting from 0) at which the view starts when the app loads.

Top Navigation with a TabBar and TabBarView

Significantly more useful and common is the TabBarView which, paired with a TabBar below the AppBar, provides the same swiping experience of a PageView combined with a nice menu at the top to select which page to switch to and to highlight the page the user is currently at.

The TabBarView and the TabBar are linked by a TabController.

An elegant way to create one is by wrapping the entire view in a DefaultTabController, and setting the entire Scaffold as its child, the number of tabs as its length, and (optionally) an initialIndex (starting from 0, which is the default).

The TabBar can be set as the AppBar's bottom option and it has a tab option where you'll add the Tab widgets, made up of a text and an optional icon, which will be the menu items which will make up the TabBar.

The TabBarView will instead be set as the Scaffold's body and you will add the pages to be displayed to its children option.

For example, this:

```
DefaultTabController(
  length: 3,
// OPTIONAL initialIndex: 0,
```

```
      child: Scaffold(
        appBar: AppBar(
          title: Text("TabBarView Example"),
          bottom: TabBar(
            tabs: <Widget>[
              Tab(
                icon: Icon(Icons.looks_one),
                text: "First Page",
              ),
              Tab(
                icon: Icon(Icons.looks_two),
                text: "Second Page",
              ),
              Tab(
                icon: Icon(Icons.looks_3),
                text: "Third Page",
              ),
            ],
          ),
        ),
        body: TabBarView(
          children: <Widget>[
            Center(
              child: Text("This is the first page")
            ),
            Center(
              child: Text("This is the second page")
            ),
            Center(
              child: Text("This is the third page")
            ),
          ],
        )
      ),
    )
```

which produces the result as shown in the screenshot on page 166.

InheritedWidgets

The DefaultTabController is a special kind of widget: an InheritedWidget, which is used to share state information between Flutter widgets, by storing them in a widget that sits at the top of the widget tree and allowing direct access to its fields and methods by its children, so that they don't need to be passed down the tree using constructor arguments.

They are usually accessed using the Widget.of(context).fieldName syntax that we used previously to get theming data from the Theme and to show snackbars

in the Scaffold. That is because both the Theme and the Scaffold are actually InheritedWidgets.

An InheritedWidget is defined in the following way:

```
class Example extends InheritedWidget {
  Example({child, this.field}):
    super(child: child);
  final String field;

  @override
  bool updateShouldNotify(Example old) => true;
}
```

updateShouldNotify() is used to determine whether the children widgets have to be rebuilt when the InheritedWidget gets rebuilt by the framework.

That will usually be true, but there you can also set it to a set of conditions to determine whether, for example, there are changes to the widget's fields and only rebuild the children in that case.

In its current state, Example.of(context).fieldName from a child of Example wouldn't work since there is actually no of() method.

Even though it is very common, it is not actually built into the framework: by default you access parent InheritedWidgets using context.inheritFromWidgetOfExact-Type(Example).

In fact, a very common static method (explained on Static Members, on page 308) defined inside InheritedWidgets is the of method which, in the case of an InheritedWidget called Example, can be defined in the following way:

```
static Example of(BuildContext context) =>
 context.inheritFromWidgetOfExactType(Example);
```

so that our entire Example class definition becomes:

```
class Example extends InheritedWidget {
  Example({child, this.field}): super(child: child);
  final String field;

  @override
  bool updateShouldNotify(Example old) => old.field != field;

  static Example of(BuildContext context) =>
    context.inheritFromWidgetOfExactType(Example);
}
```

You can use it inside an app like this:

```
Example(
  field: "An example of a string",
  child: MyCustomExternalWidget(),
)
```

And, at any point inside the definition of MyCustomExternalWidget, which takes no arguments, you could access that field you set using:

```
Example.of(context).field
```

which returns the exact String that was set earlier.

Build the App's Basic UI

We'll build an app that is going to display a ListView of ListTiles. There will be a tile for each comic and tapping on a tile should display the details of that comic.

The home is going to look like the screenshot on page 168.

Let's start by defining the classes we need for this app:

- A class for the home screen.
- A custom ComicTile class to make creating ListTiles for the comics easier.
- A class for the comic page.

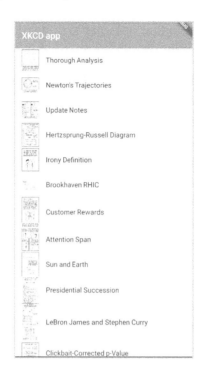

For a change, we won't be using an app class; the main() method will pass the needed data directly to the HomeScreen class we're going to create:

networking_starting/xkcd_app/lib/main.dart
```
void main() async =>
 runApp(
   new MaterialApp(
     home: HomeScreen(
       title: 'XKCD app',
       latestComic: await getLatestComicNumber(),
     )
   )
 );
```

The getLatestComicNumber() method is the one we created in A Function to Get the Latest Comic Number, on page 148, and we need to define it at the start of the file, after the library imports and outside any class definitions:

networking_starting/xkcd_app/lib/main.dart
```
Future<int> getLatestComicNumber() async =>
json.decode(
    await http.read('https://xkcd.com/info.0.json')
 )
 ["num"];
```

Define the Home Screen

At this point we need to define the HomeScreen widget. This time the app tree is very simple and we don't need a figure to get the big picture: the HomeScreen will be a normal Scaffold, with an AppBar (as always), and as a body it will have a ListView made of ListTiles.

Since we need a ListTile for each comic, we'll use the ListView.builder() constructor, as seen in The ListView, on page 44, which uses an itemBuilder function to generate each widget. In this case, the itemBuilder will be a call to a FutureBuilder, which is a kind of item builder that builds widgets based on the contents of a Future, which is what we need since http.get() is an asynchronous function that returns a Future.

Let's start writing the class definition with the basics: it will be a StatelessWidget and it needs two parameters—the title that should appear in the AppBar and the latest comic number:

networking_starting/xkcd_app/lib/main.dart
```
class HomeScreen extends StatelessWidget {
 HomeScreen({this.title, this.latestComic});
 final int latestComic;
 final String title;

}
```

At this point we'll finish doing the preparatory work on the class by defining a _fetchComic() method, just like the one we talked about in The New fetchComic, on page 148:

networking_starting/xkcd_app/lib/main.dart
```
Future<Map<String, dynamic>> _fetchComic(int n) async =>
  json.decode(
    await http.read(
      "https://xkcd.com/${latestComic-n}/info.0.json"
    )
  );
```

Now all that's left to do is the fun part: defining the UI we want for our app in the build() method. We'll start by defining the Scaffold and AppBar, as we always do:

networking_starting/xkcd_app/lib/main.dart
```
@override
Widget build(BuildContext context) {
  return Scaffold(
    appBar: AppBar(
      title: Text(title),
    ),

  );
}
```

The Scaffold's body will be, as we said, a ListView.builder()-built ListView, and we need to give it two arguments:

- An itemCount, which is the maximum number of items that will be built; in this case, it will be the latestComic number, since that's also the number of comics that have ever been published.

- An itemBuilder, which is a function called with the BuildContext and an int that starts from 0 at the top (we'll call it i).

In this case the itemBuilder is going to be, as we said before, a FutureBuilder.

The FutureBuilder, in turn, requires two arguments: a future, which is the Future that will retrieve the data needed for each tile, and a builder function, which builds the tile taking the BuildContext and the result of the Future.

The future will be a call to fetchComic(i) where i is the aforementioned progressive integer variable and the itemBuilder will return a ComicTile that takes the comic data as an argument. We'll worry about implementing the ComicTile itself later.

On the Correct Use of the FutureBuilder

The FutureBuilder's future shouldn't be a function call: it should be a previously obtained Future because setting it to a function call would result in the future being called every time the parent widget is rebuilt, but that doesn't apply in our case: the parent widget is a StatelessWidget and there are no StatefulWidgets above. You need to remember this when you build your own Flutter apps though: forgetting this could make app interactions needlessly slow and clunky.

Usually these Futures should be obtained in the initState() method of StatefulWidgets.

Here is the full body of the HomeScreen's Scaffold:

networking_starting/xkcd_app/lib/main.dart
```
body: ListView.builder(
  itemCount: latestComic,
  itemBuilder:(context, i) => FutureBuilder(
    future: _fetchComic(i),
    builder: (context, comicResult) =>
      comicResult.hasData ?
      ComicTile(comic: comicResult.data) :
      Divider();
  ),
),
```

The full HomeScreen class definition, combining all of the pieces of code we saw earlier, is:

networking_starting/xkcd_app/lib/main.dart

```
class HomeScreen extends StatelessWidget {
  HomeScreen({this.title, this.latestComic});
  final int latestComic;
  final String title;

  Future<Map<String, dynamic>> _fetchComic(int n) async =>
    json.decode(
      await http.read(
        "https://xkcd.com/${latestComic-n}/info.0.json"
      )
    );

  @override
  Widget build(BuildContext context) {
    return Scaffold(
      appBar: AppBar(
        title: Text(title),
      ),
      body: ListView.builder(
        itemCount: latestComic,
        itemBuilder:(context, i) => FutureBuilder(
          future: _fetchComic(i),
          builder: (context, comicResult) =>
            comicResult.hasData ?
            ComicTile(comic: comicResult.data) :
            Divider();
        ),
      ),
    );
  }
}
```

Define the ComicTile

Now we need to define the ComicTile class, which will be yet another StatelessWidget and it will take the comic data it needs to display as its only argument:

networking_starting/xkcd_app/lib/main.dart

```
class ComicTile extends StatelessWidget {
  ComicTile({this.comic});

  final Map<String, dynamic> comic;
```

The ComicTile will be a ListTile that has the comic image as the leading, a comic title Text as its title and, when tapped, displays a new screen just for that comic, showing the comic in a bigger format along with its *alt-text*.

We'll worry about building the comic page later: we now need to figure out how to show that screen. We talked about push/pop navigation earlier in Push/Pop Navigation Using the Navigator, on page 149, and that's what we're going to use:

```
  @override
  Widget build(BuildContext context) {
    return ListTile(
❶     leading: Image.network(
        comic["img"],
        height: 30,
        width: 30
      ),
❷     title: Text(comic["title"]),
❸     onTap: () {
        Navigator.push(
          context,
          MaterialPageRoute(
            builder: (BuildContext context) => ComicPage(comic)
          ),
        );
      },
    );
  }
```

❶ In this section we define the leading widget of the ListTile: an Image taken from the network URL provided (the comic's 'img' attribute).

We set the maximum width and height for the image preview to 30 pixels to avoid having the previews take up too much vertical or horizontal space in the list.

❷ This is the text that will appear for each tile. In this case we use the comic's title, taken from the comic's title attribute.

❸ Here we set what will happen when the user taps on the tile. In this case, it opens a ComicPage (that we'll define later) using the push operation we discussed in Push/Pop Navigation Using the Navigator, on page 149.

The full ComicTile class definition is:

networking_starting/xkcd_app/lib/main.dart
```
class ComicTile extends StatelessWidget {
  ComicTile({this.comic});

  final Map<String, dynamic> comic;

  @override
  Widget build(BuildContext context) {
    return ListTile(
      leading: Image.network(
        comic["img"],
        height: 30,
        width: 30
      ),
```

```
          title: Text(comic["title"]),
        onTap: () {
          Navigator.push(
            context,
            MaterialPageRoute(
              builder: (BuildContext context) =>
                ComicPage(comic)
            ),
          );
        },
      );
    }
  }
}
```

Building the Comic Page

The ComicPage is going to be the simplest of the widgets we talked about until now: we're going to give it an AppBar that shows the comic number, and the body is simply going to be a scrollable ListView that shows the comic's title, image and alt-text:

networking_starting/xkcd_app/lib/main.dart
```
class ComicPage extends StatelessWidget {
  ComicPage(this.comic);

  final Map<String, dynamic> comic;

  @override
  Widget build(BuildContext context) {
    return Scaffold(
      appBar: AppBar(title: Text("#${comic["num"]}")),
      body: ListView(children: <Widget>[
        Center(
          child: Text(
            comic["title"],
            style: Theme.of(context).textTheme.display3,
          ),
        ),
        Image.network(comic["img"]),
        Padding(
          padding: EdgeInsets.all(8.0),
          child: Text(comic["alt"])
        ),
      ],),
    );
  }
}
```

All of that adds up to the following main.dart:

networking_starting/xkcd_app/lib/main.dart

```
import 'package:flutter/material.dart';
import 'package:http/http.dart' as http;

import 'dart:async';
import 'dart:convert';

Future<int> getLatestComicNumber() async =>
 json.decode(
    await http.read('https://xkcd.com/info.0.json')
 )
 ["num"];


void main() async =>
 runApp(
   new MaterialApp(
     home: HomeScreen(
       title: 'XKCD app',
       latestComic: await getLatestComicNumber(),
     )
   )
 );

class ComicPage extends StatelessWidget {
 ComicPage(this.comic);

 final Map<String, dynamic> comic;

 @override
 Widget build(BuildContext context) {
   return Scaffold(
     appBar: AppBar(title: Text("#${comic["num"]}")),
     body: ListView(children: <Widget>[
       Center(
         child: Text(
           comic["title"],
           style: Theme.of(context).textTheme.display3,
         ),
       ),
       Image.network(comic["img"]),
       Padding(
        padding: EdgeInsets.all(8.0),
        child: Text(comic["alt"])
       ),
     ],),),
   );
 }
}
```

```dart
class ComicTile extends StatelessWidget {
  ComicTile({this.comic});

  final Map<String, dynamic> comic;

  @override
  Widget build(BuildContext context) {
    return ListTile(
      leading: Image.network(
        comic["img"],
        height: 30,
        width: 30
      ),
      title: Text(comic["title"]),
      onTap: () {
        Navigator.push(
          context,
          MaterialPageRoute(
            builder: (BuildContext context) =>
              ComicPage(comic)
          ),
        );
      },
    );
  }
}

class HomeScreen extends StatelessWidget {
  HomeScreen({this.title, this.latestComic});
  final int latestComic;
  final String title;

  Future<Map<String, dynamic>> _fetchComic(int n) async =>
    json.decode(
      await http.read(
        "https://xkcd.com/${latestComic-n}/info.0.json"
      )
    );

  @override
  Widget build(BuildContext context) {
    return Scaffold(
      appBar: AppBar(
        title: Text(title),
      ),
      body: ListView.builder(
        itemCount: latestComic,
        itemBuilder:(context, i) => FutureBuilder(
          future: _fetchComic(i),
```

```
      builder: (context, comicResult) =>
        comicResult.hasData ?
        ComicTile(comic: comicResult.data) :
        Divider();
    ),
  ),
);
 }
}
```

At this point we're ready to run the app, which is going to look like this:

 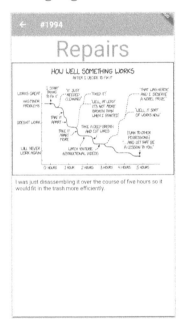

Using the CircularProgressIndicator

In those screenshots you see what the app looks like when everything has finished loading, but we also need to think about what it looks like while it's still in the process of loading: we currently display a Divider when it's loading each tile, but that isn't really visually pleasing if the user is on a slow network and will therefore look at many dividers stacked on top of each other for a few seconds.

There is a class specifically meant to be used for this placeholder task: the CircularProgressIndicator.[6] It's not the only progress indicator: there is also a LinearProgressIndicator, but it's less common and less flexible.

---

6. https://material.io/design/components/progress-indicators.html#circular-progress-indicators

You can just place its constructor (CircularProgressIndicator()) anywhere you want to display it (for example, instead of the Divider placeholder for the ComicTile), but that would make it stretch to fill the space given to it. This is fixed by restraining it to a Container with a limited width.

The builder for the FutureBuilder inside the ListView.builder in the HomeScreen becomes the following:

```
networking/xkcd_app/lib/main.dart
builder: (context, snapshot) {
  return snapshot.hasData ?
   ComicTile(comic: snapshot.data) :
   Container(
     width: 30,
     child: CircularProgressIndicator()
   );
},
```

Making Everything Faster by Caching to Local Storage

Our app works, but it is very slow because it downloads everything every time, and that wastes the user's time and data.

To make our app more efficient, we'll have to save the comics to a local cache and retrieve them from there before trying to get them from the Internet. If the needed comic isn't already saved, we'll download it from the Internet.

An Introduction to the path_provider Package

Mobile apps can store data in two directories: a temporary cache directory (which is what we'll use for this example) or a permanent Data/Documents directory (which is meant to be used for permanent storage of user data). The difference between those two directories is that the cache directory may be wiped at any time by the operating system or the user; wiping the data directory should be done only after warning the user that they may lose important data.

The path_provider package allows you to get the path where these folders are located in all of the operating systems supported by Flutter, whereas the I/O operations themselves are handled by the built-in dart:io plugin. Let's start by adding the following to the dependencies in pubspec.yaml:

```
networking/xkcd_app/pubspec.yaml
path_provider:
```

And import it in our Dart code using this at the top:

networking/xkcd_app/lib/main.dart
```
import 'package:path_provider/path_provider.dart';
```

Since they perform I/O operations (which take a considerable amount of time to complete), both path_provider and dart:io functions return Futures.

Get Down to It: Implement Caching

Since we also need to use Dart's built-in dart:io plugin to actually perform the I/O operations, we need to add the following at the top of the Dart file:

networking/xkcd_app/lib/main.dart
```
import 'dart:io';
```

The code we need to modify is the code that fetches the comics: we need the comic fetching functions to check if the comic is already saved, get it from local storage if it is, and download it and save it if it isn't already saved.

We'll create a file to store the number of the latest comic (which is going to be updated whenever the app is started with a network connection available) and each comic is going to be saved in a separate file.

Let's start with the most significant change: the change to the fetchComic() methods.

Specifically, the HomeScreen's fetchComic method, which, at the moment, looks like this:

networking_starting/xkcd_app/lib/main.dart
```
Future<Map<String, dynamic>> _fetchComic(int n) async =>
  json.decode(
    await http.read(
      "https://xkcd.com/${latestComic-n}/info.0.json"
    )
  );
```

Fat arrow syntax won't work for what we need now: before returning a value we need to get the temporary directory path, check if the comic has already been downloaded and fetch it if it hasn't.

We'll start editing it by reverting to the regular syntax, with braces and return:

```
Future<Map<String, dynamic>> _fetchComic(int n) async {
  return json.decode(
    await http.read(
      "https://xkcd.com/${latestComic-n}/info.0.json"
    )
  );
}
```

At the start of the function, we'll declare three variables: the directory that will contain the files, the comic number (since we'll use it more than once it's easier to just calculate it once and use it every time) and the File object itself.

The function that returns the directory is getTemporaryDirectory(), it is asynchronous and returns a Directory object, the path string itself is the Directory.path member.

Files are managed through the File class, which allows us to create files and perform read/write operations on them.

The File constructor is very simple: it takes one positional argument, which is the path to the file.

We can perform operations on files using two methods for each operation: we can choose between a synchronous method (like File.readAsStringSync()) which returns whatever is requested directly (no Futures involved), and an asynchronous method (like File.readAsString()) which is asynchronous, returns a Future and requires await or Future.then() to retrieve the requested data. The advantage of the synchronous method is that we don't need to convert everything to asynchronous methods and we don't need to use await all the time, while the advantage of the asynchronous method is that we can just run it and let the rest of the main thread run unaffected if we don't need the result, as would happen when we create files, for example.

The First Step: Saving the JSON Response

These three things can be done with the following three lines of code:

```
final dir = await getTemporaryDirectory();
int comicNumber = latestComic-n;
var comicFile = File("${dir.path}/$comicNumber.json");
```

Now we need to check if the file exists and isn't empty and return its decoded content:

```
if(await comicFile.exists() && comicFile.readAsStringSync() != "")
  return json.decode(comicFile.readAsStringSync());
```

If it isn't, we need to create the file and write the JSON string to it:

```
else {
  final comic =
      await http.read('https://xkcd.com/${latestComic - n}/info.0.json');
```

The entire function, when put together, ends up being:

```
Future<Map<String, dynamic>> _fetchComic(int n) async {
  final dir = await getTemporaryDirectory();
  int comicNumber = latestComic-n;
  var comicFile = File("${dir.path}/$comicNumber.json");
  if(await comicFile.exists() && comicFile.readAsStringSync() != "")
    return json.decode(comicFile.readAsStringSync());
  else {
    final comic =
        await http.read('https://xkcd.com/${latestComic - n}/info.0.json');
    /* no need to use sync methods as we
       don't have to wait for it to finish caching */
    comicFile.writeAsString(comic);
    return json.decode(comic);
  }
}
```

Since the SelectionPage should also take advantage of cached comics, we just
need to modify this function slightly to take the comic number as a string
argument:

```
Future<Map<String, dynamic>> _fetchComic(int n) async {
  final dir = await getTemporaryDirectory();
  var comicFile = File("${dir.path}/$n.json");

  if(await comicFile.exists() && comicFile.readAsStringSync() != "")
    return json.decode(comicFile.readAsStringSync());
  else {
    final comic =
        await http.read('https://xkcd.com/$n/info.0.json');
    comicFile.writeAsString(comic);
    return json.decode(comic);
  }
}
```

Saving the Latest Comic Number

In its current state, our app still depends on the latest comic number being
fetched at startup to work, but we can save that in a file when we get it and,
if at some point we can't fetch it at startup, we will try to get it from the file
instead.

We obviously want to fetch the remote one whenever we can, since we want
that number to change when new comics come out, unlike what we did in
_fetchComic(), where we fetched from files whenever possible and only resorted
to fetching from the Internet if that wasn't possible.

To do this in our app we need to change the getLatestComicNumber() top-level
function, and to achieve what we want there is a feature that will be familiar
to most programmers is catching exception using try and catch.

If the app attempts a network connection and fails (which happens when the site can't be reached by the device for any reason), it will throw an exception.

We can catch that exception and grab the comic number from local storage instead.

We'll start editing the function declaring the directory and file variables, along with a variable to store the latest comic number that will be returned:

networking/xkcd_app/lib/main.dart
```
final dir = await getTemporaryDirectory();
var file = File('${dir.path}/latestComicNumber.txt');
int n = 1;
```

Catching Exceptions

This section is an anticipation of Throwing and Catching Exceptions, on page 233, since we will deal with try-catch block to catch exceptions.

Whenever, in any programming language, a piece of code fails to perform the action that is requested to perform, the programming language allows it to *throw* an *exception*. This will result in a crash of the piece of software in question, but any exception can be handled by *catching* it and performing an action in response to the exception.

For example, if we try to get the comic number and an exception is thrown (meaning that the latest comic number couldn't be fetched, probably because no network connection is available) we can catch that exception and check if we have fetched it in a previous occasion, so that we can retrieve it from there instead.

To do that, we'll start by wrapping whatever could fail in a try block, like this:

```
try {
  // CODE THAT COULD FAIL
} catch(exceptionDetails) {
  print("Something failed");
  print(exceptionDetails);
}
```

So let's fetch the latest comic number, but in a try block:

networking/xkcd_app/lib/main.dart
```
try {
  n = json.decode(
    await http.read('https://xkcd.com/info.0.json')
  )["num"];

}
```

Since saving the number in a file doesn't affect the rest of the function's execution, we can check if the file exist, create it if it doesn't and write the number to the file in a separate thread, without making the function wait for these operations to be completed (all of this will go inside the try block and will only be executed if the previous instruction doesn't fail):

networking/xkcd_app/lib/main.dart
```
file.exists().then(
  (exists) {
    if(!exists) file.createSync();
    file.writeAsString('$n');
  }
);
```

The .then() method creates a new thread, waiting for the function to return a value.

When file.exists() returns a value, it is passed to an anonymous function that does everything we need it to do without affecting the rest of the function.

If this fails and there is a file from which we can get the number we will get the number from that file, using the catch keyword:

networking/xkcd_app/lib/main.dart
```
catch(e) {
  if(
    file.existsSync() &&
    file.readAsStringSync() != ""
  )
    n = int.parse(file.readAsStringSync());
}
```

And, regardless of how we get here, we return the number:

networking/xkcd_app/lib/main.dart
```
return n;
```

Saving the Images

Now, if you try to open the app with no network connection, you will notice that everything works, but there are no images.

This shouldn't be surprising: we are only saving their URL, and we obviously can't access the images without a network connection.

This means we need to download the images to make our app 100% usable offline and, to be able to do this, we will, once again, have to make changes to fetchComic().

The code that runs when the file already exists doesn't need to be changed: it just reads the file and saves it, we just need to ensure that we clear the cache before running the app since we'll be making changes to how the comic's JSON string is being saved and we will be making changes to the functions that use the values in the cached comics.

In the else statement's curly braces in the HomeScreen's fetchComic method we need to create the file, get the comic's JSON body, save the image to local storage, and replace the URL in the img parameter with the saved image's path.

These are all operations that have already been described by this book and, when put together, produce the following _fetchComic():

```
networking/xkcd_app/lib/main.dart
Future<Map<String, dynamic>> _fetchComic(int n) async {

  final dir = await getTemporaryDirectory();
  int comicNumber = latestComic-n;
  var comicFile = File("${dir.path}/$comicNumber.json");
  if(
   await comicFile.exists() &&
   comicFile.readAsStringSync() != ""
  )
     return json.decode(comicFile.readAsStringSync());
  else {
    comicFile.createSync();
     final comic = json.decode(
      await http.read(
       'https://xkcd.com/$comicNumber/info.0.json'
      )
     );

    File('${dir.path}/$comicNumber.png')
      .writeAsBytesSync(await http.readBytes(comic["img"]));
    comic["img"] = '${dir.path}/$comicNumber.png';
    comicFile.writeAsString(json.encode(comic));

    return comic;

  }
}
```

We are just using an asynchronous function without an await expression to write the comic file, since it isn't going to be used by the app until it is restarted, so we don't need to pause the execution to write it like we do, for example, for the image file that is going to be used by the ComicTile not long after the method returns.

The same exact changes apply to the SelectionPage's _fetchComic() method, given that this part of the function doesn't change between the two:

networking/xkcd_app/lib/main.dart

```
Future<Map<String, dynamic>> _fetchComic(String n) async {
  final dir = await getTemporaryDirectory();
  var comicFile = File("${dir.path}/$n.json");

  if(
    await comicFile.exists() &&
    comicFile.readAsStringSync() != ""
  )
    return json.decode(comicFile.readAsStringSync());
  else {
    comicFile.createSync();
    final comic = json.decode(
      await http.read('https://xkcd.com/$n/info.0.json')
    );

    File('${dir.path}/$n.png')
      .writeAsBytesSync(await http.readBytes(comic["img"]));
    comic["img"] = '${dir.path}/$n.png';
    comicFile.writeAsString(json.encode(comic));

    return comic;
  }
}
```

Since the comic["img"] value is now the path to the file that contains the comic image, we need to change (in the build methods for the ComicPage and for the ComicTile) the following line:

```
Image.network(comic["img"])
```

to:

```
Image.file(File(comic["img"]))
```

At this point opening the app with an active Internet connection, closing it and opening it again without an Internet connection will reveal that the app is now completely capable of browsing comics that have already been fetched while not being able to perform requests to the XKCD website.

Allowing the User to Click the Image and Go to the Website: The url_launcher Package

What if users want to see a comic on the XKCD website? Right now, the only way they could do that is by taking advantage of the comic number and title and searching the XKCD website themselves.

It wouldn't be too hard to provide users with the ability to do that with a tap in the app, so let's do it!

To launch URLs from Flutter apps, we'll use a handy package on Pub called *url_launcher*.

Using the url_launcher Package

Let's add the url_launcher package to the dependencies in pubspec.yaml:

networking/xkcd_app/pubspec.yaml
```
url_launcher: ^5.0.2
```

and import it in our code in main.dart:

networking/xkcd_app/lib/main.dart
```
import 'package:url_launcher/url_launcher.dart';
```

The *url_launcher* package provides two functions: canLaunch(url) and launch(url). The first returns a bool wrapped in a Future, which will be true if there is an app that can handle the URL or false if there isn't. The second actually launches the URL and returns the same value as the other function: if the launch was successfull, it returns true; if it wasn't, it returns false.

So we know how to launch the URL, but we don't actually get the comic URL when we fetch the comic's JSON. That's not actually a problem, since the URL for each comic is just *https://xkcd.com/comic_number/*: the URL to reach comic #2019 is *https://xkcd.com/2019/*.

This means that a method to launch comics, to be defined inside the ComicPage class, can be written in the following way:

networking/xkcd_app/lib/main.dart
```
void _launchComic(int comicNumber) {
  launch("https://xkcd.com/$comicNumber/");
}
```

Adding an onTap Event

We know how to launch an URL, but the Image's constructors don't provide an onTap argument, so we need to wrap it in a InkWell, which is a lot like wrapping an img HTML image tag in an a link tag: the InkWell needs two arguments: a child which, in this case, will be the Image, and the onTap argument we wanted, along with a bunch of options to customize the inksplash effect you can check out on the official Flutter documentation.[7]

All that's left to do is to find the place where we show the comic image in ComicPage and wrap it in the InkWell:

---

7. https://docs.flutter.io/flutter/material/InkWell-class.html

networking/xkcd_app/lib/main.dart
```
InkWell(
  onTap: () {_launchComic(widget.comic["num"]);},
    child: Image.file(File(widget.comic["img"])),
),
```

Showing Inksplash on the InkWell

One of InkWell's features is that it can show an inksplash effect when the user taps on the area where it is located, but that will not work in our app because of how visual effects like the inksplash are applied on Flutter widgets.

A Flutter layout is made of widgets, but the inksplash is not applied to widgets: it is applied to Material, which is the class that is also responsible for clipping and elevation effects. An Image is drawn *over* a Material, so the inksplash will be applied to the Material *below* the image, which will make it invisible.

To show the inksplash effect you'd need to overlap the Image with a transparent Material widget. The Ink widget[8] makes that simpler: it provides a Ink.image() method that allows you to set the InkWell as a child, making the image and the Material on top of it an ancestor of the InkWell.

A disadvantage of the Ink() is that it requires setting a maximum width and height. For an example of code that correctly shows the inksplash over the image and that works when replacing the code we used above, take a look at this:

networking/xkcd_app/lib/inkSplashComicLaunch.dart
```
Material(
  child: Ink.image(
    image: FileImage(File(widget.comic["img"])),
    height: 300,
    width: 200,
    child: InkWell(
      onTap: () {_launchComic(widget.comic["num"]);},
    ),
  ),
),
```
If you are not interested in the inskplash effect at all, you can use a GestureDetector instead of the InkWell. It works in the same way as the InkWell, with the same arguments, but without applying an inksplash effect on any kind of widget.

---

8. docs.flutter.io/flutter/material/Ink-class.html

Adding Comic Selection by Number

It's very easy to fetch comics by number, so it seems obvious that we should be able to let the user select comics using the comic number, especially because very often users want to go back to a comic they've seen on the Web.

To do that, we'll start by creating a page to select the comics, which will look like this:

Since it doesn't need any parameters to work, we don't need to specify the constructor, but we need to have a fetchComic() method that fetches by comic number, unlike the one we used for the HomePage:

```
class SelectionPage extends StatelessWidget {
  Future<Map<String, dynamic>> _fetchComic(String n) async =>
    json.decode(
      await http.read('https://xkcd.com/$n/info.0.json')
    );
}
```

The build() method will be more complex, using some Flutter features we've never seen before in this book:

```
@override
Widget build(BuildContext context) {
 return Scaffold(
   appBar: AppBar(
     title: Text("Comic selection"),
   ),
```

```
     body: Center(
①      child: TextField(
         decoration: InputDecoration(
           labelText: "Insert comic #",
         ),
②        keyboardType: TextInputType.number,
③        autofocus: true,
         onSubmitted: (String a) => Navigator.push(
           context,
           MaterialPageRoute(
④            builder: (context) => FutureBuilder(
               future: _fetchComic(a),
               builder: (context, snapshot) {
                 if(snapshot.hasData) return ComicPage(snapshot.data);
                 return CircularProgressIndicator();
               }
             ),
           ),
         ),
       ),
     ),
   );
}
```

❶ This is a TextField, which is a widget that allows the user to input text.

❷ keyboardType is used to set the type of information the user is supposed to input (the framework will optimize the display and/or the type of keyboad shown to the user to suit this setting). It is of type TextInputType, which can be one of the following:

- TextInputType.text (default) for regular single-line text.
- TextInputType.multiline for multiple lines of text.
- TextInputType.number, which is what we're going to use, for numbers.
- TextInputType.datetime for date and time.
- TextInputType.emailAddress for email addresses.
- TextInputType.phone for telephone numbers.

❸ This argument makes the view automatically focus on the TextField. This means the keypad will automatically open and any numbers typed on it will be sent to the TextField, without requiring the user to tap on it first.

❹ We haven't yet fetched the comic, which means we need to call the FutureBuilder to fetch the comic and use the comic as an argument for the ComicPage.

Now we need to be able to reach that page from the home page. We'll do this by using AppBar actions, which are widgets we can show on the right side of the app bar. In this case, we're going to use an IconButton:

```
  appBar: AppBar(
   title: Text(title),
   actions: <Widget>[
      IconButton(
       icon: Icon(Icons.looks_one),
       tooltip: "Select Comics by Number",
       onPressed: () =>
         Navigator.push(
           context,
           MaterialPageRoute(
             builder: (BuildContext context) => SelectionPage()
           ),
         ),
      ),
    ],
  ),
),
```

❶ This is where we are going to add a List of widgets to show on the AppBar. In this case it's going to be just one IconButton.

❷ The IconButton also needs a tooltip to help the user understand what the button does. Further on in the book there is a screenshot of what it looks like.

❸ This is just like the ComicTile's onpressed.

The updated home page, showing the overall new look of the app, looks like:

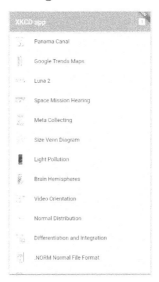

and when the user keeps the button pressed the tooltip will look like:

What If That Comic Doesn't Exist?

The user could input any number that goes through their head in the Selection-Page. While I don't actively endorse abusing innocent app features this way, the user could choose to input a number that is bigger than the latest comic's number, and we can't just let the app crash or let the CircularProgressIndicator loop forever because the user isn't supposed to do that.

We need to handle that situation, and for that we'll use the AsyncSnapshot's hasError property: if it is true, it means an error occurred during the processing of the future. If it is true, we'll show the user an ErrorPage, which we'll build later.

Meanwhile, here's the new builder for our FutureBuilder:

networking/xkcd_app/lib/main.dart
```
builder: (context, snapshot) {
  if(snapshot.hasError) return ErrorPage();
  if(snapshot.hasData) return ComicPage(snapshot.data);
  return CircularProgressIndicator();
}
```

I said we were going to build a ComicPage at some point. The moment has come to do that, so let's do it! The ComicPage needs to be just a simple StatelessWidget and the usual Scaffold and AppBar. The body will be a Column containing an icon and a Text informing the user they have done something wrong:

networking/xkcd_app/lib/main.dart
```
class ErrorPage extends StatelessWidget {
  @override
  Widget build(BuildContext context) {
    return Scaffold(
      appBar: AppBar(
        title: Text("Error Page"),
      ),
      body: Column(
            children: [
              Icon(Icons.not_interested),
              Text(
                "The comics you have selected doesn't exist"+
                "or isn't available"
              ),
            ]
          )
    );
  }
}
```

Make Your Own Changes

We have already seen quite a lot of Dart code, but have you been writing your own as well? If you haven't, here is another chance (after the one in Wrapping Up the Calculation, on page 105) for you to make a very simple and slight improvement to our XKCD app.

The ErrorPage we just wrote generically informs the user that we couldn't get that comic. This can also be used any time we can't fetch a comic (for example, if there is no Internet available and the cache was wiped).

You can do this yourself very easily by adding a snapshot.hasError condition to each FutureBuilder. You could go one step further and compare the comic number given to the SelectionPage to the latest comic number and show a different error if the user accidentally gave a comic number that is bigger than the latest comic number.

Permanent Data I/O in Flutter: Adding "Starred" Comics

Up until now we have only used the temporary cache directory, but if we want to add a feature that allows the user to save some comics to local storage permanently as a way to keep their favorite comics always available to them. To do that, we need to have access to a permanent local storage facility.

That is available to us in the form of application documents directory, which is where an app is supposed to save data that should be kept until the user consciously deletes it.

We can get the path of the application documents directory using getApplication-DocumentsDirectory(), and we can use it in the same way we use the cache directory we got through getTemporaryDirectory(): we use getApplicationDocumentsDirectory().path as part of the path we give to the File's constructor.

Let's get to implementing this feature, starting with adding a star-shaped button in the app bar in the home page to access previously saved comics and one in the comic page to save comics.

But even before we do any of that, we need to turn the ComicPage into a Stateful-Widget if we want the view to reflect the change in the comic's state triggered by the user's action. This means we need to do two things: change the definition of the ComicPage to be a subclass of StatefulWidget and turn what was up until now the ComicPage into a State<ComicPage> definition, inside which the same build() method will reside:

networking/xkcd_app/lib/main.dart
```
class ComicPage extends StatefulWidget {
  ComicPage(this.comic);

  final Map<String, dynamic> comic;

  @override
  _ComicPageState createState() => _ComicPageState();
}

class _ComicPageState extends State<ComicPage> {

  @override
  Widget build(BuildContext context) {
    // return Scaffold(...)
  }
}
```

The next step is to decide what kind of file we should use for storing the starred comics. We have used two different kind of files until now:

- A JSON-encoded text file to store the comic data and a simple text file to store the latest comic number.

- A binary file to save the image data.

The choices have been dictated by the nature of the data we needed to save: images are binary data, whereas we get the comics in a textual JSON format, meaning they can easily be saved in that format to local storage. A single number can be stored as binary data or text-based data without too many differences.

The starred comics will be a list of numbers, and there are advantages and disadvantages to each approach:

- Saving in a binary format (using writeAsBytes()) is simpler to implement and requires less computing overhead, but will generate files that are not readable by the user, but more efficient on storage.

- Saving it in a JSON list makes it possible for the user to read and edit the file directly, but results in a less efficient use of computing power and storage space.

We are going to use binary format in this case since that seems to be the optimal solution for this problem. We'll start by implementing an _addToStarred() in the ComicPageState to add a comic to the starred comics list:

networking/xkcd_app/lib/main.dart
```
void _addToStarred(int num) {
  var file = File("$docsDir/starred");
  List<int> savedComics = json.decode(
    file.readAsStringSync()
```

```
  ).cast<int>();
  if(isStarred) {
    savedComics.remove(num);
  }
  else {
    savedComics.add(num);
  }
  file.writeAsStringSync(json.encode(savedComics));
}
```

which depends on the existence of isStarred as a ComicPage member variable:

networking/xkcd_app/lib/main.dart
```
bool isStarred;
```

We need to determine whether or not the comic is starred when we load the ComicPage for the first time, since we will be changing that variable's value whenever the user taps on the star button. Since we can't have an async init-State(), we'll use .then():

networking/xkcd_app/lib/main.dart
```
void initState() {
  super.initState();
  getApplicationDocumentsDirectory().then(
    (dir) {
      docsDir = dir.path;
      var file = File("$docsDir/starred");
      if(!file.existsSync()) {
        file.createSync();
        file.writeAsStringSync("[]");
        isStarred = false;
      }
      else {
        setState((){isStarred = _isStarred(widget.comic["num"]);});
      }
    }
  );
}
```

This depends on an onStarred() method that finds out if the comic have been starred by opening the file containing the starred comic numbers, casting it from a List of dynamic (which is a data type that can contain anything) to a List of integers and checking whether the comic number is contained in the list:

networking/xkcd_app/lib/main.dart
```
bool _isStarred(int num) {
  var file = File("$docsDir/starred");
  List<int> savedComics = json.decode(
    file.readAsStringSync()
  ).cast<int>();
```

```
  if(savedComics.indexOf(num) != -1)
    return true;
  else
    return false;
}
```

Adding the AppBar Action to the Comic Path

Now we need to implement a way to add each comic to the starred. The way we'll do it in this case is by showing a star-shaped icon in the app bar that, when tapped, calls the _addToStarred() method on the current comic, adding it to the starred comics list. To do that, we'll add yet another AppBar action to our app in the ComicPage's build() method:

networking/xkcd_app/lib/main.dart
```
actions: <Widget>[
  IconButton(
    icon: isStarred == true ?
      Icon(Icons.star) :
      Icon(Icons.star_border),
    tooltip: "Star Comic",
    onPressed: () {
      _addToStarred(widget.comic["num"]);
      setState(() {
        isStarred = !isStarred;
      });
    }
  ),
],
```

This is what our new ComicPage looks like:

and what its app bar will look like if the current comic has been starred:

Implementing a Starred Comics List

We need a way for the user to find all of the comics they add to their favorite comics, and we'll be doing that by creating a new widget: a new page in our app that will be just like the HomeScreen, but only showing starred comics.

Let's define yet another widget and a fetchComic() just like the one in the Selection Page (one that fetches by comic number):

networking/xkcd_app/lib/main.dart

```dart
class StarredPage extends StatelessWidget {

  StarredPage();

  Future<Map<String, dynamic>> _fetchComic(String n) async {
    final dir = await getTemporaryDirectory();
    var comicFile = File("${dir.path}/$n.json");

    if(
      await comicFile.exists() &&
      comicFile.readAsStringSync() != ""
    )
      return json.decode(comicFile.readAsStringSync());
    else {
      comicFile.createSync();
      final comic = json.decode(
        await http.read('https://xkcd.com/$n/info.0.json')
      );

      File('${dir.path}/$n.png')
        .writeAsBytesSync(await http.readBytes(comic["img"]));
      comic["img"] = '${dir.path}/$n.png';
      comicFile.writeAsString(json.encode(comic));

      return comic;
    }
  }

}
```

While we're at it, let's also write a method to retrieve all of the saved comics and return a List containing all of the data, taking advantage of the _fetchComic() method we just wrote:

```
Future<List<Map<String, dynamic>>> _retrieveSavedComics() async {
  Directory docsDir = await getApplicationDocumentsDirectory();
  File file = File("${docsDir.path}/starred");
  List<Map<String, dynamic>> comics = [];

  if(!file.existsSync()) {
    file.createSync();
    file.writeAsStringSync("[]");
  } else {
    json.decode(file.readAsStringSync()).forEach(
      (n) async =>
        comics.add(await _fetchComic(n.toString()))
    );
  }
  return comics;
}
```

❶ Here we define the needed variables and fetch the application documents directory and use it to define the file which we wil be operating on.

❷ We need to check whether the starred comics file exists; if it doesn't, we just create the file and end up returning an empty list (we'll work with that later when we build the UI for the starred comics page).

❸ If the file exists, we fetch all of the comics listed in the file and return them.

Now we'll build the UI for the StarredPage:

networking/xkcd_app/lib/starredPageUI.dart

```
@override
Widget build(BuildContext context) {
  var comics = _retrieveSavedComics();

  return Scaffold(
    appBar: AppBar(
      title: Text("Browse your Favorite Comics")
    ),
    body: FutureBuilder(
      future: comics,
      builder: (context, snapshot) =>
        snapshot.hasData && snapshot.data.isNotEmpty ?
        ListView.builder(
          itemCount: snapshot.data.length,
          itemBuilder: (context, i) =>
            ComicTile(comic: snapshot.data[i],),
        )
        :
```

```
        Column(
          children: [
            Icon(Icons.not_interested),
            Text("""
              You haven't starred any comics yet.
              Check back after you have found something worthy of being here.
              """),
          ]
        )
      )
    );
}
```

❶ The build() method will be called just once, so adding this call anywhere wouldn't change anything, but this is how you're supposed to do it: put the call returning a Future anywhere it will be called just once and then use the value returned by that call as the FutureBuilder constructor's future argument.

❷ We need to check whether there are any starred comics. If there are any, we'll show a ListView of ComicTiles as we do in the home page.

❸ If there are no starred comics, we'll just show a notice to the user. We are using multi-line strings as explained in the Dart appendix to this book (Characters and Strings, on page 286).

The entire StarredPage code we've seen is combined into the following class definition:

networking/xkcd_app/lib/main.dart
```
class StarredPage extends StatelessWidget {

  StarredPage();

  Future<Map<String, dynamic>> _fetchComic(String n) async {
    final dir = await getTemporaryDirectory();
    var comicFile = File("${dir.path}/$n.json");

    if(
      await comicFile.exists() &&
      comicFile.readAsStringSync() != ""
    )
      return json.decode(comicFile.readAsStringSync());
    else {
      comicFile.createSync();
      final comic = json.decode(
        await http.read('https://xkcd.com/$n/info.0.json')
      );
```

```dart
      File('${dir.path}/$n.png')
        .writeAsBytesSync(await http.readBytes(comic["img"]));
      comic["img"] = '${dir.path}/$n.png';
      comicFile.writeAsString(json.encode(comic));

      return comic;
    }
}

Future<List<Map<String, dynamic>>> _retrieveSavedComics() async {
  Directory docsDir = await getApplicationDocumentsDirectory();
  File file = File("${docsDir.path}/starred");
  List<Map<String, dynamic>> comics = [];

  if(!file.existsSync()) {
    file.createSync();
    file.writeAsStringSync("[]");
  } else {
    json.decode(file.readAsStringSync()).forEach(
      (n) async =>
        comics.add(await _fetchComic(n.toString()))
    );
  }
  return comics;
}

@override
Widget build(BuildContext context) {
  var comics = _retrieveSavedComics();

  return Scaffold(
      appBar: AppBar(
        title: Text("Browse your Favorite Comics")
      ),
      body:
      FutureBuilder(
        future: comics,
        builder: (context, snapshot) =>
          snapshot.hasData && snapshot.data.isNotEmpty ?
          ListView.builder(
            itemCount: snapshot.data.length,
            itemBuilder: (context, i) =>
              ComicTile(comic: snapshot.data[i],),
          )
          :
          Column(
            children: [
              Icon(Icons.not_interested),
```

```
        Text("""
          You haven't starred any comics yet.
          Check back after you have found something worthy of being here.
          """),
      ]
    )
  )
);
  }
}
```

This is what our starred comics' list will look like:

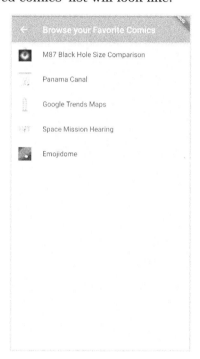

Adding a Link to the HomeScreen's App Bar

Now we need the user to be able to reach this page from the rest of the app. We'll make this possible by adding an AppBar action to the HomeScreen. This will be very similar to previous app bar actions we added earlier: when the user taps on the icon we show the user the StarredPage on top of the current view:

networking/xkcd_app/lib/main.dart
```
IconButton(
 icon: Icon(Icons.star),
 tooltip: "Browse Starred Comics",
 onPressed: () {
   Navigator.push(
     context,
     MaterialPageRoute(
       builder: (BuildContext context) =>
         StarredPage()
     ),
   );
 }
),
```

This is what the HomeScreen's app bar will look like:

Where We're Going Next

In this chapter we've seen how to interact with the network and local storage by building an XKCD comic browser app. In the next chapter, we're going to explore how to test Flutter apps.

CHAPTER 6

Testing and Debugging Flutter Apps

Up until now we have discussed how a Flutter app is built, with all the different UI, I/O, and state management features the framework offers. That's all very nice when everything goes according to plan and the code does exactly what you think it will do, but that's not always the case and testing can simplify the development process, especially on larger projects, by making sure each piece of code does what it's supposed to.

It's not the only thing we're going to talk about in this chapter: when things go wrong in your app and there's nothing the method you're writing can do about it, exceptions are there to make sure you can notify the rest of your app that something has gone wrong, letting a calling function make a decision about what to do about the issue. This is especially necessary when apps make I/O operations that, as they operate on things outside the control of the user and/or the developer, are bound to fail at some point if the required conditions to execute the operation aren't met.

Testing

There are multiple kinds of automated tests that can be applied to Flutter apps:

- Unit testing, the most common, which tests a smaller piece of code and should comprise the majority of the testing you should do on an app.

- Integration testing, which tests a big section of integrated pieces of code and, in the case of Flutter, runs the app in an emulator or physical device to check whether it behaves as it should when the user interacts with it in a certain way.

- Widget testing, which tests UI elements without firing up the app on an emulator or device, instead just keeping track of everything that is supposed to be on screen and letting us interact with it in a way that is much simpler and faster than is done in integration tests.

In this section we are going to use as an example the calculator app we built earlier in the book (Chapter 3, Building a Calculator App, on page 77) and write some tests that make sure each section of the app is working correctly. We are then going to test the XKCD comic browsing app built in the previous chapter to introduce you to mock objects and dependency injection in Flutter.

Dart Unit Testing

Unit testing is really simple: you run a piece of code (for example, a class constructor and a few member methods) and check whether the return value is what is expected.

To perform unit testing, we need to add the test package to pubspec.yaml's dev_dependencies, which is the section where we list dependencies only needed for development and debugging/testing and not needed for the execution of the app on an user's device.

Writing Unit Tests for the Calculator App

Let's start by taking a look at the app tree created by flutter create: it contains a directory called test. That's where we're going to add any tests we want to be performed by Flutter.

Here we'll create a file called calculation_test.dart, inside which, as the name says, we are going to test the Calculation class which, if you remember (or go back to Implement the Calculations, on page 98), allows us to add little pieces of an expression (as Strings) at a time and then get either the result as a double number or a String representing the expression.

There are multiple tests that can be done: we'll test whether it performs all the different operations and return the right result, then whether it can handle multiple operations and then whether it respects operator precedence. Additionally, we need to check both string values and numeric values returned by it.

We'll start writing the test by importing the needed classes. In this case we'll need to import the test package and the calculator.dart file in which we have defined the Calculation class:

layout/calculator/test/calculation_test.dart
```
import 'package:flutter_test/flutter_test.dart';
import 'package:calculator/calculator.dart';
```

Then we call the Calculation constructor to get an object on which to operate:

layout/calculator/test/calculation_test.dart
```
var calc = Calculation();
```

Everything else will go into the main() function:

layout/calculator/test/calculation_test.dart
```
void main() {

}
```

The first thing to do is to define a setUp() function that will get called before each test, creating a brand-new calculation object by calling the constructor in order to make sure each test is run in isolation.

layout/calculator/test/calculation_test.dart
```
setUp(() {
  calc = Calculation();
});
```

We are going to call the test() function, which takes a string and a callback function as positional arguments. The string is a text description of the test, so that we know what tests failed (if any fail) and the callback is the code that is going to be run when that test is fired. Inside the callback we'll use the expect() function to specify what value a certain instruction should return. For example, if we wanted to test a simple addition operation in our Calculation we could write the following:

layout/calculator/test/calculation_test.dart
```
test('simple addition', () {
  calc.add("5");
  calc.add("+");
  calc.add("6");
  calc.add("5");
  expect(calc.getResult(), 70.0);
});
```

If we want to test more than one addition/subtraction operation in the same test, we just add the following after it:

layout/calculator/test/calculation_test.dart
```
test('more sums', () {
  calc.add("5");
  calc.add("5");
  calc.add("-");
  calc.add("5");
  calc.add("+");
  calc.add("50");
  expect(calc.getResult(), 100.0);
});
```

We also need to test whether multiplication works, as we do in the following:

layout/calculator/test/calculation_test.dart
```
test('simple multiplication', () {
  calc.add("5");
  calc.add("x");
  calc.add("6");
  expect(calc.getResult(), 30.0);
});
```

Division is also important, and we also get a chance to check whether we can properly return floating-point values with a decimal part:

layout/calculator/test/calculation_test.dart
```
test('division', () {
  calc.add("5");
  calc.add("÷");
  calc.add("2");
  expect(calc.getResult(), 2.5);
});
```

Operator precedence can't be taken for granted, so we need to check whether it is respected:

layout/calculator/test/calculation_test.dart
```
test('precedence', () {
  calc.add("5");
  calc.add("+");
  calc.add("6");
  calc.add("x");
  calc.add("5");
  expect(calc.getResult(), 35.0);
});
```

The last thing to check is whether the getString() operation works correctly:

layout/calculator/test/calculation_test.dart
```
test('string', () {
  calc.add("5");
  calc.add("x");
  calc.add("6");
  calc.add("+");
  calc.add("7");
  expect(calc.getString().toString(), "5x6+7");
});
```

The entire calculation_test.dart file adds up to the following:

layout/calculator/test/calculation_test.dart
```
import 'package:flutter_test/flutter_test.dart';
import 'package:calculator/calculator.dart';

var calc = Calculation();
```

```
void main() {
  setUp(() {
    calc = Calculation();
  });
  test('simple addition', () {
    calc.add("5");
    calc.add("+");
    calc.add("6");
    calc.add("5");
    expect(calc.getResult(), 70.0);
  });
  test('more sums', () {
    calc.add("5");
    calc.add("5");
    calc.add("-");
    calc.add("5");
    calc.add("+");
    calc.add("50");
    expect(calc.getResult(), 100.0);
  });
  test('simple multiplication', () {
    calc.add("5");
    calc.add("x");
    calc.add("6");
    expect(calc.getResult(), 30.0);
  });
  test('division', () {
    calc.add("5");
    calc.add("÷");
    calc.add("2");
    expect(calc.getResult(), 2.5);
  });
  test('precedence', () {
    calc.add("5");
    calc.add("+");
    calc.add("6");
    calc.add("x");
    calc.add("5");
    expect(calc.getResult(), 35.0);
  });
  test('string', () {
    calc.add("5");
    calc.add("x");
    calc.add("6");
    calc.add("+");
    calc.add("7");
    expect(calc.getString().toString(), "5x6+7");
  });
}
```

Make Your Own Changes

If you have implemented parentheses in the calculator app, you should consider writing a unit test for that too.

It is very easy to write unit tests: you actually only need to split calc.add() calls when you want to add an operator, but it's recommended you add numbers one digit at a time at least in some tests since that's how the actual calculator app does it and there might be an issue that only manifests itself when doing it that way (or maybe adding more than one digit at a time would break an implementation that would work in the real calculator, but that's not the case for how we implemented it).

At this point, every time you try to build your app these tests will be run. You can also run the tests using flutter test on the command line. However, probably the best way to run tests is by using Visual Studio Code, which shows a *Run* button for each test, allowing you to run each test and get the results shown in an intuitive UI. Android Studio also shows a *right arrow* button next to the line number to run a test, but I found its UI slightly less intuitive and consistent. You might feel differently, though, especially if you prefer the Android Studio/IntelliJ UI over the Visual Studio UI; opt for whichever you're more comfortable using.

Flutter Widget and Integration Testing

Unit testing was simple and straight-forward enough, but widget and integration testing need more attention since they rely on UI, which isn't exactly as dry and simple as the calculation processing code.

Each little piece of low-level logic in our app may be correct, but there might be something wrong in the UI or the combination of some of the pieces of code we already tested. This is why widget testing and integration testing exist. It's to test whether a single widget or a bigger part of the app work correctly.

Flutter Widget Testing

Flutter provides a way to test whether widgets work correctly and to programmatically interact with widgets in our app.

This might be really hard to imagine if you're not used to similar testing infrastructure, so here's an example of how you might test whether pressing the 5 button will actually make the 5 number appear on the calculator screen after importing main.dart:

```
layout/calculator/test/widget_test.dart
```
```
testWidgets('5 press test', (WidgetTester tester) async {
  await tester.pumpWidget(new MyApp());

  expect(find.text('5'), findsOneWidget);

  await tester.tap(find.text('5'));
  await tester.pump();

  expect(find.text('5'), findsNWidgets(2));
});
```

❶ The testWidgets() function is very similar to the test() function, but with a big difference: it passes a WidgetTester object to its callback, and that object is what makes widget testing special.

❷ *pump* means *build* or *render*. tester.pumpWidget() renders a widget for which we have a definition.

It's important to keep in mind that, even though the pumpWidgets() gives the impression that it allows to pump any kind of widget, if you have a Scaffold in your widget it needs to be wrapped in a MaterialApp (or the more generic WidgetsApp class, which doesn't rely on the Material Design classes) because it needs to have a MediaQuery widget in its scope, and such a widget is provided by the aforementioned classes.

❸ This is the first expect() call. When we build the app for the first time, just one widget containing the 5 string should exist (the 5 button).

find is a constant. We'll look at its use in more detail later in this section.

find.text() is a Finder and findsOneWidget is a *flutter_test*-provided Matcher constant.

We'll list all Finders and Matchers in more detail in the next two paragraphs after this code's explanation. All you need to know now is that a Matcher is used to judge the results delivered by a Finder, which looks for widgets based on a certain characteristic.

❹ This is quite self-explanatory: we tap that widget.

❺ When testing, Flutter widgets aren't rebuilt automatically when setState() is called: to do that, we need to call tester.pump(), which re-renders the next frame the app is waiting to render.

There is also another method called tester.pumpAndSettle(), which keeps rendering frames until there is no re-render waiting to happen. This is useful when certain actions trigger an animation that takes several frames to complete.

❻ This is just like the other find.text() check, but this time there should be two widgets with that text: one is the button, and the other is the screen, which should now show that number.

As you can see, the interface is quite flexible and intuitive, and it is really useful to check whether the UI actually functions correctly.

All of the Finders

Let's get a bigger picture of Flutter widget testing: there are multiple ways to find widgets using the find constant, which is a collection (of class CommonFinders[1]) of the most commonly used Finders:

- find.text(text), which finds Text widgets that display a string that is *equal* to its text argument.

- find.byIcon(icon), which looks for Icon widgets that show an IconData (something such as Icons.not_interested) equal to its icon argument.

- find.byKey(key), which takes us back to The Key, on page 74: it matches the widget that has the Key you give it as an argument.

- find.byElementPredicate(predicate), which is very flexible: the predicate argument (of type WidgetPredicate) is simply a callback that receives a Widget as its argument, and returning either true or false will, respectively, consider the widget being examined as matching or not matching the requirements to be included in the Finder's result, which gives the developer significantly more freedom in deciding matching conditions than the other Finders.

- find.byWidget(widget), which is the most specific of the Finders: it matches just the Widget given as an argument.

There are other, less common Finder provided by the find constant:

- find.byTooltip();
- find.byElementType();
- find.byType();
- find.widgetWithIcon();
- find.widgetWithText();
- find.byDescendant().

All of the Matchers

In addition to findsNothing, findsOneWidget, and findsNWidgets(n) there is also findsWidgets, which is the opposite of findsNothing (equal to !findsNothing).

---

1.   https://docs.flutter.io/flutter/flutter_test/CommonFinders-class.html

Offstage Widgets

All of the Finders we have talked about allow you to set a named boolean skipOffstage argument which, if set to true, will skip any widgets contained in the rarely used Offstage widget, which is a class that allows you to get some widgets (set as the Offstage's child) to get laid out and occupy space without actually being shown.

More Calculator Testing

Let's actually get into a more complete and realistic example of widget testing our calculator app.

Checking the Grid

The first part of the *5 press test* can actually be turned into something very useful: checking whether all of the grid is actually being rendered and the user has a button for each button. The numbers, the deletion buttons, the . button and all of the operation buttons except the division button contain a Text to show their use. This means that we can match them using find.text():

```
layout/calculator/test/widget_test.dart
testWidgets('grid existence test', (WidgetTester tester) async {
    await tester.pumpWidget(new MyApp());

❶  expect(find.text('0'), findsNWidgets(2));

❷      for(int i = 1; i < 10; i++) {
            expect(find.text('$i'), findsOneWidget);
        }

        ['+', '-', 'x', '<-', 'C'].forEach(
        (str) => expect(find.text(str), findsOneWidget)
❸  );

❹  expect(find.byElementPredicate((element) {
        if(!(element.widget is Image))
          return false;
        else if(
          (element.widget as Image).image
          ==
          AssetImage("icons/divide.png")
        )
          return true;
        else return false;
    }), findsOneWidget);

});
```

❶ There should be two widgets containing the *0* string: the calculator screen at the start and the zero button.

❷ The numbers from 1 to 10 can be found by simply using a for loop.

❸ We haven't used forEach() much in this book, but it is very useful: it executes the same callback on each member of a List or Iterable. In this case, it is a good replacement for a for loop iterating over the list of symbols or just writing the instruction to look for each symbol separately.

❹ We can't use find.text() for images obviously, and find.byWidget() might come up as a viable alternative. The issue with that, though, is that it doesn't actually work in our case: it looks for an *exact* match, and it wouldn't find our image if we tried since the resulting object usually contains extra arguments that control widget position and other properties that we don't set directly while creating the widget.

That's where find.byElementPredicate() comes to our rescue: we can judge ourselves whether the widget matches what we want, which means we can focus just on what we need: we need the widget in question to be an image and we want it to be displaying icons/divide.png from the assets.

What gets passed to the callback closure is an Element (an instance of a widget along with some context on its position in the widget tree, which we don't need for what we're doing right now). We can access the Widget that Element was spawned from by accessing its widget member property, so that's what we're doing when using element.widget.

If the widget isn't an instance of an Image (that's what is is for, it's checking whether the widget is an instance of an Image or a subclass), we need to ignore it (return false to exclude it from the found widgets). If it is, we need to check whether the ImageProvider it's taking the image from is actually the icons/divide.png file from the assets.

Please note that accessing assets in unit and widget tests is only available starting from Flutter version *1.5*.

Flutter Integration Testing

Integration testing is a level above widget testing: for mobile apps, it is performed in an emulator and is meant to test whether a big part of app functionality works correctly. The calculator app is really simple and we don't really get much from integration testing when compared with widget testing, whereas one app that requires integration testing is the previous chapter's XKCD comics app.

Before we get to running integration tests on it, we need to figure out how to also run unit tests and widget tests on it without being dependent on a network connection to the XKCD servers being available and without being able to access the filesystem, as is the case during unit and widget testing.

Testing the XKCD App: Using Mock Objects

Testing the XKCD app presents a challenge: the app relies on external variables: an Internet connection needs to be present and the app needs to be able to connect to the XKCD servers (which need to be up) to work. The issue with that is that we may need to only test a small part of our app (especially during unit testing) without needing to interface with anything else, and we need to mock files since we can't access them anyway. To do this, developers usually resort to building *mock objects*, which are objects that simulate the features provided by the external interface while not requiring that interface.

Building mock objects isn't language or framework specific, but Google has developed a Flutter package that allows developers to simplify the creation of mock objects: the Mockito library.

The Mockito Library

The Google-developed *mockito* package on Pub[2] allows you to write classes that reproduce a behavior you choose by using the when() function.

Writing a Mock Object

As an example, let's write a replacement for the http constant we use in the XKCD app to make requests so that we can test the getLatestNumber() and fetchComic() methods. It is an object of the class Client, so we write an empty class that extends (extends, on page 309) Mock and implements (Writing a Class That implements an Interface, on page 310) Client's members:

```
testing/xkcd_app/test/unit_test.dart
import 'package:http/http.dart' as http;

class MockHTTPClient extends Mock implements http.Client {}
```

Let's define two comics we can return:

```
testing/xkcd_app/test/unit_test.dart
const comics = [
"""
  {
    "month": "",
    "num": 1,
    "link": "",
    "year": "",
```

---

2. https://pub.dartlang.org/packages/mockito

```
      "news": "",
      "safe_title": "The First Comic",
      "transcript": "",
      "alt": "first comic alt-text",
      "img": "https://example.com/1.png",
      "title": "The First Comic",
      "day": ""
    }
    """,
    """
    {
      "month": "",
      "num": 2,
      "link": "",
      "year": "",
      "news": "",
      "safe_title": "The Second Comic",
      "transcript": "",
      "alt": "second comic alt-text",
      "img": "https://example.com/2.png",
      "title": "The Second Comic",
      "day": ""
    }
    """
];
```

At this point we need to think about the calls we make to http.read(). The first of them is http.read('https://xkcd.com/info.0.json'), which is supposed to return a String containing the comic in a JSON format, so we'll return the second comic:

```
when(mockHttp.read('https://xkcd.com/info.0.json')).thenReturn(
  comics[1]
);
```

The same also needs to apply for /$num/info.0.json, so we also need the following:

```
when(mockHttp.read('https://xkcd.com/2/info.0.json')).thenReturn(
  comics[1]
);
```

We need to be ready to return comic number 1 since that's going to be fetched at some point and we need to be ready for that:

```
when(mockHttp.read('https://xkcd.com/1/info.0.json')).thenReturn(
  comics[0]
);
```

We also need to worry about when http.readBytes()() gets called to fetch an image. The issue with that is that it should return an Uint8List, which is a list of 8-bit integers (each of them is a byte). To create an Uint8List we need first import the dart:typed_data library. The simplest way to create an Uint8List is by calling the Uint8.fromList(list) and passing it a list literal.

After that, we need to worry about what to return. In this case, we don't really care that the data actually represents an image, since we don't need to render it, we just need it to be something we can predict—in this case, the list will be just the comic number:

```
when(mockHttp.readBytes('https://example.com/1.png')).thenReturn(
  Uint8List.fromList([1])
);

when(mockHttp.readBytes('https://example.com/2.png')).thenReturn(
  Uint8List.fromList([2])
);
```

File Mock Object

We need to also create mock objects for files and images.

In this case, even though we are calling the classes directly in the app, we need to implement file objects to pass to the functions. An example will be given when we see Testing, on page 218.

Using the Mock Object

We need to make changes to the functions that use the objects we created mock objects for so that they can be passed the mock object and use it instead of the real object they currently use.

This means that the getLatestComicNumber() function you see in the following code needs to instead take the Client and custom File as a parameter:

```
networking/xkcd_app/lib/main.dart
Future<int> getLatestComicNumber() async {
  final dir = await getTemporaryDirectory();
  var file = File('${dir.path}/latestComicNumber.txt');
  int n = 1;

  try {
    n = json.decode(
      await http.read('https://xkcd.com/info.0.json')
    )["num"];
    file.exists().then(
      (exists) {
        if(!exists) file.createSync();
        file.writeAsString('$n');
      }
    );
  }
```

```
  catch(e) {
    if(
      file.existsSync() &&
      file.readAsStringSync() != ""
    )
      n = int.parse(file.readAsStringSync());
  }
  return n;
}
```

The updated code should look as follows:

testing/xkcd_app/lib/main.dart

```
Future<int> getLatestComicNumber
({http.Client httpClient, File latestComicNFile}) async
{
  if(httpClient == null) {
    httpClient = http.Client();
  }

  if(latestComicNFile == null) {
    final dir = await getTemporaryDirectory();
    latestComicNFile = File('${dir.path}/latestComicNumber.txt');
  }

  int n = 1;

  try {
    n = json.decode(
      await httpClient.read('https://xkcd.com/info.0.json')
    )["num"];
    latestComicNFile.exists().then(
      (exists) {
        if(!exists) latestComicNFile.createSync();
        latestComicNFile.writeAsString('$n');
      }
    );
  }
  catch(e) {
    if(
      latestComicNFile.existsSync() &&
      latestComicNFile.readAsStringSync() != ""
    )
      n = int.parse(latestComicNFile.readAsStringSync());
  }
  return n;
}
```

This method works just like the older one when no additional named arguments are provided (they would be equal to null, triggering the fallback if clauses), which would happen during normal app use. If they are provided, though, they are used in place of the real file and HTTP client.

Obviously fetchComic() also needs to change. Let's start with the SelectionPage's, which was the following in the original app:

networking/xkcd_app/lib/main.dart
```
Future<Map<String, dynamic>> _fetchComic(String n) async {
  final dir = await getTemporaryDirectory();
  var comicFile = File("${dir.path}/$n.json");

 if(
    await comicFile.exists() &&
    comicFile.readAsStringSync() != ""
 )
    return json.decode(comicFile.readAsStringSync());
  else {
    comicFile.createSync();
    final comic = json.decode(
      await http.read('https://xkcd.com/$n/info.0.json')
    );

    File('${dir.path}/$n.png')
      .writeAsBytesSync(await http.readBytes(comic["img"]));
    comic["img"] = '${dir.path}/$n.png';
    comicFile.writeAsString(json.encode(comic));

    return comic;
  }
}
```

and needs to become the following to allow for testing by using the clients and files given as arguments if they are given and reverting back to the default when they aren't (in normal app usage) just like we did for getLatestComicNumber():

testing/xkcd_app/lib/main.dart
```
Future<Map<String, dynamic>> fetchComic
(
  String n,
  {
    http.Client httpClient,
    File comicFile,
    File imageFile,
    String imagePath
  }
) async
{
  Directory dir;
  if(httpClient == null) {
    httpClient = http.Client();
  }
```

```
if(comicFile == null) {
  dir = await getTemporaryDirectory();
  comicFile = File("${dir.path}/$n.json");
}

if(imageFile == null) {
  if(dir == null) dir = await getTemporaryDirectory();
  imagePath = '${dir.path}/$n.png';
  imageFile = File(imagePath);
}

if(
  await comicFile.exists() &&
  comicFile.readAsStringSync() != ""
)
  return json.decode(comicFile.readAsStringSync());
else {
  comicFile.createSync();
  final comic = json.decode(
    await httpClient.read(
      'https://xkcd.com/$n/info.0.json'
    )
  );

  imageFile.writeAsBytesSync(
    await httpClient.readBytes(comic["img"])
  );
  comic["img"] = imagePath;
  comicFile.writeAsString(json.encode(comic));

  return comic;
}
}
```

The StarredPage's _fetchComic() is the same as the SelectionPage's, so the same changes apply to it.

The HomeScreen's _fetchComic() needs similar changes (it's just like the other, but this time we first worry about finding out the comic number by subtracting the n argument to the latest comic number):

testing/xkcd_app/lib/main.dart
```
Future<Map<String, dynamic>> fetchComic
(
  int n,
  {
    http.Client httpClient,
    File comicFile,
    File imageFile,
    String imagePath
  }
) async
```

```
{
  int comicNumber = latestComic-n;
  Directory dir;
  if(httpClient == null) {
    httpClient = http.Client();
  }
  if(comicFile == null) {
    dir = await getTemporaryDirectory();
    comicFile = File("${dir.path}/$comicNumber.json");
  }
  if(imageFile == null) {
    if(dir == null) dir = await getTemporaryDirectory();
    imagePath = '${dir.path}/$comicNumber.png';
    imageFile = File(imagePath);
  }

  if(
    await comicFile.exists() &&
    comicFile.readAsStringSync() != ""
  )
    return json.decode(comicFile.readAsStringSync());
  else {
    comicFile.createSync();
    final comic = json.decode(
      await httpClient.read(
        'https://xkcd.com/$comicNumber/info.0.json'
      )
    );

    imageFile.writeAsBytesSync(
      await httpClient.readBytes(comic["img"])
    );
    comic["img"] = imagePath;
    comicFile.writeAsString(json.encode(comic));

    return comic;
  }
}
```

By making the additional arguments that allow us to provide mock objects optional we can call those methods inside the app without being forced to pass the extra arguments and we keep the function as close to the original as possible while allowing for the usage of mock objects.

Writing the Tests

We have made the necessary changes and now we need to write the tests for the XKCD app.

XKCD App Unit Tests

We need to test whether the app correctly fetches the latest comic number which, in this case, is 2. We also need to test whether both _fetchComic() method run as expected.

Let's start by adding the mock classes we defined earlier and importing everything we need

The last thing we need outside main() is the list of comic data strings, while all of the calls to when() go inside the main() function definition.

Testing getLatestComicNumber()

Let's start by writing a test for getLatestComicNumber(): for it we'll need to define the mock objects for the latest comic number file and for the http client.

We need to define behavior for both asynchronous and synchronous calls, since we need the test to work with a different implementation too:

```
testing/xkcd_app/test/unit_test.dart
test("get latest comic number test", () async {
  var latestComicNumberFile = MyFile();
  var latestComicNumberExists = false;
  String latestComicNumberString;
  var mockHttp = MockHTTPClient();

  when(mockHttp.read('https://xkcd.com/info.0.json')).thenAnswer(
    (_) => Future.value(comics[1])
  );

  when(latestComicNumberFile.createSync()).thenAnswer(
    (_) {
      latestComicNumberExists = true;
    }
  );

  when(latestComicNumberFile.create()).thenAnswer(
    (_) {
      latestComicNumberExists = true;
      return Future.value(latestComicNumberFile);
    }
  );

  when(latestComicNumberFile.writeAsStringSync("2")).thenAnswer(
    (_) {
      latestComicNumberExists = true;
      latestComicNumberString = "2";
    }
  );
```

```
⑥   when(latestComicNumberFile.writeAsString("2")).thenAnswer(
      (_) {
        latestComicNumberExists = true;
        latestComicNumberString = "2";
        return Future.value(latestComicNumberFile);
      }
    );
⑦   when(latestComicNumberFile.existsSync()).thenReturn(
      latestComicNumberExists
    );
⑧   when(latestComicNumberFile.exists()).thenAnswer(
      (_) =>
        Future.value(latestComicNumberExists)
    );
⑨   when(latestComicNumberFile.readAsStringSync()).thenAnswer(
      (_) {
        // if we try to read from a file that doesn't exist we've made a mistake
        assert(latestComicNumberExists, true);
        return "2";
      }
    );
⑩   when(latestComicNumberFile.readAsString()).thenAnswer(
      (_) {
        assert(latestComicNumberExists, true);
        return Future.value(latestComicNumberString);
      }
    );
⑪   expect(
      await getLatestComicNumber(
        httpClient: mockHttp,
        latestComicNFile: latestComicNumberFile,
      ),
      2
    );
  });
```

❶ This is where we declare the mock objects and some data they operate on: a mock File that uses a bool to keep track of whether it has been created and a String to simulate the storage of a string. We also declare a mock HTTP client.

❷ This is the first of our when() calls and it's the only one for the mock HTTP client: it returns our fake latest comic when we try to access it.

❸ Now we need to define the latestComicNumberFile's behavior: we'll start with the synchronous method to create the file, which will change the latestComic-NumberExists boolean to true. This is going to be important when we try to read from the file or run the exists() or existsSync() methods.

In the parentheses we used _, which is meant to be used for unused arguments (it may be used in catch blocks as well). If we had chosen to use that argument and give it a name instead, it would be an Invocation.

An invocation has a few properties that are interesting to us:

- namedArguments, which is a Map of the named arguments supplied by the caller;
- positionalArguments, which is a List of the positional arguments supplied by the caller.

❹ We are doing the same thing for the asynchronous method to create files, which is supposed to return the file (in a Future, since it is an async method).

❺ At some point getLatestComicNumber() is supposed to try to write the number 2 to a file. We'll simulate writing it by storing it in latestComicNumberString. We also simulate creating the file at the same time, just like what the real methods to write to files do.

❻ This is just like the previous one, but asynchronous. We return the file for the same reason we return it in create().

❼ getLatestComicNumber() checks whether the file exists at some point, so we need to be able to implement that method too.

❽ Having mock objects that implement methods that may be used in the method we're trying to test even if they aren't used allows the mock object to be used without change for more tests and it makes it so we don't have to change the test if at some point we change the functions used in the method we're testing. In this case, we implement both asynchronous and synchronous methods even when we only use one of them.

❾ This simulates reading from a file. We have an assertion that interrupts execution if we try to read from a file we haven't yet created (either by running create() or by writing to it.

❿ The asynchronous version of the previous method.

⓫ Finally we get to expect(), passing the mock HTTP client and file and expecting it to return 2.

Testing Fetching the Latest Comic

The fetchComic() method has an important feature: it isn't actually defined as fetchComic() but, instead, it's called _fetchComic(), which makes it private: it's only accessible within the class itself. It's good practice to define all class members as private if they aren't supposed to be accessed from outside the class, but we need to call it directly to perform unit tests on it. This means we need to change its definition from:

```
Future<Map<String, dynamic>> fetchComic
(
  String n,
  {
    http.Client httpClient,
    File comicFile,
    File imageFile,
    String imagePath
  }
) async
{
```

to:

```
testing/xkcd_app/lib/main.dart
Future<Map<String, dynamic>> fetchComic
(
  String n,
  {
    http.Client httpClient,
    File comicFile,
    File imageFile,
    String imagePath
  }
) async
{
```

This also means that we need to change any call to _fetchComic() to calls to fetchComic(). In this case, it is just one and it is set as the future argument of the FutureBuilder in the build() method.

Given that we also need to test the SelectionPage's and the HomeScreen's fetchComic(), the same changes need to be made to those classes. The StarredPage's fetchComic() is called only inside _retrieveSavedComics() and the HomeScreen's is set as the future of a FutureBuilder inside the build() method.

Testing fetchComic

This is the code to test the SelectionPage fetchComic()'s ability to fetch comic number 2:

testing/xkcd_app/test/unit_test.dart
```dart
test("SelectionPage fetchComic latest", () async {
  var latestComicFile = MyFile();
  var latestComicExists = false;
  String latestComicString;
  var latestImageFile = MyFile();
  Uint8List latestImageData;
  var latestImageExists = false;
  var mockHttp = MockHTTPClient();

  when(mockHttp.read('https://xkcd.com/2/info.0.json')).thenAnswer(
    (_) => Future.value(comics[1])
  );

  when(mockHttp.readBytes("https://example.com/2.png")).thenAnswer(
    (_) => Future.value(Uint8List.fromList([2]))
  );

  when(latestComicFile.createSync()).thenAnswer(
    (_) {
      latestComicExists = true;
    }
  );

  when(latestComicFile.create()).thenAnswer(
    (_) {
      latestComicExists = true;
      return Future.value(latestComicFile);
    }
  );

  when(latestComicFile.writeAsStringSync(comics[1])).thenAnswer(
    (_) {
      latestComicExists = true;
      latestComicString = comics[1];
    }
  );

  when(latestComicFile.writeAsString(comics[1])).thenAnswer(
    (_) {
      latestComicExists = true;
      latestComicString = comics[1];
      return Future.value(latestComicFile);
    }
  );

  when(latestComicFile.existsSync()).thenReturn(
    latestComicExists
  );

  when(latestComicFile.exists()).thenAnswer(
    (_) =>
      Future.value(latestComicExists)
  );
```

```dart
  when(latestComicFile.readAsStringSync()).thenAnswer(
    (_) {
      /*
       * if we try to read from a file that doesn't
       * exist it's because we've made a mistake
       */
      assert(latestComicExists, true);
      return latestComicString;
    }
  );

  when(latestImageFile.readAsBytes()).thenAnswer(
    (_) {
      assert(latestImageExists, true);
      return Future.value(latestImageData);
    }
  );

  when(
    latestImageFile.writeAsBytesSync(
      Uint8List.fromList([1])
    )
  ).thenAnswer(
    (_) {
      latestImageExists = true;
      latestImageData = Uint8List.fromList([1]);
    }
  );

  when(latestComicFile.writeAsString(comics[1])).thenAnswer(
    (_) {
      latestImageExists = true;
      latestImageData = Uint8List.fromList([1]);
      return Future.value(latestImageFile);
    }
  );

  var selPage = SelectionPage();

  expect(
    await selPage.fetchComic(
      "2",
      httpClient: mockHttp,
      comicFile: File("latestComicFole"),
      imageFile: File("latestComicFile"),
      imagePath: "https://example.com/2.png"
    ),
    json.decode(comics[1])
  );
});
```

It's nothing new: we use Mockito to define expected behavior for all functions that may be called by the fetchComic() method to fetch the comic: reading and writing from image and comic files and performing HTTP requests.

Defining new tests for other fetchComic() methods only requires changes for the HomeScreen: it needs an integer for the comic number, which is a number that starts from 0 and can be, at most, 1 less than the latest comic number.

Grouping Together Tests

Multiple tests can be grouped together using the group() method, which works exactly like test():

```
group("group name", () {
  test("first test in group", () {
    // First test in group
  });
  test("second test in group", () {
    // Second test in group
  });
  // any other tests you want to add
});
```

For example, we can group all tests that involve fetchComic() methods, or maybe we can group together all tests that fetch a specific comic if you decide to structure tests differently. Inside groups we can, for example, define variables and mock objects that are needed for more than one test, so that they are accessible by all tests in a group but not outside of the group, but you need to keep in mind that the group's callback closure can't be async.

A Few Words on Widget Testing More Complicated Apps

We have already covered widget testing in the section about testing the calculator, so we won't have examples of widget tests for the XKCD apps, which would be redundant.

Widget testing the XKCD app involves testing whether or not the UI actually works, so we don't actually need to be necessarily design mock objects that perfectly emulate the behavior of the network or file system: we just need to know the UI we need exists and is correctly interacting with our app's backbone.

Widget tests rely on mock objects to work, so reducing the scope of these tests to just testing whether the widgets call the functions they are supposed to call is all that should be done in widget tests: doing anything more than that will only make the tests more complicated and make the integration tests partially redundant.

More Unit Tests: Comic Starring

Testing comic starring in the StarredPage doesn't introduce particularly challenging situations, except for the fact that the retrieveSavedComics() method calls fetchComic(), which means that the mock objects need to be passed first to retrieveSavedComics() which will, in turn, pass it to fetchComic().

The overall structure of the test should be the following: the addToStarred() method (in the ComicPage) should be called on the same file that will then be used by retrieveStarred-Comics() to get the starred comics list. The main difference between this test and the fetchComic() test is that this one needs two mock text files: one of them needs to contain the comic file, whereas the other one will store the list of saved comics numbers, so it needs to predict the data it will be asked to store, just like we did earlier for the comic and latest number files.

Writing these tests as someone who is trying to understand Flutter will also help you understand the inner workings of our app in more detail and test your own understanding of it. If you can't write a test for it, you probably don't understand how it's working and that means you need to try to first understand how the app works.

Verifying Whether a Method Has Been Called: Mockito's verify

Mockito includes a function to verify whether or not a method has been called, making it possible to reduce the scope of tests to only verifying whether methods get called instead of necessarily checking whether a given method returns a given value. For example, if you want the test to fail if myObj.run-Method()() hasn't been called, you'd add:

```
verify(myObj.runMethod());
```

If you replaced verify with verifyNever you'd have the opposite effect.

You can also specify the amount of times a method should get called:

```
verify(myObj.runMethod()).called(5);
```

requires the method to have been called 5 times and:

```
verify(myObj.runMethod()).called(greaterThan(4));
```

requires it to have been called *at least* 5 times.

Calling verify(myObj.runMethod()).called(0) will fail. You have to use verifyNever(myObj.run-Method()) for that.

XKCD App Integration Test

Integration tests are just like widget tests, but they are run on a real device or emulator by using the flutter_driver package.

Modifying the App: Using a TextEditingController

Integration testing requires us to make modifications to the app. One of the main modifications is the addition of keys to any widgets we want to be interacting with, especially if they don't contain text or we need to check the text they contain.

Meeting an Old Friend Again: The Need for a Key

That is because widget testing and integration testing Finders are very similar, but not the same: integration testing uses SerializableFinders, which are a lot fewer, and only allow us the following operations:

- find.byValueKey(value), which finds object with Keys or ValueKeys attached to them that are generated using that value.

- find.text(text), which finds Text widgets containing the given text.

- find.byType(tyoe), which finds widgets of the given type.

- find.byTooltip(tooltip), which finds widget showing the given tooltip when long-pressed.

- find.pageBack(), which finds the button to go to the previous page.

This means the best way to find widgets with features that don't conform to any of the others, we have to equip the widget with a key and use find.byValueKey() to find it.

The reason why they are so few is because integration tests shouldn't have access to the app's resources or the Flutter UI framework's widgets and classes in general.

Adding a Button to Submit the TextField's Input

Additionally, we need to make a change to the SelectionPage: at the moment the user can only sumbit using the number using the submit button on the on-screen keyboard or the Enter key on a physical keyboard. This is, unfortunately, not supported by Flutter's integration testing infrastructure (at the time of writing), which means we have to create a TextEditingController and a separate FlatButton to submit the TextField's contents.

Defining a TextEditingController

A TextEditingController is a class that stores the data inserted in a TextField or a similar widget and makes it possible to access that data from outside the onSubmitted callback we give to the TextField itself, allowing us to create a button that opens the comic the user asked for, and giving us something to tap to do that when performing integration tests.

Let's declare a TextEditingController as a private member variable of the SelectionPage:

testing/xkcd_app/lib/main.dart
```
final TextEditingController _controller = TextEditingController();
```

Using the TextEditingController

Let's pass it as the controller argument to the TextField:

testing/xkcd_app/lib/main.dart
```
TextField(
 controller: _controller,
 decoration: InputDecoration(
   labelText: "Insert comic #",
 ),
```

Adding the FlatButton

We now need to turn the Center widget in the body of the Scaffold into a Column, which will also require changing the child argument to children, which needs to be a List literal (we need to enclose the TextField definition in square brackets, in which we'll also add the FlatButton).

The FlatButton we're going to add needs a key to be used in integration testing, and it needs to perform the same actions performed by the TextField's onSubmit, but by taking the number of the comic requested by the user from _controller.text. The entire body of the Scaffold ends up being the following:

testing/xkcd_app/lib/main.dart
```
body: Column(
  mainAxisAlignment: MainAxisAlignment.center,
  children: [
    TextField(
      controller: _controller,
      decoration: InputDecoration(
        labelText: "Insert comic #",
      ),
      keyboardType: TextInputType.number,
      autofocus: true,
      onSubmitted: (String a) => Navigator.push(
        context,
        MaterialPageRoute(
          builder: (context) => FutureBuilder(
            future: fetchComic(a),
```

```
        builder: (context, snapshot) {
          if(snapshot.hasError)
            return ErrorPage();
          if(snapshot.hasData)
            return ComicPage(snapshot.data);
          return CircularProgressIndicator();
        }
      ),
    ),
  ),
  key: Key("insert comic")
),
FlatButton(
  key: Key("submit comic"),
  child: Text("Open".toUpperCase()),
  onPressed: () => Navigator.push(
    context,
    MaterialPageRoute(
      builder: (context) => FutureBuilder(
        future: fetchComic(_controller.text),
        builder: (context, snapshot) {
          if(snapshot.hasError)
            return ErrorPage();
          if(snapshot.hasData)
            return ComicPage(snapshot.data);
          return CircularProgressIndicator();
        }
      ),
    ),
  ),
)
],
),
```

Using the flutter_driver to Test the Selection Page

Integration testing requires a package called flutter_driver. The entire pubspec.yaml file containing all of the dependencies required to test Flutter apps (along with the other dependencies we need to run the XKCD app) is the following:

testing/xkcd_app/pubspec.yaml
```
name: xkcd_app
description: An app to display XKCD comics.

dependencies:
  http: "^0.12.0+1"
  path_provider:
  url_launcher: ^5.0.2
  flutter:
    sdk: flutter
```

```
dev_dependencies:
  flutter_driver:
    sdk: flutter
  mockito:
  test:

flutter:
  uses-material-design: true
```

To use it, let's create a new directory in the root of our app's source tree called test_driver. Inside it, we need to create a file that will run the app with the Flutter driver extensions enabled, and another that will connect to that running app and perform some tests on it.

As an example, we're going to explore how we can interact with the SelectionPage and see what it's possible to do with the Flutter integration testing framework.

Creating a selectionpage.dart File

Let's start by creating a file that enables the Flutter driver extensions:

testing/xkcd_app/test_driver/selectionpage.dart

```
❶ import 'package:flutter_driver/driver_extension.dart';
  import 'package:xkcd_app/main.dart' as app;
  import 'package:flutter/material.dart';

  void main() {
❷   enableFlutterDriverExtension();

❸   runApp(
      MaterialApp(
        home: app.SelectionPage(),
      )
    );
  }
```

❶ *package:flutter_driver/driver_extension.dart* is the part of *flutter_driver* that allows us to enable *driver extensions*, which need to be enabled when running an app we want to run integration tests on.

We also need to import the app's main.dart because we need to be able to run the app and we need to import Flutter's Material Design library because we only want to run the SelectionPage in this case so we need access to runApp() and the MaterialApp class.

❷ enableFlutterDriverExtension() actually enables the driver extensions. This function is contained in *package:flutter_driver/driver_extension.dart*.

❸ We want to test the selection page, so we run it just like we run regular app home screens when we build Flutter apps, but selecting the SelectionPage instead.

This is the only file that will have access to your app or to Flutter's UI classes at all. The actual test file mustn't import any of that.

Creating a selectionpage_test.dart File

This file name needs to be the same as the previous one, but with _test added to the name before the .dart extension. In this case, it has to be called selectionpage_test.dart.

This test will be very simple and will simply try to open a comic and check whether it is correctly opened by the app:

```
testing/xkcd_app/test_driver/selectionpage_test.dart
import 'package:flutter_driver/flutter_driver.dart';
import 'package:test/test.dart';

void main() {
  group('Selection Page', () {
    FlutterDriver driver;
    SerializableFinder appBarText = find.byValueKey("AppBar text");

    setUpAll(() async {
      driver = await FlutterDriver.connect();
    });

    tearDownAll(() async {
      if (driver != null) {
        driver.close();
      }
    });

    test('Verify Page is Loaded', () async {
      await driver.waitFor(appBarText);
      expect(await driver.getText(appBarText), "Comic selection");
    });

    test('Open Comic', () async {
      await driver.tap(find.byValueKey("insert comic"));
      await driver.enterText("1");
      await driver.tap(find.byValueKey("submit comic"));
      await driver.waitFor(find.text("#1"));
      expect(await driver.getText(appBarText), "#1");
    });
  });
}
```

❶ Here we need to import the main flutter_driver.dart file, along with the regular test package.

❷ Let's define some of the variables we are going to use more than once: the FlutterDriver we're going to use to interact with the running Flutter app, and the SerializableFinder looking for a Key created with the string *AppBar text*, that you should add to every AppBar Text widget in the app.

❸ This section is used to connect to the running app when starting the test.

❹ Here we disconnect from the app when testing is over.

❺ This first test is very simple: we wait for the page to load and then we check that the AppBar text is correct (so that we know that the app has loaded the right page).

❻ This test is more important: we find the TextField to insert the comic, we tap it (to select it, just in case), we enter the text *1*, we press the newly created *submit* button, wait for the comic page to load, and check that comic number 1 has actually been loaded (the AppBar Text should be *#1*).

To start the test, run the following command with an emulator or device connected:

```
flutter drive --target=test_driver/selectionpage.dart
```

and you'll see the app open and do everything you asked it to do automatically. In the command line, you'll get the confirmation that all tests have passed.

Testing More

In our integration testing example, we are only testing the SelectionPage. That's because it allows us to combine many interesting flutter_driver features and it doesn't require repeating the same instructions many times, which would not be very interesting for an example that aims to help you learn new things.

We haven't done integration testing on the calculator app, but it may be used to test executing calculation using the keypad, testing both the Calculation and the UI, and that is simply a combination of tests we have already done: it is useful on a real app, but you already know how to do that. That's what integration testing is for, just like the test we wrote for our XKCD app: it tests both the UI and the logic.

Testing the codebase is essential and should be done as much as possible. When writing your own apps, it's important you design and write all three kinds of tests for every aspect of the app: our XKCD app needs tests for the HomeScreen, for the ComicPage, perhaps testing whether the ErrorPage is shown when it's needed. Additionally, more unit tests and widget tests for the basic UI elements are useful (for example, testing the AppBar controls on the Home-Screen).

Code examples of those test cases look a lot like the previous ones, and thus I have not reproduced them here; however, you need to keep in mind the importance of testing.

When We Have to Mock and When We Don't

Testing using mock objects can be repetitive and feels like an useless exercise in pedantry and correctness, often begging the question: *is this really necessary?*

Testing software looks like an easy task when no mocking is involved: we just run a method and check whether it returns the correct value, or we simulate user interaction and check whether the app behaves correctly: it's simple, intuitive, and doesn't involve writing too many lines of code for simple things.

Writing mock objects isn't as simple and straight-forward: we need to consider every single interaction of the app with the outside world and simulate the response of the outside world: it is, in many respects, a chore and it seems to detract from time that could be spent developing a new feature, without actually achieving anything new.

The problem with mocking is that it's not just about protecting from unpredictable outside variables: it is about making the tests actually work. Even though the test will actually work correctly if we don't mock the HTTP client (even though we won't really be able to test the app's functionality based on its result), any attempt to call the functions provided by path_provider to access the paths where to store app files will result in exceptions being thrown.

If we want to know whether the fetchComic() method works, we can't just make the part that works with files optional: it's integral to the correct functioning of the app and that means we need to test it. The best way to test it in tests not run inside an emulator is by mocking files, so that's what we do.

This use case, as we've seen, may be made easier by just using real files on the physical machine that runs the tests: just running the File() constructor will create a file on the machine you're using to run the tests, and that's a way to make testing easier, but not really too predictable or controlled, since it relies on the local machine's file system, which may be inaccessible in case the test is run on a server that doesn't allow the code to have write access to the file system.

Also, an important feature that absolutely requires mock objects even in integration tests is authentication: an app that requires authentication to work makes testing impossible unless tests takes advantage of mocking to overcome the issue of authenticathing.

Mockito Versus Do-It-Yourself Mock Objects

Mockito doesn't always make it easier to create mock objects: on the contrary, sometimes you might find it easier to just write a class that implements the methods you need. You can make them work by defining those classes as subclasses (extends, on page 309) or as classes that implement (Writing a Class That implements an Interface, on page 310) the interface you want to mock.

Throwing and Catching Exceptions

We already used exceptions in some of the previous chapters, but we'll go through the Flutter implementation in more detail in this section.

Exceptions are used in a piece of code as a way to signal that something's gone wrong, the current function(or Anonymous Functions and Closures, on page 297)'s execution is interrupted and the calling function is supposed to deal with it by catching it.

Throwing an Exception

In Dart exceptions are thrown using the throw keyword (in Python you'd call this raising an exception, in case you never got to see what the world looks like outside of Python). You can create your own exception by creating a class that Writing a Class That implements an Interface, on page 310 the Exception class error:

```
class MyOwnPersonalException implements Exception {
  MyOwnPersonalException(this.myOwnPersonalMember);

  String myOwnPersonalMember;
}
double myPersonalDivision(double a, double b) {
  if(b == 0) {
    throw MyOwnPersonalException("Failed to divide a number by 0.");
  }
  return a/b;
}
```

Catching an Exception

Whenever we call a function or use an operation that may fail under certain circumstances we're not checking for, we should be catching the exception:

```
void responsibleFunction() {
  int a, b;
// ...
  b = 0;
```

```
  try {
    int d = myPersonalDivision(a, b);
    // ...
  }
  catch(exception) {
    // Deal with the exception
  }
// ...
}
```

You can substitute exception in catch's parentheses with whatever you want (it is usually just e). It contains the name of the exception that was thrown. You can print it to the debug console by using print(exception). Additionally, you can pass a stack trace of the source of the error, which you can also print.

For example, the following:

```
try {
  int.parse("Flutter");
} catch(e, stacktrace) {
  print(e);
  print(stacktrace);
}
```

will trigger a FormatException and print the following to the debug console:

```
FormatException: Invalid radix-10 number (at character 1)
Flutter
^

#0   int._throwFormatException (dart:core/runtime/lib/integers_patch.dart:131:5)
#1   int._parseRadix (dart:core/runtime/lib/integers_patch.dart:142:16)
#2   int._parse (dart:core/runtime/lib/integers_patch.dart:100:12)
#3   int.parse (dart:core/runtime/lib/integers_patch.dart:63:12)
#4   main (file:///home/carmine/flutter/example_app/lib/main.dart:21:9)
```

on SomeException catch()

What if that called function had thrown another kind of exception, which didn't have myOwnPersonalMember or maybe you needed to deal with different exceptions in different ways? That's what on is for.

For example, let's say we have a function that takes two numbers in a string format, parses them, and performs integer division on them. This means two different kinds exceptions can be thrown during its execution: a FormatException if it can't parse the numbers, or a IntegerDivisionByZeroException exception if we try to divide by zero.

Dart by default performs floating-point division and returns a double number. To perform integer division we need to use the ~/ operator instead of just /. This means the function definition will be the following:

```
int jsonDivide(String a, String b) =>
  int.parse(a)~/int.parse(b);
```

Seen like that, it's no wonder why a function like this is a good example: it is very short but it could throw two different kinds of exceptions: for example, calling it as jsonDivide("5", "0") will return an IntegerDivisionByZeroException, whereas calling it as jsonDivide("Flutter", "10") will return a FormatException. Let's pretend we need to tell the user to correct the bad data they entered, so we need to handle each exception differently, which isn't to hard to do in Dart:

```
try {
  jsonDivide(firstString, secondString);
}
on IntegerDivisionByZeroException {
  // tell the user to not divide by 0
}
on FormatException {
  // tell the user to insert valid numbers
}
```

So that each of the two on blocks will be executed only when the corresponding exception is thrown.

An alternative syntax for on blocks is on ExceptionName catch(e) {}, which will pass the exception to the block, just like what happens in regular catch blocks.

You can, optionally, add a catch block after the on blocks to handle any exceptions that aren't handled by the on blocks.

Finally

When using a regular try-catch construct without throwing new exceptions in the process, the execution will continue by executing the instructions placed after the end of the catch block, but if you are only using on blocks instead of generic catch blocks or you're throwing new exceptions inside catch blocks, the execution will be interrupted and those instructions won't be executed. If, instead, you want to execute some instructions regardless of anything that happens in the try block and in the catch and on block, you'd use a finally block:

```
try {
  // code that could fail
}
on SomeException {
  // handle SomeExceptin
}
finally {
  // code that will surely be executed
}
```

Assert Statements

Somewhere in the middle of the use case of testing and the use case of exceptions you'll find assert() statements, which are a way for the developer to define conditions that must be met during the app's execution or to have an effective way to test the result of a certain condition.

An assert statement can be added anywhere inside an app's code and will terminate the app's execution by throwing an AssertionError exception when a condition doesn't return true:

```
int a = 3;
assert(a == 3);
```

These two lines of code will not affect the app's execution and similar syntax is often used in documentation when demonstrating a programming language's features in code examples, including Google's official Dart Language Tour.[3]

On the other hand, having code such as this:

```
int a = (6+9/3)/3;
assert(a != 3);
```

will terminate the app's execution by throwing an exception *while debugging*. Assert statements do *not* have any effect on production code and are only considered while debugging code.

It is possible to include a string to desctibe the assertion by passing it as the second named argument to assert():

```
assert(condition, "The condition wasn't met");
```

Where We're Going Next

In the next chapter we're going to talk about Firebase and how it can make building a chat app very simple.

---

3.   https://www.dartlang.org/guides/language/language-tour

CHAPTER 7

Build a Chat App Using Firebase

Google Firebase is a collection of tools to ease the development of some kinds of apps. In this chapter, we are going to build a chat app using it.

What Is Firebase?

The traditional way to build web and mobile apps is by having a front end and a back end. The front end is what is built using tools like Flutter, platform-specific native SDKs, *React* or *HTML* and it's run on a the users' client device, whereas the back end is ran on a server and is built with tools like *PHP*, *Spring* or *Node.js*.

Firebase aims to replace most of the features run on server-side software with their own services that connect directly to apps using Google's own API instead of using standard HTTP requests. Apps built using Firebase are usually simpler to set up and less complicated to maintain. There is a free plan (called *Spark*) that allows a limited number of connections and only offers limited storage and computing, but you don't need anything more to complete the tasks described in this chapter.

Getting Started

Let's start by navigating to the Firebase Console,[1] logging into Google and creating a new project:

---

1.   https://console.firebase.google.com/

after that, you'll get the following popup window:

Choose a project name (for this example, we'll use *ChatOnFire* from now on for all project/app names) and the closest servers to your location in the world. Now you need to connect your app to Firebase, and this has to be done separately for the Android and iOS configuration of the app by following the instructions provided on screen, keeping in mind that you can find the plat-form-specific configuration for each platform the app runs on in the android and ios directories of your app tree.

After completing the platform-specific configuration, we need to start connecting Firebase to Flutter, and there are a bunch of Google-developed Flutter packages on Dart Pub that help us build apps using Flutter and Firebase.

Firebase for Flutter

After installing the *firebase_core* package[2] (you know the drill, there's no need for further explanations, remember to run flutter packages get after editing pub-spec.yaml) we need to worry about the specific features we need for our app. There is a complete list of Flutter Firebase packages on GitHub's official Flutter account.[3]

---

2.   https://pub.dartlang.org/packages/firebase_core
3.   https://github.com/flutter/plugins/blob/master/FlutterFire.md

Let's start with the most commonly used Firebase tool: the Cloud Firestore database.

The Firebase Cloud Firestore

The Firebase Cloud Firestore is ideal for data that is subject to frequent additions and needs to be accessed in real time. This means it is perfectly suited to the creation of a chat app.

For this example, navigate to Database -> Rules in the Firebase Console and change the rules to the following so that we don't need to authenticate (we'll worry about that Authentication, on page 242).:

```
service cloud.firestore {
  match /databases/{database}/documents {
    match /{document=**} {
      allow read, write;
    }
  }
}
```

What is commonly referred to in any SQL DBMS as a table is called a collection in Cloud Firestore. Let's create one. Since we're going to build a chat app, we'll create one to store messages sent by the users.

Creating a Collection

Since our example is going to be a simple public chatroom, we just need to store three pieces of data about the message:

- Who sent the message, which will be a string that we'll initially set to *Anonymous* for each message, but that will be the user ID of the sender (which is a string) after we implement authentication.

- The message body itself (another string).

- The date and time at which the message was sent, which can be set to the Firestore data type timestamp, which is converted to a DateTime object in Dart.

So, let's go to Databases -> Data in the Firebase Console, click the *Add collection* button, which will prompt you to enter a name for the collection. We'll use *Messages* as the collection name. After that, you'll be prompted to enter the data for the first document to be added to the collection.

The Document ID doesn't have to be anything in particular, so you can click the *Auto-ID* button to get it automatically filled for you by random characters; We also need to add all of the fields we mentioned earlier, choosing the appropriate types and setting an appropriate value for each field to be used for the creation of the first message. For our example, let's set the fields in the following way:

- A string called *from* to identify the sender, with *Anonymous* as the value.

- A string called *msg*, which will be the body of the message, the value of which we you could set simply to *Hi*, as a test.

- A timestamp called *when*, which you should set to your current time converted to UTC time.

We are using UTC time for the when field because we want the date and time to be in the user's local time, so we keep the UTC time in the database and convert it to the local time in the app. We'll have to keep this in mind when sending messages from the app because in that occasion we'll have to convert the local time to UTC.

Interacting with Cloud Firestore in Flutter Apps

To use Firestore in our Flutter app, we'll take advantage of the *cloud_firestore* package.

Let's start by adding the cloud_firestore package to the dependencies in pubspec.yaml:

firebase/chatonfire/pubspec.yaml
```
dependencies:
  flutter:
    sdk: flutter
  firebase_core:
  cloud_firestore:
```

and importing it into main.dart:

firebase/chatonfire/lib/main.dart
```
import 'package:cloud_firestore/cloud_firestore.dart';
```

We interact with Cloud Firestore using an instance of the Firestore class created using Firestore.instance. We can access a collection with Firestore.instance.collection("collectionName") where *collectionName* is the name of the collection we want to access. The type of data returned by that is CollectionReference, and we will explore how to use that in this section.

Reading from the Cloud Firestore

If we want to access a certain document directly, we use the:

```
CollectionReference.document(path)
```

simple query method (where) path is actually the ID of the document, which corresponds with the path leading to the document within the collection. This returns a DocumentReference, and doesn't actually fetch the document. To fetch it, we need to call DocumentReference.get(), which returns a Future<DocumentSnapshot>. After awaiting or otherwise getting the DocumentSnapshot itself, we can access the data contained in the document by accessing the DocumentSnapshot.data property, which contains a Map of the data contained in the document.

For example, if we had the name of a collection stored in a variable called collectionName and we wanted to access document with ID docPath, and in particular its property "myMember" and set it to the data variable, we would need to write the following:

```
var firestore = Firestore.instance;
var data = (
  await firestore
    .collection(collectionName)
    .document(docPath)
    .get()
).data["myMember"];
```

Querying a single document is useful for some purposes, but what we really want in a chat app when fetching messages is a way to access the list of all of the documents that have been stored in the collection.

To do that, we can use the CollectionReference.getDocuments() method, which returns all of the documents in the given collection in a Future, but its disadvantage is that we need to fetch it again every time we want to update the list of messages, which doesn't really go well with the real-time nature of instant messaging.

What we want is to get the messages as a Stream that is changed in real time to yield the list of all messages updated in real time. This is done using the CollectionReference.snapshots() method, meaning we can use it to get a Stream of the messages by writing:

```
Firestore.instance.collection("Messages").snapshots()
```

Adding Data to the Cloud Firestore

We can add a document to a Firestore collection by using CollectionReference.add(doc) where doc is a Map assigning a value for each of the document's fields, like in the following example, which sends an anonymous message to be stored in the collection:

```
Firestore.instance.collection("Messages").add(
  {
    "from": "Anonymous",
    "when": DateTime.now().toUtc(),
    "msg": "Hi There From The App",
  }
);
```

In a real app we need to authenticate users, so we'll start by discovering how we can authenticate users to our Flutter apps using Firebase Authentication.

Deleting or Changing Data from the Cloud Firestore

Given a DocumentReference (the object we get from Firestore.instance.collection(collection).document(document)()), we can, in addition to getting the data using the DocumentReference.get() as we said earllier, perform some actions on the document:

- Delete it using DocumentReference.delete().
- Change some fields by passing a Map to DocumentReference.updateData().
- Set the contents of the document, creating it if doesn't exist, by passing a Map to DocumentReference.setData().

All of these methods run asynchronously but don't return anything.

Authentication

Authentication requires its own *firebase_auth* package[4] and can be configured in Flutter's console by going to Develop -> Authentication -> Sign-in method. In our example we'll authenticate users using their email address and password, which is made very easy by Firebase and is representative of the majority of apps. After selecting it, you'll be warned that more platform-specific setup is required: specifically, we need to add:

```
implementation 'com.google.firebase:firebase-auth:16.2.1'
```

to the app-level build.gradle dependencies for Android, and:

```
pod 'Firebase/Auth'
```

to the iOS Podfile you should have from the CocoaPods configuration that was needed to connect the iOS app to Firebase.

---

4. https://pub.dartlang.org/packages/firebase_auth

Using the firebase_auth Package

Let's import the *firebase_auth* package, which provides an intuitive Flutter interface to the Firebase Authentication tools:

firebase/chatonfire/pubspec.yaml
```
firebase_auth: ^0.6.2
```

As always, we need to import the firebase_auth package in main.dart:

firebase/chatonfire/lib/main.dart
```
import 'package:firebase_auth/firebase_auth.dart';
```

The FirebaseAuth

Firebase authentication is achieved using an instance of the FirebaseAuth class, obtained using:

```
var auth = FirebaseAuth.instance;
```

After this, we can use the auth object to handle most authentication-related actions.

Among them, we find:

```
createUserWithEmailAndPassword(email, password)
```

which creates a user with the given email and password, and:

```
signInWithEmailAndPassword(email, password)
```

which signs in the user with the given email and password.

The Many Authentication Methods Available in Flutter

There are many authentication methods available to use with Firebase. Here is a list of the most common ones:

- Phone Authentication, which relies on two phases: running FirebaseAuth.instance.verifyPhoneNumber(), which takes methods to be run when the code is sent, it's automatically retrieved, or there was an issue during verification. If it is auto-retrieved, we should consider the user authenticated and move on. If it is not, we need to provide the user a way to insert the code they received via SMS and use and use an AuthCredential to log in, as described in the aside *Package and Library Versions* that follows this sidebar.

- Google Sign-In Authentication, using FirebaseAuth.instance.signInWithGoogle().

Package and Library Versions

The *FlutterFire* packages (as Google likes to call the Firebase-related Flutter packages), just like the testing interface, are sometimes incompatible with some versions of Flutter or of the platform-specific API (the one we import in the Gradle/CocoaPods configuration) or don't work at all. Additionally, they tend to have breaking changes from one version to another, meaning the same code has a high change of not working after one or two major releases.

 For our example, I used *firebase_auth* version 0.6.X because that was the only version that consistenly worked with the current Flutter version (1.5) and native API version. If, in the future, you need to use a newer version because of security concerns about the older versions or any other reason. One thing to keep in mind is that the package is slowly switching to using the generic auth.signInWithCredential() method, which takes as a positional argument a AuthCredential object.

An AuthCredential object can be generated by calling the getCredential() of each AuthProvider, providing to each the arguments it needs to perform the authentication.

You can look at all of the AuthProviders available and the methods you can use to get AuthCredentials on the official *firebase_auth* API reference.[5] That's also where you should look in case you upgrade the package version and have issues in general.

The FirebaseUser

The final result of an authentication process is the generation of a FirebaseUser variable, which will also be stored. This represents the user account and stores the following information as properties:

- Its uid, a string equivalent to a typical numerical User ID.

- Its phoneNumber and/or email address.

- An isEmailVerified to establish whether a user's email address has been verified, which is useful when doing email and password authentication.

- A displayName and photoUrl we can set by changing these properties directly.

---

5. pub.dev/documentation/firebase_auth/latest/firebase_auth/AuthCredential-class.html

To make changes to these properties (for example to set the display name), we need to create an UserUpdateInfo object, which will have all of these properties. Change any properties you want to change and then run user.updateProfile(userUpdateInfo), where userUpdateInfo is the UserUpdateInfo object containing the changed properties.

To change the user's email address, you can use user.updateEmail(newEmail), whereas to change the user's password you can use user.updatePassword(newPassword). You can reload the local profile to match the remote one using user.reload(). Keep in mind that this will only have an effect if you reassign the user variable to auth.currentUser().

Firebase's authentication tools can do a lot: other than just creating and deleting accounts, resetting passwords and changing email address, it allows you to also verify email addresses. Verification happens by calling user.sendEmailVerification(), which sends an email containg a verification link to the user. When the user clicks the link, the email will be considered as verified.

The only difference this makes to Firebase itself is that users with a verified email addresses have the user.isEmailVerified boolean property set to true instead of false. You get to decide what to do with unverified users: whether to supply all features, only some of them, or no features at all.

You also get to decide what the email sent to the user will look like: by going to Authentication -> Templates you can choose the sender name, some aspects of the sender email address and the entire body of the email sent to the user.

Writing Log-In and Sign-Up Methods

That's the theory, here are two examples of how you can use those methods to write an interface to the Firebase Authentication API for our app.

This is what a sign-up method for email and password authentication could look like:

```
firebase/chatonfire/lib/main.dart
Future<FirebaseUser> signUp(
  String email, String password
) async =>
  _auth.createUserWithEmailAndPassword(
    email: email,
    password: password
  );
```

and this is how we could write a log-in method

firebase/chatonfire/lib/main.dart
```
Future<FirebaseUser> logIn(
  String email, String password
) async =>
  _auth.signInWithEmailAndPassword(
      email: email,
      password: password
  );
```

Checking Whether the User is Logged-In and Getting Information on the Current user

Running:

```
auth.currentUser();
```

will return (asynchronously) the currently logged in FirebaseUser.

If we haven't performed log-in yet, it will return null, meaning there is an easy way to check whether log-in has happened.

Log-In Persistency in Local Cache

Firebase will preserve login information in local storage, meaning we don't have to worry about persistence of user data on the local user's device since Firebase will take care of that for us as well.

Sign Out

Given that the user data is kept by Firebase indefinetly, to sign out a user you need to run:

```
auth.signOut();
```

which is an asynchronous method that doesn't return anything.

Combining Authentication and Database Access

Firebase is great: you just need to authenticate the user and then any operation you try to execute on a Firebase database will be executed on behalf of that user. You don't even need to think about it: Firebase does it on its own and Flutter supports it perfectly. That's what we're going to take advantage of when we build our chat app in Building the Chat App, on page 260.

Animations and Transistions

There are two ways to animate widgets in Flutter: animating them *within* a given screen and animating them *between* different screens.

Animating Within a Screen: the AnimatedContainer and Similar Widgets

The AnimatedContainer is one of the simplest widgets to start animating your Flutter app: it's a regular Container but it animates to when a property is changed, giving a nicer transition to a different state. For example, changing its height or width will make the widget shrink or expand gradually, and similar effects can be had by changing the border or color properties of the widget. The duration of the animation can optionally be changed using the duration argument and its curve (whether or not and how much the animation slows down or speeds up over time) can be changed using the curve argument.

The duration is of type duration, so you'd use the Duration we used earlier during authentication, while the curve is of type Curve. A collection of the most common curves is found in the Curves class. It is a big collection, so you might consider reading the full list on the official Flutter reference manual[6] in the *Constants* section if the following basic curves aren't enough for you or if you want to know the mathematical function that produces each curve:

- Curves.easeIn, which starts out slowly and quickens over time.
- Curves.easeOut, which starts out fast and slows down over time.

If you want to animate just some padding, you can replace a Padding widget with some AnimatedPadding, and if you want to anymate changes in TextStyle you can use the animated version of the DefaultTextStyle (which is a class that applies its style TextStyle arguments to all of the descendants of its child), called the AnimatedDefaultTextStyle (which animates the change in the style) by providing, optionally, a curve and a duration to these animated widgets.

Those are all interesting, but the most useful is certainly the AnimatedList, which animates additions made to a list or deletions of elements of a list.

AnimatedList

The AnimatedList starts out as a normal ListView, but its state object can be used (via a GlobalKey) to insert or delete items, showing a transition when one of these operations is performed.

We can construct an AnimatedList just like a ListView.builder()-constructed ListView, but we have to set a key that we'll use to interact with it later, which has to be a GlobalKey<AnimatedListState>, and the itemCount will instead be called initialItemCount.

---

6. https://docs.flutter.io/flutter/animation/Curves-class.html

The itemBuilder gets an extra animation argument, which provides the current state of the animation, which can be used by a SizeTransition widget inside the itemBuilder to actually visually create the transition when an item is inserted by increasing the size of the widget (clipping it at the start and gradually showing it all) to animate the insertion of a widget.

All of that adds up to the following:

```
AnimatedList(
  key: key,
  initialItemCount: n,
  itemBuilder(context, i, animation) =>
    SizeTransition(
      sizeFactor: animation,
      child: WidgetToShow()
    )
)
```

The SizeTransition isn't the only widget that can perform similar transitions (for example the similar ScaleTransition scales the widget up and down instead of clipping it), but it's the most effective for the purpose of animating a list.

Having the same key stored somewhere allows us to get the AnimatedListState object relative to that AnimatedList by writing:

```
var listState = key.currentState as AnimatedListState;
```

which allows us to add a list item by wrapping the following in a call to setState():

```
listState.insertItem(position);
```

keeping in mind that the AnimatedList needs to be able to build the new element at that position: if it's taking elements from a List, make sure there is actually new data to build the new item from.

A full example of a widget (or, more accurately, a stateful widget's state) that takes advantage of an AnimatedList to dynamically add items to a list when a floating action button is pressed is the following:

```
GlobalKey _key = GlobalKey<AnimatedListState>();
int _nextWidget = 3;
var _strings = [
  "First",
  "Second",
  "Third"
];

@override
Widget build(BuildContext context) {
```

```
  return Scaffold(
    appBar: AppBar(title: Text("Animated List")),
    body: AnimatedList(
      key: _key,
      initialItemCount: _nextWidget,
      itemBuilder: (context, i, animation) =>
        SizeTransition(
          sizeFactor: animation,
          child: ListTile(title: Text(_strings[i]),),
        ),
    ),
    floatingActionButton: FloatingActionButton(
      child: Icon(Icons.add),
      onPressed: () {
        setState(() {
          (_key.currentState as AnimatedListState).insertItem(
            _nextWidget++
          );
          _strings.add(
            "${_nextWidget}th"
          );
        });
      },
    ),
  );
}
```

These widgets provide the simplest kind of animation available in Flutter: the most interesting animations are provided by the Hero widget, which allows you to animate the movement of a widget across different screens.

Hero Animation

Hero animations are performed by the Flutter framework on Hero widgets. An Hero widget needs a tag that identifies it and a child (which is the widget to animate). Adding the same tag to two Hero widgets in two different screens, one of which is pushed from the other, will make the widget animate to move to its new position on the screen.

A simple example that demonstrates the use of the Hero widget is the following: there are two pages that have in common a widget (I used FlutterLogo as an example) that is wrapped in an Hero widget with the same tag. Switching between the views by clicking the floating action button will cause the widget to animate between its centered position in the first page to a top-left position in the second page and vice versa:

```
class FirstPage extends StatelessWidget {
  @override
  Widget build(BuildContext context) =>
    Scaffold(
      body:Center(
        child:Hero(
          tag: "Flutter Logo Hero",
          child: FlutterLogo(),
        )
      ),
      floatingActionButton: FloatingActionButton(
        child: Icon(Icons.looks_two),
        onPressed: () => Navigator.pushReplacement(
          context,
          MaterialPageRoute(
            builder: (context) => SecondPage()
          )
        ),
      ),
    );
}
class SecondPage extends StatelessWidget {
  @override
  Widget build(BuildContext context) =>
    Scaffold(
      body:Hero(
        tag: "Flutter Logo Hero",
        child: FlutterLogo(),
      ),
      floatingActionButton: FloatingActionButton(
        child: Icon(Icons.looks_one),
        onPressed: () => Navigator.pushReplacement(
          context,
          MaterialPageRoute(
            builder: (context) => FirstPage()
          )
        ),
      ),
    );
}
```

Custom Shapes and Drawing in Flutter Apps Using Painters

With Canvas and Paint we can change the look of a certain widget. That is done using a CustomPainter, which is a class that allows us to draw lines and shapes on a virtual Canvas.

CustomPaint

CustomPaint is the widget that allows us to insert the custom shapes we'll create using a CustomPainter into the widget tree. It takes two arguments: a CustomPainter as the named painter and a child widget, which will be the widget on which the effect will be applied. For example, if we wanted to paint a Flutter logo widget using a custom painter we'll create called LogoPainter, we'd insert the following into the widget tree:

```
CustomPaint(
  painter: LogoPainter(),
  child: FlutterLogo(),
),
```

Creating a CustomPainter

The painter needs to be a subclass of the CustomPainter widget we have to define ourselves by overriding the paint() and shouldRepaint() methods.

The paint Method

The paint() method takes two arguments: a Canvas and a Size.

The Canvas is the object on which we will perform drawing operations, such as:

- Drawing lines, using canvas.drawLine(point1, point2, paint), where the points are represented by Offsets (that we'll discuss later) and paint is of type Paint and decides the color and appearance of the line and will be discussed later.

- Drawing circles using canvas.drawCircle(center, radius, paint), where center is an Offset, radius is a double and paint is a Paint object.

- Inserting an Image using canvas.drawImage(image, point, paint), where image is the dart:ui library's Image class, about which there will be a sidebar at the end of this section.

- Drawing rectangles, using canvas.drawRect(rect, paint), where rect is of class Rect, about which we're going to talk later in this section;

- Drawing ellipses using canvas.drawOval(rect, paint), where the arguments are the same as the rectangle's, but will result in an oval being drawn instead of a rectangle.

The Offset class is used to represent a point in the absolute virtual plane of the app screen by using two double numbers (for example (Offset(0.0, 0.0) is the origin of the virtual plane). You can choose offsets relative to various properties of the Paint widget using the properties and methods that are passed along with the Canvas to the paint() method as part of the Size widget, as described in the official API reference.[7] Most of the time, you're going to use Offset like vectors to define shapes relative to some other points using Size as we'll see later.

The Paint class is used to define styling features (such as the color or the width) of the lines and shapes drawn on the canvas. The main ones are color and painting style: paint.color can be set to any color (for example Colors.green) and paint.style can be set to either PaintingStyle.fill or PaintingStyle.stroke, where the first one fills the shape with paint, whereas the second one only draws the edge. If you choose the latter, you may set paint.strokeWidth to any double value.

The Rect class is used to describe a rectangle in the plane. It is created from either two points (using the Rect.fromPoints(point1, point2) constructor), which will generate the smallest possible rectangle that encloses the two points, from the left and right X coordinates and top and bottom and top Y coordinates (using Rect.fromLTRB(left, top, right, bottom), where the arguments are all double values), or from a couple of edges, width and height (using Rect.fromLTWH(left, top, width, height), the arguments are all double values just like with the previous constructor). Rect.fromCircle(center, radius), with the same arguments as Canvas.drawCircle(), is used to get a square from a circle.

The Size is used to generate Offset based on the size and positioning of the CustomPaint's child. This can be done using methods such as Size.center(offset), which will return an Offset that is obtained by considering the center of the widget we're painting as the origin of the plane and considering. Another way to see that is as the point obtained from the translation of the center of the widget by the vector offset. Other methods, such as Size.bottomRight(offset) can be used if you need to draw a point relative to other points of the widget.

The shouldRepaint Method

The shouldRepaint() method has to be implemented, and it's an important optimization factor when talking about complex and resource-intensive CustomPainters.

It returns a boolean value that tells the framework whether or not the widget needs to be repainted. It is called whenever a CustomPaint object attempts to get painted with a new instance of a CustomPainter class. This method gets the old custom painter instance as an argument, so you can compare it with the new one to decide whether anything worthy of a re-render has changed.

In our case, we're just going to return false because the same object never gets called with different CustomPainters. For performance reasons, you should start with that and, if there are problems, try to make it more and more common

---

7.   https://api.flutter.dev/flutter/dart-ui/Size-class.html

Using ui.Image

The image passed to drawImage() isn't a regular Flutter Image widget: it's the Image class found in the dart:ui library.[a]

An ui.Image (usually referred to with the 'ui.' prefix in documentation because 'dart:ui' is typically imported 'as ui' to differentiate it from the Flutter Image widget) is obtained as the 'image' property of an ui.FrameInfo object.

A FrameInfo can be obtained by running (and awaiting) ui.Codec's getNextFrame() method. Finally, an ui.Codec can be obtained using 'dart:ui''s instantiateImageCodec() function. This data can be obtained from an image file by using dart:io's regular File.readBytes() method.

---

a.   api.flutter.dev/flutter/dart-ui/Image-class.html

that shouldRepaint() returns true until all issues are fixed and the widgets get painted according to how you want them to be painted.

An Example of a CustomPainter

CustomPainters allow a great degree of customization, so they are best described with an example to show you how to put together the basic concepts we talked about, so that you can get an idea of how it's done, keeping in mind that only the official API reference[8] can comprehensively list all of the possible transformations and shapes available:

```
class LogoPainter extends CustomPainter {
  @override
  void paint(Canvas canvas, Size size) {
    var greenPaint = Paint()
      ..style = PaintingStyle.fill
      ..color = Colors.green;
    var redPaint = Paint()
      ..style = PaintingStyle.fill
      ..color = Colors.red;
    var whitePaint = Paint()
      ..style = PaintingStyle.fill
      ..color = Colors.white;
    canvas.drawColor(Colors.blue, BlendMode.color);
    canvas.drawOval(
      Rect.fromPoints(
        size.topLeft(Offset(-40, -100)),
        size.bottomRight(Offset(15, 10))
      ),
      greenPaint
    );
```

---

8.   https://api.flutter.dev/flutter/dart-ui/Canvas-class.html

```
    canvas.drawOval(
      Rect.fromPoints(
        size.topLeft(
          Offset(-15, -10)
        ),
        size.bottomRight(Offset(40, 100))
      ),
      redPaint
    );
    canvas.drawCircle(size.center(Offset(0, 0)), 40.0, whitePaint);
  }
  @override
  bool shouldRepaint(CustomPainter old) {
    return false;
  }
}
```

This example takes advantage of cascade notation (covered in Cascade Notation, on page 306), which is a way to call multiple methods on an object or alter some of its properties without having to repeat the name of the object by returning the altered object and not the result of the method (whitePaint.. color=Colors.white returns whitePaint, meaning we can add another two dots with another instruction, and it will be executed on the whitePaint object).

It results in the following being drawn when painting a FlutterLogo:

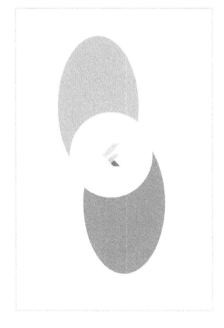

Hero Animations Combined with CustomPaint

The combination of these canvas painting abilities with hero animation could make for interesting user interaction animation in Flutter apps: let's imagine having two widgets similar to the one we've seen in the previous section, but in different colors and that serve as links to different views or different versions of the same view.

Let's start by defining the painters: a red, green and white one just like the previous one:

```
class GreenWhiteRedPainter extends CustomPainter {
  @override
  void paint(Canvas canvas, Size size) {
    var greenPaint = Paint();
    greenPaint.style =PaintingStyle.fill;
    greenPaint.color = Colors.green;
    var redPaint = Paint();
    redPaint.style =PaintingStyle.fill;
    redPaint.color = Colors.red;
    var whitePaint = Paint();
    whitePaint.style =PaintingStyle.fill;
    whitePaint.color = Colors.white;
    canvas.drawColor(Colors.blue, BlendMode.color);
    canvas.drawOval(
      Rect.fromPoints(
        size.topLeft(Offset(-40, -100)),
        size.bottomRight(Offset(15, 10))
      ),
      greenPaint
    );
    canvas.drawOval(
      Rect.fromPoints(
        size.topLeft(Offset(-15, -10)),
        size.bottomRight(Offset(40, 100))
      ),
      redPaint
    );
    canvas.drawCircle(size.center(Offset(0, 0)), 40.0, whitePaint);

  }

  @override
  bool shouldRepaint(CustomPainter old) {
    return false;
  }
}
```

and a blue and white one:

```
class BlueWhiteBluePainter extends CustomPainter {
  @override
  void paint(Canvas canvas, Size size) {
    var bluePaint = Paint();
    bluePaint.style =PaintingStyle.fill;
    bluePaint.color = Colors.blue;
    var whitePaint = Paint();
    whitePaint.style =PaintingStyle.fill;
    whitePaint.color = Colors.white;
    canvas.drawColor(Colors.blue, BlendMode.color);
    canvas.drawOval(
      Rect.fromPoints(
        size.topLeft(Offset(-40, -100)),
        size.bottomRight(Offset(15, 10))
      ),
      bluePaint
    );
    canvas.drawOval(
      Rect.fromPoints(
        size.topLeft(Offset(-15, -10)),
        size.bottomRight(Offset(40, 100))
      ),
      bluePaint
    );
    canvas.drawCircle(size.center(Offset(0, 0)), 40.0, whitePaint);

  }

  @override
  bool shouldRepaint(CustomPainter old) {
    return false;
  }
}
```

We'll use them in an app for two different widgets in a Row that will each pass themselves to a second view:

```
class FirstPage extends StatelessWidget {

  final widgets = [
    Hero(
      tag: "Blue White Red",
      child: CustomPaint(
        painter: BlueWhiteBluePainter(),
        child: Text("1"),
      ),
    ),
    Hero(
      tag: "Green White Red",
      child: CustomPaint(
        painter: GreenWhiteRedPainter(),
        child: Text("2"),
```

```
        ),
      ),
    ];

    @override
    Widget build(BuildContext context) =>
      Scaffold(
        body:Center(
          child:Row(
            mainAxisAlignment: MainAxisAlignment.spaceEvenly,
            children: <Widget>[
              Hero(
                tag: "Green White Red",
                child: CustomPaint(
                  painter: BlueWhiteBluePainter(),
                  child: GestureDetector(
                    child: Text("1"),
                    onTap: () => Navigator.pushReplacement(
                      context,
                      MaterialPageRoute(
                        builder: (context) => SecondPage(
                          widgets[0]
                        )
                      )
                    ),
                  ),
                ),
              ),
              Hero(
                tag: "Blue White Red",
                child: CustomPaint(
                  painter: GreenWhiteRedPainter(),
                  child: GestureDetector(
                    child: Text("2"),
                    onTap: () => Navigator.pushReplacement(
                      context,
                      MaterialPageRoute(
                        builder: (context) => SecondPage(
                          widgets[1]
                        )
                      )
                    ),
                  ),
                ),
              ),
            ],
          )
        ),
      );
}
```

that other view shows the widget in the top left corner of the screen, as a way to show what choice has been made and provides a way to go back:

```
class SecondPage extends StatelessWidget {
  SecondPage(this.topLeft);

  final Widget topLeft;

  @override
  Widget build(BuildContext context) =>
    Scaffold(
      body: Padding(
        padding: EdgeInsets.only(left: 50.0, top: 150.0),
        child: topLeft,
      ),
      floatingActionButton: FloatingActionButton(
        child: Icon(Icons.looks_one),
        onPressed: () => Navigator.pushReplacement(
          context,
          MaterialPageRoute(
            builder: (context) => FirstPage()
          )
        ),
      ),
    );
}
```

The first view will look like this:

When clicking the number 1 the view will animate to show the following:

and when clciking the number 2 the view will animate to show the following:

Clicking the floating action button in the second page will animate to the initial page with both buttons.

The StreamBuilder

The StreamBuilder works just like a FutureBuilder, but it updates its content in real time to match the content of a given stream, instead of simply displaying the result of a given future like the FutureBuilder does:

```
StreamBuilder(
  stream: myStream(),
  builder: (context, snapshot) {
    if(!snapshot.hasData) return CircularProgressIndicator();
    return MyWidget(
      data: snapshot.data
    );
  }
)
```

Building the Chat App

Now that we know how to use Firebase for what we need (authentication and database) and we have some more advanced UI notions, we can start building the chat app I promised we would work on.

Planning Our App's UI

A chat app needs the user to perform multiple actions when they first start the app:

- We need the user to insert an email address and password and either log into an existing account or create a new one if they don't have one yet, at this point the user should also receive an email asking him to verify his user account, but we're not going to make distinctions between verified and unverified users at this point.

- We need the user to choose a *display name* to use to identify themselves to other users in the app.

- If the user has done all of this, they should get to the page showing all messages sent by other users.

Building the UI

We'll build the UI by creating each piece in the order in which the user will interact with it. Let's start with the Sign-Up/Sign-In page!

Login/Signup Page

As we did in the previous chapter, we are going to use a TextEditingController to be able to access text entered into a TextField from outside its own onSubmitted.

The UI is going to be the following (we'll implement the logIn() and signUp() methods later in Authentication, on page 270):

firebase/chatonfire/lib/main.dart
```dart
@override
Widget build(BuildContext context) {
  if(_verificationComplete) {
    Navigator.pushReplacement(
        context,
        MaterialPageRoute(
          builder: (context) => ConfigPage()
        )
    );
  }
  return Scaffold(
    appBar: AppBar(
      title: Text("ChatOnFire Login"),
    ),
    body: ListView(
      children: <Widget>[
        Padding(
          padding: EdgeInsets.all(15.0),
          child: Text(
            "Log In Using Your Phone Number",
            style: Theme.of(context).textTheme.display1,
          ),
        ),
        Padding(
          padding: EdgeInsets.all(10.0),
          child: TextField(
            keyboardType: TextInputType.emailAddress,
            controller: _emailController,
            decoration: InputDecoration(
              labelText: "Email Address",
            ),
            autofocus: true,
          )
        ),
        Padding(
          padding: EdgeInsets.all(10.0),
          child: TextField(
            keyboardType: TextInputType.text,
            obscureText: true,
            controller: _passwordController,
```

```
        decoration: InputDecoration(
          labelText: "Password",
        ),
      )
    ),
    Padding(
      padding: EdgeInsets.all(10.0),
      child: FlatButton(
        color: Theme.of(context).accentColor,
        textColor: Colors.white,
        child: Text("Log In".toUpperCase()),
        onPressed: () {
          logIn(
            _emailController.text,
            _passwordController.text
          ).then(
            (user) {
              _user = user;
              if(!_user.isEmailVerified) {
                _user.sendEmailVerification();
              }
              _verificationComplete = true;
              Navigator.pushReplacement(
                context, MaterialPageRoute(
                  builder: (context) => ConfigPage()
                )
              );
            }
          ).catchError(
            (e) {
              Scaffold.of(context).showSnackBar(
                SnackBar(
                  content: Text(
                    "You don't have an account. Please sign up."
                  )
                )
              );
            }
          );
        },
      ),
    ),
    Padding(
      padding: EdgeInsets.all(10.0),
      child: FlatButton(
        color: Theme.of(context).hintColor,
        textColor: Colors.white,
        child: Text("Create an Account".toUpperCase()),
```

```
              onPressed: () async {
                try {
                  _user = await signUp(
                    _emailController.text,
                    _passwordController.text
                  );
                  if(!_user.isEmailVerified) {
                    _user.sendEmailVerification();
                  }
                  _verificationComplete = true;
                  Navigator.pushReplacement(
                    context, MaterialPageRoute(
                      builder: (context) => ConfigPage()
                    )
                  );
                }
                catch(e) {
                  Scaffold.of(context).showSnackBar(
                    SnackBar(
                      content: Text("An error occurred")
                    )
                  );
                }
              },
            ),
          ),
        ],
      )
    );
}
```

At this point no guidance should be needed to understand these widgets, all of which we have already used at some point.

An exception is Navigator.pushReplacement(), which is just like Navigator.push(), but it provides no way for the user to go back to the previous page. In this case each screen means that some progress has been done, so the previous screen was a worry of the past we don't want the user to accidentally go back to.

Config Page

After logging in, the user has to enter a display name, so we need a screen called ConfigPage specifically meant to achieve that, since it's a step that requires authentication to have happened and is a prerequisite to using the chat page:

```
firebase/chatonfire/lib/main.dart
@override
Widget build(BuildContext context) {
  return Scaffold(
    appBar: AppBar(title: Text("Configure you account's basic information")),
```

```
    body: ListView(
      children: <Widget>[
        TextField(decoration: InputDecoration(
            labelText: "Display Name"
          ),
          onSubmitted: (displayName) =>
            setNameAndGoToChatPage(displayName, context),
          controller: _controller,
        ),
        FlatButton(
          child: Text("Submit"),
          onPressed: () =>
            setNameAndGoToChatPage(_controller.text, context),
        )
      ],
    ),
  );
}
```

Once again, we're going to implement setNameAndGoToChatPage() later. All we need to know about it is that it's certainly going to push a new screen, loading a widget called ChatPage, which we'll implement now.

Chat Page

Here's what we're going to build in this section:

The ChatPage is going to consist of a Column that shows an Expanded-wrapped ListView built using the messages passed to the StreamBuilder and a Row(shown at the bottom of the screen, since the ListView is going to be expanded by the

Expanded widget) showing a TextField and an IconButton to send the message, making use of a TextEditingController as always:

firebase/chatonfire/lib/main.dart
```
@override
Widget build(BuildContext context) {
  return Scaffold(
    appBar: AppBar(
      title: Text("ChatOnFire"),
    ),
    body: Column(
      children: <Widget>[
        Expanded(
          child: StreamBuilder(
            stream: getMessages(),
            builder: (context, snapshot) =>
              snapshot.hasData ?
                MessagesList(snapshot.data as QuerySnapshot)
              :
                Center(child: CircularProgressIndicator())
          ),
        ),
        Row(
          children: <Widget>[
            Expanded(
              child: Padding(
                padding: const EdgeInsets.all(8.0),
                child: TextField(
                  controller: _messageController,
                  keyboardType: TextInputType.text,
                  onSubmitted: (txt) {
                    sendText(txt);
                    _messageController.clear();
                  }
                ),
              ),
            ),
            IconButton(
              icon: Icon(Icons.send),
              onPressed: () {
                sendText(_messageController.text);
                _messageController.clear();
              }
            )
          ],
        )
      ],
    ),
  );
}
```

As always, getMessages() and the MessagesList will be defined later, when we implement an interface with the Cloud Firestore in Database, on page 271.

The List of Messages

In the MessagesList widget, we'll take the list of messages and create a ListView using the ListView.builder() constructor, passing the data needed to show the message (sender, text, and timestamp) to a Message widget we'll build later.

The ListView's reverse argument makes the list *start from the bottom*, meaning the first element will be shown at the bottom, which will be the scrolling view's default position, which will be held when new messages are added. This is the typical behavior of chat apps and we want to replicate it, so we'll set that to true:

```
firebase/chatonfire/lib/main.dart
class MessagesList extends StatelessWidget {
  MessagesList(this.data);

  final QuerySnapshot data;

  bool areSameDay(Timestamp a, Timestamp b) {
    var date1 = a.toDate().toLocal();
    var date2 = b.toDate().toLocal();
    return
      (date1.year == date2.year)
      &&
      (date1.month == date2.month)
      &&
      (date1.day == date2.day);
  }

  @override
  Widget build(BuildContext context) =>
    ListView.builder(
      reverse: true,
      itemCount: data.documents.length,
      itemBuilder: (context, i) {
        var months = [
          "January",
          "February",
          "March",
          "April",
          "May",
          "June",
          "July",
          "August",
          "September",
          "October",
          "November",
          "December"
        ];
```

```
        DateTime when = data
                      .documents[i]
                      .data["when"]
                      .toDate()
                      .toLocal();
        var widgetsToShow = <Widget>[
          Message(
            from: data.documents[i].data["from"],
            msg: data.documents[i].data["msg"],
            when: when
          ),
        ];
        if(i == data.documents.length-1) {
          widgetsToShow.insert(
            0,
            Padding(
              padding: const EdgeInsets.symmetric(vertical: 10.0),
              child: Text(
                "${when.day} ${months[when.month-1]} ${when.year}",
                style: Theme.of(context).textTheme.subhead,
              ),
            )
          );
        } else if(
          !areSameDay(
            data.documents[i+1].data["when"],
            data.documents[i].data["when"]
          )
        ) {
          widgetsToShow.insert(
            0,
            Padding(
              padding: const EdgeInsets.symmetric(vertical: 10.0),
              child: Text(
                "${when.day} ${months[when.month-1]} ${when.year}",
                style: Theme.of(context).textTheme.subhead
              ),
            )
          );
        }
        return Column(
          children: widgetsToShow
        );
      }
    );
}
```

You might have noticed that we are building the ListView using a Column that allows us to show the date on which a message was sent if it is different than the previous message's date. This is the preferred approach of many chat apps since it allows us to show the date only when it matters to the user.

One disadvantage is that doing it that way is a bit unintuitive and verbose: we need to have an if and an else if necessarily because having both conditions in the first if will cause the app to crash if we try to access the document at index documents.length, but it's made even worse by the fact that the list is created in two steps, making the contents less clear at first glance.

Dart 2.3 helps with that by allowing us to integrate if statements in list literals, allowing us to bypass the widgetsToShow variable completely and return a Column that has, at the start of the list of children, the following:

```
return Column(
  children: [
    if(i == data.documents.length)
      Padding(
        padding: const EdgeInsets.symmetric(vertical: 10.0),
        child: Text(
          "${when.day} ${months[when.month-1]} ${when.year}",
          style: Theme.of(context).textTheme.subhead
        ),
      )
    else if(
      !areSameDay(
        data.documents[i+1].data["when"],
        data.documents[i].data["when"]
      )
    )
      Padding(
        padding: const EdgeInsets.symmetric(vertical: 10.0),
        child: Text(
          "${when.day} ${months[when.month-1]} ${when.year}",
          style: Theme.of(context).textTheme.subhead
        ),
      ),
```

This is more intuitive, but it requires you to change pubspec.yaml's environment section to the following, requiring Dart version 2.3.0 or higher:

firebase/chatonfire2/pubspec.yaml
```
environment:
  sdk: ">=2.3.0 <3.0.0"
```

In case you wondered, for loops can be used inside list literals in a similar way starting from Dart version 2.3.2.

Showing Each Message

firebase/chatonfire/lib/main.dart

```dart
@override
Widget build(BuildContext context) {

  return FutureBuilder(
    future: FirebaseAuth.instance.currentUser(),
    builder: (context, snapshot) {
      if(snapshot.hasData) {
        FirebaseUser user = snapshot.data;
        return Container(
          alignment: user.displayName == from
            ?
            Alignment.centerRight
            :
            Alignment.centerLeft,
          child: Container(
            width: MediaQuery.of(context).size.width/3*2,
            child: Card(
              shape: StadiumBorder(),
              child: ListTile(
                title: user.displayName != from
                  ? Padding(
                    padding: const EdgeInsets.only(
                      top: 8.0,
                      left: 5.0
                    ),
                    child: Text(
                      from,
                      style: Theme.of(context).textTheme.subtitle
                    ),
                  )
                  : Padding(
                      padding: EdgeInsets.only(left: 5.0),
                      child: Text(
                        "You",
                        style: Theme.of(context).textTheme.subtitle
                      ),
                    ),
                subtitle: Padding(
                  padding: const EdgeInsets.only(
                    bottom: 10.0,
                    left: 5.0
                  ),
                  child: Text(
                    msg,
                    style: Theme.of(context).textTheme.body1
                  ),
                ),
```

```
                    trailing: Text("${when.hour}:${when.minute}"),
                )
              ),
            )
          );
        } else {
          return CircularProgressIndicator();
        }
      }
    }
  );
}
```

Implementing an Interface with Firebase

The emphasis on email/password authentication in the previous section was spefically meant to prepare you to implement this kind of authentication method in our chat app.

We're going to follow the flow of user interaction for this section as well and start with implementing an interface for authentication purposes.

Authentication

In Writing Log-In and Sign-Up Methods, on page 245, we saw how to implement a log-in method:

firebase/chatonfire/lib/main.dart
```
Future<FirebaseUser> logIn(
  String email, String password
) async =>
  _auth.signInWithEmailAndPassword(
      email: email,
      password: password
  );
```

and a sign-up method:

firebase/chatonfire/lib/main.dart
```
Future<FirebaseUser> signUp(
  String email, String password
) async =>
  _auth.createUserWithEmailAndPassword(
    email: email,
    password: password
  );
```

What we're missing is a method that sets the display name and redirects to the chat page, as needed by the ConfigPage.

That's something that you shouldn't find too hard since we have already seen how to change data such as the display name when we've covered The FirebaseUser, on page 244:

firebase/chatonfire/lib/main.dart
```
void setNameAndGoToChatPage(String name, BuildContext context) {
  FirebaseAuth.instance.currentUser().then(
    (user) {
      var newUserInfo = UserUpdateInfo();
      newUserInfo.displayName = name;
      user.updateProfile(newUserInfo);
    }
  );
  Navigator.pushReplacement(
    context,
    MaterialPageRoute(
      builder: (_) => ChatPage(),
    )
  );
}
```

Database

Sending a message is done using the CollectionReference.add() we mentioned when we talked about adding documents to the Cloud Firestore in Adding Data to the Cloud Firestore, on page 241:

firebase/chatonfire/lib/main.dart
```
void sendText(String text) =>
  FirebaseAuth.instance.currentUser().then(
    (user) =>
      Firestore.instance.collection("Messages").add(
        {
          "from": user != null ? user.displayName : "Anonymous",
          "when": Timestamp.fromDate(DateTime.now().toUtc()),
          "msg": text,
        }
      )
  );
```

Among the methods discussed at the start of the chapter (Reading from the Cloud Firestore, on page 241) to read data from the Cloud Firestore, we need to get a Stream to use with a StreamBuilder, so we use CollectionReference.snapshots():

```
firebase/chatonfire/lib/main.dart
Stream<QuerySnapshot> getMessages() =>
  Firestore
    .instance
    .collection("Messages")
    .orderBy("when", descending: true)
    .snapshots();
```

Adding a Profile Page: Storing User Data in the Cloud Firestore

There are some issues with our app: two users with the same display name would create confusion, since we are only storing a user's display name in the database, and not their ID, so our app would think a user was the sender of a message even if the user who sent the message was a completely different user that happened to have the same display name.

Additionally, the app doesn't really provide any way to distinguish between these two users, so that would be a confusing situation for everyone. A good start would be to provide users with a way to set a short string to customize their profile (usually called a status or a bio) and a way to contact another user of the chat app via email since we're already asking for that information.

Creating a Collection for User Data

Let's create another collection! We'll call it *Users*, and it'll be structured the following way:

- The user's uid will be the document's ID, to make it easier to access the document corresponding to each user.

- The user's displayName will be a string called displayName.

- The user's email address will be another string called email.

- The user's bio will be stored as a string called bio.

Changing the Documents and the App

We need to create entries to the user data collection for each existing user of our app and change every entry in the collection of messages and substitute the display name with the user ID. Then, we'll worry about making the app work with the changed messages in the database, make it display the display name fetched from the Firestore, and then we'll work on building a profile page.

Changing the Data

Creating the users' collection has to be done manually and it's a good idea generally to have a collection containing user data: that's how it is in most "traditional" databases and it's worth it to replicate it in Firebase, except for the fact we don't need (and shouldn't, and especially not in plain text) to store passwords in the database we can access.

Let's start with dealing with the changing data: to change each message in the database and substitute the values is easy enough when there aren't many messages since we can just change them manually in the Firebase console, but with bigger databases you'd have to write some code that (using the interfaces we learned about in this chapter) fetches the messages, finds the user with the given display name and substitutes the display name with the user ID.

Making Smooth Transitions

During initial development (and in our case) an app has no users, so we can make changes to the database that stop a previous version of the app from working at any moment, but that's not the case when an app is already on the market and a significant change is made to the way data is stored.

Certainly, one of the first steps would be to inform the user of a previous version that their version of the app doesn't work anymore instead of just crashing the app, but giving the user a window of time to perform the update would also be something good, and that would be done, in our case, by storing the user ID as an additional property of a message, instead of replacing the previously used one, and then removing the (now useless) display name property after giving some time for the users to upgrade, showing users of the previous version a notice that they shouldn't use that version anymore.

Additionally, for other users who have updated their version of the app before many have had a chance to set a bio, you'd have to set every existing user's bio to some default value (which could be a blank "" or something different like the ones other chat apps use).

Changing the App

The changes we need to make to our app start, as always, before the user even gets to the chat page. After log-in or sign-up, when we ask the user for a display name, we need to prompt the user to enter a bio.

We'll change the setNameAndGoToChatPage(name, context) to a generic setDataAndGoToChatPage(name, bio, context). This addition means we need to define another TextEditingController and change the UI to this:

firebase/chatonfire2/lib/main.dart
```
TextField(
  decoration: InputDecoration(
    labelText: "Display Name"
  ),
  controller: _nameController,
),
```

```
TextField(
  decoration: InputDecoration(
    labelText: "Bio"
  ),
  controller: _bioController,
),
FlatButton(
  child: Text("Submit"),
  onPressed: () =>
    setDataAndGoToChatPage(
      _nameController.text,
      _bioController.text, context
    ),
)
```

The method itself will do the same things setNameAndGoToChatPage() did, but it will also add a document to the Users collection:

firebase/chatonfire2/lib/main.dart

```
void setDataAndGoToChatPage(
  String name,
  String bio,
  BuildContext context
) {
  FirebaseAuth.instance.currentUser().then(
    (user) {
      var newUserInfo = UserUpdateInfo();
      newUserInfo.displayName = name;
      user.updateProfile(newUserInfo);
      Firestore
        .instance
        .collection("Users")
        .document(user.uid)
        .setData(
          {
            "bio": bio,
            "displayName": name,
            "email": user.email,
          }
        );
    }
  );
  Navigator.pushReplacement(
    context,
    MaterialPageRoute(
      builder: (_) => ChatPage(),
    )
  );
}
```

Another place where things need to change is the chat page, more specifically, the list of messages should pass the entire user to the Message class, so that it has all of the information about it that will also be needed by the ProfilePage, but it should also pass the user ID, which isn't actually included in the Map that contains the user data, since the ID actually represents the path where to find the user data in the Firestore collection.

This requires changing the Message constructor and properties:

firebase/chatonfire2/lib/main.dart
```
Message({this.from, this.msg, this.when, this.uid});

final Map<String, dynamic> from;
final String uid;
final String msg;
final DateTime when;
```

and the call from the MessagesList:

firebase/chatonfire2/lib/main.dart
```
? Message(
    from: (snapshot.data as DocumentSnapshot).data,
    msg: data.documents[i].data["msg"],
    when: when,
    uid: data.documents[i].data["from"]
  )
```

The Message itself doesn't need to change a lot: it just needs to align widgets left or right by checking the UID we got from the MessagesList with the current user's ID instead of comparing display names, everything else will be supplied by the from argument. The other change is that the display name's Text widget (the title of each ListTile) will now be wrapped in an InkWell to make it possible for the user to tap it and go to the profile page:

firebase/chatonfire2/lib/main.dart
```
@override
Widget build(BuildContext context) {
  return FutureBuilder(
    future: FirebaseAuth.instance.currentUser(),
    builder: (context, snapshot) {
      if(snapshot.hasData) {
        FirebaseUser user = snapshot.data;
        return Container(
          alignment: user.uid == uid
          ? Alignment.centerRight
          : Alignment.centerLeft,
          child: Container(
            width: MediaQuery.of(context).size.width*2/3,
            child: Card(
```

```
          shape: StadiumBorder(),
          child: ListTile(
            title: user.uid != uid
              ?
              InkWell(
                child: Padding(
                  padding: EdgeInsets.only(
                    top: 8.0,
                    left: 5.0
                  ),
                  child: Text(
                    from["displayName"],
                    style: Theme.of(context).textTheme.subtitle
                  ),
                ),
                onTap: () =>
                  Navigator.push(
                    context,
                    MaterialPageRoute(
                      builder: (context) => ProfilePage(from)
                    )
                  ),
              )
              :
              InkWell(
                child: Padding(
                  padding: EdgeInsets.only(left: 5.0),
                  child: Text(
                    "You",
                    style: Theme.of(context).textTheme.subtitle
                  ),
                ),
                onTap: () =>
                  Navigator.push(
                    context,
                    MaterialPageRoute(
                      builder: (context) => ProfilePage(from)
                    )
                  ),
              ),
            subtitle: Padding(
              padding: const EdgeInsets.only(
                bottom: 10.0,
                left: 5.0
              ),
              child: Text(
                msg,
                style: Theme.of(context).textTheme.body1
              ),
            ),
```

```
          trailing: Text("${when.hour}:${when.minute}"),
        )
      ),
    )
  );
  } else {
    return CircularProgressIndicator();
  }
  }
 }
);
}
```

Creating a Profile Page

The profile page, as we said previously, needs to show three things: the user's display name, the bio, and a button to send an email. To do the latter we need a new package: the *url_launcher* package, which allows us to launch an URL from the app.

Using url_launcher to Launch an URL and Send an Email

Since an URL can also be used to create an email by prefixing the email address to which to send the email with mailto:, we need to add the url_launcher package to the dependencies in pubspec.yaml and import it into main.dart:

firebase/chatonfire2/lib/main.dart
```
import 'package:url_launcher/url_launcher.dart';
```

The package provides two functions:

- canLaunch(url), which returns a Future<bool> and checks whether there are any apps that are capable of handling the URL we're trying to launch.

- launch(url), which launches the URL asynchronously, throwing a PlatformException if no app was able to handle the URL.

The profile page UI itself is going to be very simple: a Column (with evenly spaced children) with two Text widgets (one for the display name and one for the bio) and a FlatButton to allow the user to send an email.

More specifically, the FlatButton is going to have an icon as well as text as shown in the screenshot on page 278.

The code is the following:

firebase/chatonfire2/lib/main.dart
```
class ProfilePage extends StatelessWidget {
  ProfilePage(this.user);

  final Map<String, dynamic> user;
```

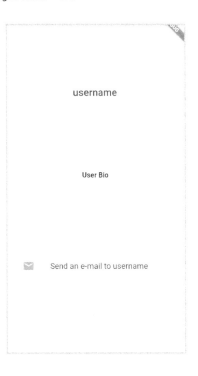

```
@override
Widget build(context) {
  return Scaffold(
    body: Center(
      child: Column(
        crossAxisAlignment: CrossAxisAlignment.center,
        mainAxisAlignment: MainAxisAlignment.spaceEvenly,
        children: <Widget>[
          Text(
            user["displayName"],
            style: Theme.of(context).textTheme.title
          ),
          Text(
            user["bio"],
            style: Theme.of(context).textTheme.subtitle
          ),
          FlatButton.icon(
            icon: Icon(Icons.email),
            label: Text("Send an e-mail to ${user["displayName"]}"),
            onPressed: () async {
              var url =
                "mailto:${user["email"]}?body=${user["displayName"]},\n";
              if(await canLaunch(url)) {
                launch(url);
              } else {
                Scaffold.of(context).showSnackBar(
```

```
                        SnackBar(
                          content: Text("You don't have any e-mail app"),
                        )
                      );
                    }
                  }
                )
              ],
            ),
          )
        );
      }
    }
```

Allowing Users to Edit Their Bio

A user might want to edit their bio in the future. For that, we'll provide an
AppBar action in the chat page that fires up a new page called ChangeBioPage:

firebase/chatonfire2/lib/main.dart

```
appBar: AppBar(
  title: Text("ChatOnFire"),
  actions: [
    IconButton(
      tooltip: "Change your bio",
      icon: Icon(Icons.edit),
      onPressed: () =>
        Navigator.push(
          context,
          MaterialPageRoute(
            builder: (context) => ChangeBioPage()
          )
        ),
    )
  ],
),
```

The page itself is going to be very similar to the ConfigPage:

firebase/chatonfire2/lib/main.dart

```
class ChangeBioPage extends StatelessWidget {
  final _controller = TextEditingController();

  void _changeBio(String bio) =>
    FirebaseAuth.instance.currentUser().then(
      (user) {
        Firestore
          .instance
          .collection("Users")
          .document(user.uid)
          .updateData(
```

```
                    {
                       "bio": bio
                    }
                );
        }
    );

  @override
  Widget build(context) =>
    Scaffold(
      appBar: AppBar(
        title: Text("Change your bio"),
      ),
      body: Center(
        child: Column(
          children: <Widget>[
            Padding(
              padding: const EdgeInsets.all(8.0),
              child: TextField(
                controller: _controller,
                decoration: InputDecoration(
                  labelText: "New Bio"
                ),
                onSubmitted: (bio) {
                  _changeBio(bio);
                  Navigator.pop(context);
                }
              ),
            ),
            FlatButton(
              child: Text("Change Bio"),
              onPressed: () {
                _changeBio(_controller.text);
                Navigator.pop(context);
              }
            )
          ],
        ),
      )
    );
}
```

Making the App More Secure by Locking Down Access to the Firestore

Since we've implemented authentication, we shouldn't keep the Cloud Firestore database rules as open as they are now because, even though we allow anyone to sign up, we should try to constrain access to the minimum necessary for the app to work.

What We're Going to Do

More specifically we need to do the following:

- Only allow users authenticated with a given uid to add or edit a user with that uid to the users' collection, letting everybody read user data, but allowing nobody to delete users (at the moment we're not offering that option).

- Only allow users authenticated with a given uid to add a message that declares to be from that uid, letting everybody access the messages, but allowing nobody to edit or delete them (for the same reason: we're not offering that option to users at the moment).

Implementing the Restriction

All of that is achieved by the following Cloud Firestore configuration (to be inserted in *Database -> Rules* in the Firebase console):

```
service cloud.firestore {
  match /databases/{database}/documents {
    match /Users/{userId} {
      allow create, update: if request.auth.uid == userId;
      allow read: if request.auth != null;
    }

    match /Messages/{messageId} {
      allow create: if request.auth.uid == request.resource.data.from;
      allow read: if request.auth != null;
    }
  }
}
```

matching Documents

match /databases/{database}/documents makes it so the root path of everything in the curly braces after that statement is at collection-level, meaning that, for example, /Users/ABCD is the document of the collection *Users* that has ID *ABCD*.

Inside that, we have other two match statements:

- match /Users/{userId}, where we're going to regulate access to the *Users* collection.

- match /Messages/{message}, where we're going to worry about access to the Messages collection.

allowing Access

allow statements are used in the following way:

```
allow operation: if condition;
```

The operation can be either just read or write, or a more specific aspect of write, like create, update and delete. It can also be a comma-separated list of operations.

The condition can be just true or false (like we did at the start), but it should take into consideration both what document the user is trying to access and who the user is (whether they're authenticated, what their UID is, etc.).

In our case, for each condition, we can use three pieces of data: whatever is in the curly braces in the path of any match statement that encloses it (for example, in the case of the *Users* match statement, {userId}, which is the path of the user document, in other words its ID), the request interface and the resource interface.

Let's start with the latter: the resource interfaces contains data about the resource we're trying to read, update, or delete. For example, if we wanted to access the from field of a message, we would write resource.data.from.

Very similar to resource is request.resource, which is the incoming data from the request. For example, if the request is trying to add a user, we would access that user's bio with request.resource.data.bio. Another important proprty of the request interface is request.auth, which tells us whether the user who's trying to acess the Firestore is authenticated, and what their credentials are. For example, if the user is not authenticated request.auth will be equal to null; if, instead, the user is authenticated request.auth.uid will return the UID of the user who's trying to access the Firestore.

Combining all of these aspects and our requirements gives us the following for the *Users*:

```
match /Users/{userId} {
  allow create, update: if request.auth.uid == userId;
  allow read: if request.auth != null;
}
```

and the following for the *Messages*:

```
match /Messages/{messageId} {
  allow create: if request.auth.uid == request.resource.data.from;
  allow read: if request.auth != null;
}
```

A Few Words on Making Data in the Firestore More Secure

Now the data is inaccessible to anonymous users and, in the case of a public chat, it's fine. But what about one-on-one or group chat apps? For one, you would need to separate messages from different conversations, which would be rather simple, but a really important issue is that of privacy and confidentiality: the messages would be stored in plain text in the database, allowing those who run the app to spy on conversations, which would all be revealed in case of a security incident. That is the reason why most one-on-one chat apps implement some sort of encryption, storing in the database encrypted messages that can only be encrypted using keys stored on each user's device.

Password Reset and Verifying Email Addresses

For the purposes of our chat app, we don't really need to differentiate users who have verified their email address and those who haven't, since we're not even offering password reset via email (which is achieved by running _auth.sendPasswordResetEmail()). You could, though, choose to make those who haven't yet verified their email appear in the list of messages differently (changing their display name text to a different color, for example, or showing an approval icon next to users with verified email addresses), but it's not really needed.

In the case of other apps the ability to do all of this without having to rely on anything other than Firebase and in such a simple way is certainly a good reason to be interested in Firebase as a tool to help create apps that would otherwise have to rely on servers and separate back-end code to work.

Where You're Going Next

You're done, congratulations! Now all that's left to do is to apply the knowledge you've acquired to the real world. There is a great community of Flutter-related content online, starting from the great and comprehensive official API reference I mentioned so many times during the course of this book. Navigating that requires some knowledge of the overall structure and inner-workings of a Flutter app and I hope you've been able to get that from reading this book.

If you don't feel comfortable writing Flutter apps because you feel like you need to learn more about Dart, Appendix 1, Introduction to Dart, on page 285 might be just what you need.

Perhaps after that you will find something more interesting: the body of this book has been focused on building Material Design UIs, interacting with packages and plugins, and writing Dart code. In Appendix 2, Apple-Like Look and Additional App Configuration, on page 315 you will find out how to write apps that look like native iOS apps using Cupertino widgets and how to make your app fit in with each OS's typical style; it also contains some useful information regarding additional app configuration, contained in both pubspec.yaml and the platform-specific android and ios directories. For example, the platform-specific configuration allows you to change the launcher icon and the app name to whatever you want (since by default you can only set lower-case names without spaces with Flutter, but you can edit the platform-specific configuration to set the app name to be whatever can be a regular Android/iOS app name).

Because of all of that, it's strongly recommended that you read the second appendix.

Anyway, this book can't possibly contain all of the different widgets, features, and options that Flutter offers you: now it's up to you to find what you need. After having seen so much of how Flutter works and what it can do, you're well positioned to navigate the vast array of official and community-created content about whatever niche aspect of Flutter you'd like to explore next.

Introduction to Dart

Dart is a new language, and you might not be aware of its syntax and some of its features. Here I'll provide an overview of Dart so that you can have a better grasp on how it works.

Dart, in many ways, resembles C, C++, and Java, so developers with good knowledge of those languages shouldn't have too many issues understanding the code in the book, but there are also differences that I'll point out along the way.

This appendix is also a good starting point for people who don't have much programming experience.

Comments in Dart

Comments are sections of code that won't be evaluated by the compiler and won't be executed. Just like in C, Java, JavaScript, and similar languages, comments are created in two ways:

- Single-line comments are created by adding // before the comment.
- Multi-line comments are created by adding /* before the comment and */ after it.

For example:

```
// this is a comment
int a = 3; // this is also a comment
/* this is also
   a long, long
   comment */
```

where int a = 3; is regular code (not a comment) and will be evaluated by the compiler and executed.

Variables and Conditions

Variables can be declared in two ways in Dart:

- In the *traditional* C-like way, by prefixing the variable name with the data type:

  ```
  int a = 3;
  ```

- By prefixing the variable name with 'var':

  ```
  var a = 3;
  ```

A list of some of the most common data types is provided at the end of this appendix.

Characters and Strings

In some languages there are `char` types for single characters and arrays of `chars` or separate types for strings. In Dart, the `String` type is the only character/string type, and it can contain one or more characters. For that reason, unlike in other languages, you can use single or double quotes to enclose what you assign to the string (called a *string literal*):

```
String greeting = "Hi!";
```

will work just as well as:

```
var greeting = 'Hi!';
```

Like in many other modern languages, two strings can be concatenated using the same + operator you use for addition between numbers:

```
var firstGreeting = "Hi" + "!";
assert(firstGreeting == 'Hi!');
```

What's assert? It's something you will get used to seeing reading this appendix: its effect in compiled code is that, in a testing/debugging situation (it does nothing on production code), it terminates the execution if the condition in its parentheses isn't true, but it's widely used in programming language tutorials and documentation to explain language features. Whenever you see one in this appendix, you should expect the condition inside its parentheses to always be true.

The Backslash

Just like in many other languages, the backslash can be used to escape some characters or insert special characters.

For example, if you wanted to have quotes inside a string, you have two ways to do it:

- You use different kind of quotes to enclose the string (for example 'He said: "Hi!"').

- You escape the quotes (for example, "He said: \"Hi!\"").

For the special characters part, this will be familiar especially to C developers; the \n character can be used to go to a new line:

```
Text("First line\nSecond line")
```

will render *Second line* below *First line*.

Obviously, the backslash itself has to be escaped to be used as part of a string:

```
Text("\\ is the backslash character")
```

will display \ is the backslash character.

String Interpolation

String interpolation allows you to insert one or more variables' value into a string. Let's first explore how things would be done *without* string interpolation.

For example, if you wanted to display the value of an int with a Text, you can't just write:

```
int number;
// (...)
Text(number)
```

because Text expects a String. This means you need to change that to:

```
Text(number.toString())
```

What if you want to display a string and the number? Then you would need to write something like this, using string concatenation:

```
"You tapped the button" + number.toString() + "times"
```

What string interpolation allows you to do is write this instead:

```
"You tapped the button $number times"
```

By prefixing a variable's name with $ you can insert its value into the string. If you need to access an element of a List, the member of a class, or write any kind of expression, you need to enclose the statement in curly braces. If you had a list like the following:

```
List numbers = [1, 2, 3];
```

you would use string interpolation like this:

```
"There are ${numbers.length} and second element is number ${numbers[1]}"
```

Multi-Line Strings and Raw Strings

Like in many other languages, you can make multi-line strings by using triple quotes and you can make raw strings by prefixing the opening quotes with the letter "r".

A multi-line string makes it so that you can turn this:

```
"First line\nSecond line";
```

or this:

```
"First line\n" +
"Second line"
```

into this:

```
"""
First line
Second line
"""
```

A raw string treats any special characters inside it ($, \, and so on) like any other character, without giving it any special meaning that you can write just:

```
r"\ is the backslash character"
```

Conditions: Boolean Algebra in Dart

Dart conditions will look exactly like the conditions you find in C, Java or JavaScript: you use ==, !=, >, <, <= and >= to compare values, and you use && as the AND operator, || as the OR operator and ! as the NOT operator.

Immutable Variables: final and const

If the variable doesn't need to vary at all, there are two keywords that can make sure the compiler knows your wish: final and const:

- A final variable's value can't be changed: you initialize it with a value and that value is stored there forever, this is needed for all widget properties in Flutter because widgets themselves are immutable.

- const is used to create compile-time constants: the compiler will evaluate the value of the constant when you build your app, so you can't have const arguments.

You use these two keywords by replacing the word var with them:

```
const a = 3;
```

or by prefixing the variable data type with one of them:

```
final String greeting = "Hi!";
```

Lists and collection literals

A List is what is commonly referred to as an array: an ordered collection of data, the elements of which are indexed with the values from 0 to length-1 where the length of a List is the number of elements it contains. A List can be initialized with a list literal, which is a comma-separated list of values enclosed in square brackets:

```
var list = [30, 20, 500];

assert(list[0] == 30);
assert(list[1] == 20);
assert(list[2] == 500);
```

If and For in List Literals

List literals in Dart can do more than that, though—you can have if statements in them:

```
bool condition;

// ...

var list = [
  if(condition)
    "First"
  else
    "First, alternative",
  "Second"
];

assert(list[1] == "Second");

if(condition)
  assert(list[0] == "First");
else
  assert(list[0] == "First, alternative");

/*
 * As in other languages, these latest two assert() calls could become one:
 * assert((condition && list[0] == "First") ||
 *        (!condition && list[0] == "First, alternative"))
 */
```

Adding and Removing Items from Lists

An item can be added to the end of a list by using List.add():

```
var l = [1, 2, 3];

l.add(4);

assert(l[3] == 4);
```

An item can be removed in two main ways (there are others, feel free to check out all List methods at the official Dart language reference[1]). One of them is by passing the value you want to remove with List.remove() (which will only remove the first occurence):

```
var l = ["Test", "test", "Test"];

l.remove("Test");

assert(l[0] == "test");
assert(l[1] == "Test"); // The second occurrence won't be removed
```

The other is by passing the index at which you want to remove an element to List.removeAt():

```
var l = [5, 6, 7];

l.removeAt(1);

assert(l[1] == 7);
```

Generating Lists

One of the ways to create lists is by using the List.generate() constructor, which takes two arguments: the number of elements the list will have and a callback function (a function to be run by another function in certain conditions and with certain arguments) that generates each element based on its index.

For example, this is how you'd create a list from the concatenation of the strings contained in two lists:

```
var l1 = ["First", "Second", "Third"];
var l2 = ["1", "2", "3"];

var l = List.generate(3, (index) => l1[i]+l2[i]);
```

If this example wasn't clear to you, check out the section about functions (Functions, on page 295) and the one about classes (Classes, on page 306).

---

1.   https://api.dartlang.org/stable/2.3.2/dart-core/List-class.html

Iterating Over Lists: for, map, and forEach

We've found out how to generate lists, now what about how to iterate over the elements of a list? There are multiple ways to do that:

- The for in loop.
- The .forEach() method.
- The .map() method.

The for in Loop

Present in most modern languages, it's a special kind of Loops: while, do while, and for, on page 305 that iterates over the elements of a list:

```
var listName = [
  "First",
  "Second",
  "Third",
  "Fourth"
];

for(var elName in listName) {
  print(elName);
}
```

map and forEach

Particularly loved by some for their functional style, the Iterable's map() and forEach() methods are alternatives to the for in loop.

forEach() is the most similar to the for loop, as it is used to execute an operation on (or for) each of the elements of a list. The callback closure you use is of type void, so you can't return anything. Here's an example, showing how to print each element of a list:

```
listName.forEach((el) {
  print(el);
});
```

map() is different: it is used to create an Iterable from calling a function on each element of the List, here's an example:

```
var numbers = [
  1,
  2,
  3,
  4,
  5,
  6
];

var iter = numbers.map((el) => "#$el");
```

iter is an Iterable, not a proper List. If you want to access the elements directly just like you do with a list, you need to use the toList() method:

```
var list = numbers.map((el) => "#$el").toList();
```

The underscore

You might have seen in many code examples that we have prefixed some variable or class names with an underscore (_). It is used to make them *library private*.

For example, when we write:

```
class MyWidget extends StatefulWidget {
  // (...)
}
class _MyWidgetState extends State<MyWidget> {
  // (...)
}
```

We are making the MyWidgetState class *library private*, meaning it is only accessible from within the current package: if you are working on a library and you want to make a class or top-level function inaccessible to users of that library, you us the underscore this way.

Using the underscore for class members is used to make it inaccessible from outside its class definition, like in the following example:

```
class CounterClass {
  int _counter = 0;

  void _setCounterTo(int n) {
    _counter = n;
  }

  int getCounter() => _counter

  void increaseCounter() => _setCounterTo(_counter+1);
}
```

which is obviously a lot more complicated than it needs to be (_setCounterTo() adds unnecessary complication) in order to show how different kinds of methods may be chosen to be set as private: if we are making a counter class, we want to be able to get the current value of the counter, but we don't need to change it to any value other than it incremented by 1, so we only give access to a method that does exactly that and another that returns the value of the counter.

Other Iterable Data Structures: Maps, Sets, and More

The `Map` is a key/value collection, similar to JSON objects and often used as the way to handle JSON objects in Dart as a simpler alternative to defining a class for each kind of object the app works with. A `Map` literal is enclosed in curly braces and looks something like this:

```
var user = {
  "userId": 1,
  "firstName": "Carmine",
  "lastName": "Zaccagnino"
};
```

You can access and add elements to a `Map` by using the same [] and [] you'd use to access and modify elements of a `List`:

```
var name = "${user["firstName"]} ${user["lastName"]}";
user["password"] = "my!!Very!!own!!Very!!safelpassWordstr";
```

A Set a linear collection of different values:

```
var G8 = {
  "United States",
  "Japan",
  "Germany",
  "United Kingdom",
  "France",
  "Italy",
  "Canada",
  "Russia"
};
```

You can remove an item from a `Set` by value using `remove()` and add one using `add()`:

```
var G7 = G8
  ..remove("Russia")
  ..add("European Union");
```

Set Literals

Set literals using curly braces are supported starting from Dart version 2.2, in earlier versions the most similar way was to use the Set.from() method, which takes a List:

```
var countriesByGDP = Set.from(["USA", "PRC", /*...*/]);
```

There are many more Iterables. A very common one in computer science is the linked list, which can be implemented using LinkedList, but there is also a Queue class and the unordered hash table-based alternatives to the Map and Set called HashMap and HashSet.

Numbers: The num Type and Its Subclasses

The num class is a generic number class, and its subclasses are int for integers and double for floating-point numbers. There's no float in Dart; floating-point numbers are all 64-bit doubles.

Keeping with the mathematical notation used in the UK and the United States, the decimal separator is a dot (.). You can specify powers of 10 by using e:

```
var a = 5.2e2;
assert(a == 520);
```

double numbers can be rounded using round() (which rounds away from 0 with the decimal part starting from .5), rounded down by using floor() or rounded up using ceil():

```
var a = 5.2;
assert(a.round() == 5);
assert(a.floor() == 5);
assert(a.ceil() == 6);

var b = 5.5;
assert(a.round() == 6);
```

An hexadecimal integer is obtained by prefixing it with 0x:

```
assert(0x7E3 == 2019);
```

Lists of Bytes and More: the dart:typed_data library

When reading binary data, using a List of 64-bit ints is extremely inefficient if all each of those integers is doing is clearly less than optimally efficient. That's why the dart:typed_data contains the Uint8List class, which works exactly like the regular List, but with 8-bit integers.

Type Casting

Type casting in Dart is done in one of the following two ways.

You can use an as expression to cast a value to one of its subtypes:

```
num a = 5;

var a_int = a as int;

assert(a_int is int);
```

or use cast() to cast all values of List to a specified type:

```
List<num> l = [1, 2, 3];

var l_int = l.cast<int>();

assert(l_int[0] is int);
```

Functions

Dart supports top-level functions, meaning you can define functions outside any class definition that can be called from anywhere in the code.

A Dart function is defined in the following way:

```
returnType functionName(parameters) {
  blockOfInstructions;
  return returnValue;
}
```

where:

- returnType is the data type, see the section Conversion Between Native Java/Apple and Dart Data Types, on page 313, the function will return.

- The parameters, explained in the next paragraph, which will be the data the function will use to do what it needs to do. Parameters are variables and their value is set using function call arguments. If you are not familiar with functions and function calls, the example that follows is designed to give a real, working example of a few functions that take advantage of other functions.

- In the curly braces is where you add the block of instructions (one or more lines) which, if the function has any return type other than void, includes a return instruction, which is used to return a value to the calling code.

For example, the following function is very simple:

```
double square(double n) {
  return n*n;
}
```

but it can be used inside a function to calculate gravitational attraction, which is slightly more complex, with more parameters:

```
// We'll see how to set all of those arguments soon
double calculateGravitationalAttraction(double mass1, double mass2, double distance)
{
  const G = 6.67e-11;  // universal gravitation constant
  /*
   * Calling the square function using distance as
   * the only argument (n will be equal to
   * the value in the distance variable)
   * and saving the return value
   * to the squaredDistance variable
   */
  const squaredDistance = square(distance);
  return G*mass1*mass2/squaredDistance;
}
```

and it, in turn, can be used to calculate, for example, the force of attraction between the earth and the sun, potentially wrapped inside another function:

```
double calculateSunEarthAttraction() {
  const earthMass = 5.97e24; // mass of the Earth
  const sunMass = 1.99e30;   // mass of the Sun
  const dist = 1.496e8; // distance between the Earth and the Sun
  /*
   * Calling the calculateGravitationalAttraction
   * function setting the arguments one by one
   * in the order of the parameters in the
   * function's definition and returning
   * its return value to any other function
   * that needs the value of the force of
   * attraction between the Sun and the Earth
   */
  return calculateGravitationalAttraction(earthMass, sunMass, dist);
}
```

Function Parameters

Up until now, we have only used positional parameters: you define them like variables, one after another, and you set the arguments in the same way, following the same order.

Now, though, you need to know about *named* parameters, which allow the calling function to set the arguments in a different order (or even for just some of the parameters) by specifying a name for each parameter. If you wrap the parameters in curly braces, you'll make them *named* and *optional*, like in the following example:

```
double calculateSunPlanetAttraction({})
```

The Arrow

If the function will be simply composed of one instruction, you can use the arrow notation, so that:

```
int square(int n) {
  return n*n;
}
```

becomes:

```
int square(int n) => n*n;
```

usually written, especially when the expression is longer, as:

```
int square(int n) =>
  n*n;
```

Anonymous Functions and Closures

Closures are what we use to define callbacks. They are functions defined as variables or, more specifically, variables of type Function or Typedef and Callbacks, on page 311.

main

Main is the function that gets called when we start any kind of Dart program, including Flutter apps. It has a void return type and it takes no arguments. It can be async.

Asynchronous Code in Dart: The dart:async Library

At some point during your Dart development process, you might need to call a method without affecting the execution of your code, or call a library method that has been declared as an async method.

That's when you realize the necessity for asynchronous code and the dart:async built-in Dart library, which allows async functions to return either a Future or a Stream.

The Future

The Future is the most basic object type related to asynchronous methods—it is the return type of all async functions, including void ones:

```
Future<void> doSomethingThatTakesLong() async {
  // do something
}
```

```dart
void callingSyncFunction() {
  doSomethingThatTakesLong();
  /* the code won't wait for the function to
   * finish its execution and it will carry on
   * in its regular order, executing
   * the next instruction
   */
}
```

If you need to wait for the function to stop executing (perhaps because you need the returned value), you need to choose between using await or .then().

await

await is useful when you actually need to wait for an async function to finish its execution, often because you need its return value. It converts a Future into the value returned by the function by waiting for the code that returned the future to finish its execution:

```dart
Future<int> getValue() async {
  return 5;
}

Future<int> callingFunction() async {
  var n = await getValue();
  return n+5;
}
```

then(), catchError(), and whenComplete()

If there are some actions you want to take when the Future returns a value, but it doesn't affect the rest of the current code block's execution or its return value, you can use the Future's .then() method, which allows you to add a call-back function to be called with the Future's return value when it is available:

```dart
Future<int> getValue() async {
  return 5;
}

void main() {
  getValue().then((n) {
    assert(n == 5);
  });
  /* something else that
   * won't wait for getValue
   * to return to execute
   */
}
```

What if there's a runtime error in the execution of the future? That's when we use catchError():

```dart
void printValue() {
  getValue()
    .then(print)
    .catchError((err) {
      // handle error
    });
}
```

You can add a whenComplete() call (a lot like a finally block) for code that needs to be executed regardless of anything that happens.

Streams and StreamSubscriptions

There are certain kinds of data that are subject to frequent change, like the battery and connectivity status we saw in Chapter 4, Beyond the Standard Library: Plugins and Packages, on page 119 or the documents in the Firebase Cloud Firestore we saw in Chapter 7, Build a Chat App Using Firebase, on page 237. For this kind of data, we use special asynchronous methods that yield different values at different times or many different values at once.

Creating a Stream

The most basic way to create a Stream is to return multiple values from an asynchronous generator function (async*) using the yield keyword.

yielding Values from a Generator Function

A function that generates a Stream looks something like this:

```dart
Stream<String> myStream() async* {
  var returnValues = [
    "This is The First String You'll See",
    "After 2 Seconds You'll See This",
    "Then This"
  ];
  for (int i = 0; i < 3; i++) {
    await Future.delayed(Duration(
      seconds: 2
    ));
    yield returnValues[i];
  }
}
```

Future.delayed() allows you to define a Future that can be used to pause execution (by waiting for it to be done) for a specified amount of time.

yield is just like return, but it doesn't move the execution outside the asynchronous generator function: it yields a value to the calling function and then resumes execution inside the generator function, allowing it to yield another value later.

Using a StreamController

A StreamController is a more advanced way of generating Streams: it allows you to generate a Stream with a regular synchronous function and in more complex scenarios in which yield just doesn't cut it.

Once you define a StreamController variable in a function, you can use StreamController.add() anywhere within the function (perhaps in a callback) and have an effect similar to yield. Another very important StreamController method is StreamController.close(), which causes listening functions to stop listening to the Stream.

The StreamController has two constructors: StreamController() (which is the default) and StreamController.broadcast().

The StreamController() constructor, which is used for streams that are only supposed to have one listener, takes four callback functions as arguments:

- onListen(), which is fired when a listener starts listening for objects and should trigger the start of the yielding of values to avoid creating memory leaks by firing events that no listener is listening to, causing Dart to buffer them, using up memory for events that may never be listened to anywhere.

- onPause(), which is fired when the listener requests the Stream to temporarily not yield anything using StreamSubscription.pause(), for the same reason onListen().

- onResume(), which is fired when the listener requests the Stream to resume the yielding of values after a pause by calling StreamSubscription.resume(), it should be obvious at this point that this function should cause the stream to resume firing events.

- onCancel(), which is fired when the listener cancels its subscription by calling StreamSubscription.cancel() and is supposed to make the Stream stop trying to yield values.

The StreamController.broadcast() constructor, which is used for *broadcast streams*, can be listened to by multiple listeners. It takes only onListen() and onCancel() as arguments.

Using a Stream

We've seen the basics of how to use Streams in Getting the Battery and Connectivity Data: Asynchronous Programming Using Streams, on page 124. That example followed this structure:

```
class MyWidget extends StatefulWidget {
  // ...
}

class MyState extends State<MyWidget> {
  // ...
  StreamSubscription<Type> _streamSub;

  @override
  void initState() {
    // ...
    _streamSub = stream.listen(
      (Type res) {
        // do something with the response, setState()
      }
    );
  }

  @override
  Widget build(BuildContext context) {
    // ...
  }

  @override
  dispose() {
    // ...
    _streamSub.cancel();
  }
}
```

In that case, the stream was provided directly by a library, and we used setState() to update some variables when new data was available and rebuild the widget.

All of that is inefficient if the StatefulWidget that is rebuilt every time the stream changes isn't just the part that's showing the data from that Stream.

The StreamBuilder

Building a separate StatefulWidget for that isn't necessary because, just like the FutureBuilder exists to build UI elements based on the results of Future, the StreamBuilder is the Flutter widget that builds its contents based on the data returned by a Stream.

The StreamBuilder's constructor requires, just like the FutureBuilder, a data type and two arguments, but with a few differences.

The basic structure of a StreamBuilder widget is the following:

```
StreamBuilder<Type> {
  stream: stream,
  builder: (context, snapshot) {
    if(snapshot.hasData)
      // display snapshot.data
    else
      // display an error or some indication that the data is loading
  }
}
```

One of the differences between the StreamBuilder and the FutureBuilder lies in the snapshot.connectionState value. When working with a Future in a FutureBuilder, it could only assume the following values:

- ConnectionState.none if the future argument is set to null (not set at all).

- ConnectionState.waiting if the FutureBuilder is waiting for the future to return a value.

- ConnectionState.none if the future has returned a value, meaning snapshot.hasData is true.

This is why we only used snapshot.hasData and not snapshot.connectionState when working with Futures and FutureBuilders. When working with Streams, though, there's more to it—the connection state could also be ConnectionState.active, meaning that the Stream has already returned a value, but it hasn't terminated, meaning it could return another value at any time.

snapshot.hasError and the snapshot.error exist for both in case you need to handle errors.

The await for Loop

The Stream can be interacted with in an alternative way to using the listen() method: the await for loop.

It's just like a for-in loop but, instead of iterating over known values in a list, it waits for new values returned by the stream and only terminates when the stream terminates:

```
await for(var value in stream) {
  // do something with the value
}
```

For example, we can print to the console the strings returned by the myStream() function we defined earlier as soon as it yields them with the following loop:

```
await for(var res in myStream()) {
  print(res);
}
```

Instead of printing results the await for can be used, for example, to take an existing Stream, change the data or use it as an argument for some other function, and then yield a changed value, creating a new Stream.

Error Handling Within Streams

When using a StreamBuilder, the snapshot you get in the builder has the same snapshot.hasError and snapshot.error you get with FutureBuilders so you can use those if you need to handle errors within a FutureBuilder or a StreamBuilder

The listen() method optionally takes two more callbacks as arguments:

- onError, which is run when there is an error is thrown by the asynchronous function that generates the Stream.

- onDone, which is run when the Stream terminates.

Conditional Constructs and Expressions

Some languages (such as Rust) treat conditional constructs as expressions. Dart only does this when they are inside a list literal; in other places you'd need to use a conditional expression with the conventional C-like syntax using the ternary ?: operator.

The if-else Construct

The if-else construct in Dart is very similar to that of many other languages; it can be expressed using curly braces:

```
if(condition) {
  // Instructions to execute when the condition is true
} else {
  // Instructions to execute when the condition is false
}
```

and, if there is only one instruction to execute for each, without curly braces (executing true_instruction when the condition is true and false_instruction when it is false), usually written without line breaks:

```
if(condition) true_instruction;
else          false_instruction;
```

else if

If there is a condition to check inside the else clause you can use the else if construct:

```
int a;
// (...)
if(a>10) {
  // (...)
} else if(a == 10) {
  // (...)
} else {
  // (...)
}
```

Conditional Expressions

If you need to test a condition to decide between two values for an assignment, an expression or a return statement you can use a conditional expression. It is an expression containing the ?: ternary operator, and it can be used in the following way:

```
var a = condition ? true_value : false_value;
```

in which the value of a will be true_value if the condition is true and false_value if the condition is false. This is extremely useful for replacing simple functions such as the following:

```
num max(num a, num b) {
  if(b > a) return b;
  else return a;
}
```

with even simpler one-liners:

```
num max(num a, num b) => b > a ? b : a;
```

Switch

Switch is one of the features of Dart that might look most archaic: it works just like C's or Java's. They are used when you need to compare a variable to a certain number of constant values and are not recommended for use in Flutter apps. Its structure is the following:

```
var a;
// (...)

switch(a) {
  case 1:
    // instructions to execute if a is equal to 1
    break;
```

```
  case 2:
    // instructions to execute if a is equal to 2
    break;
  default:
    // instructions to execute if a is neither equal to 1 nor 2
}
```

If you omit the break instructions, the cases defined after the case triggered by the value of the variable will be executed as well. This effect (*fall-through*) allows for multiple values to be handled by a single case:

```
switch(a) {
  case 1: // this is supposed to fall through
  case 2:
    // instructions for values 1 and 2
    break;
  case 3:
    // instructions for the value 3
    break;
  default:
    // (...)
}
```

Fall-through obtained by omitting break is not allowed if you have instructions in the case and will generate an error. If you mean to do that, you should use the continue instruction with a label:

```
switch(a) {
  case 1:
    // additional instructions for 1
    continue caseTwo;
  caseTwo:
  case 2:
    // instructions for 1 and 2
    break;
  default:
    // (...)
}
```

Loops: while, do while, and for

Dart supports the most common loop constructs, the for loop supports the for in notation and it can be used inside list/collection literals starting from Dart 2.3:

```
var list1 = [
  for(int i = 0; i < 100; i++)
    i,
];
```

```
var list2 = [
  for(var element in list1)
    "#$element",
];
```

Classes

Classes in Dart work a lot like classes in other object-oriented languages, but here's most of what you need to know to get started.

Members: Properties and Methods

Properties are variables declared as members of a class:

```
class User {
  int id;
  String username;
  String password;
}
```

Methods are functions defined inside classes. They are defined just like top-level functions, but inside the body of a class definition:

```
class User {
  int id;
  String username;
  String password;

  void setId(int newId) {
    id = newId;
  }
}
```

Accessing Members: Dot Notation

Members can be accessed using dot notation. If you wanted to get the id property of the user object and assign it to the a variable, you'd write:

```
var a = user.id;
```

and you'd run the setId() method like this:

```
user.setId(1000)
```

Cascade Notation

If you need to run multiple methods or change many properties of an object, you can use cascade notation, which allows you to write something like this, which will create a User with the given username, password, and ID:

```
var a = User()
  ..username="yourUsername"
  ..password="Actually1veryComplicatedPass!"
  ..setId(1000);
```

Constructors

Dart allows us to define just the constructor's signature and it will automatically assign the arguments to the corresponding properties and create an instance of the class automatically. The parameters are defined just like any function's parameters, but pointing to a property of the class:

```
class ClassExample {
  ClassExample(
    this.var1, // positional argument
    {
      @required this.var2, // named arguments
      this.var3
    }
  );

  int var1;
  String var2;
  Function var3;
}
```

You can define the constructor for a class inheriting from a superclass in the following way:

```
class ClassExample extends SuperClass {
  ClassExample(parameters) :
        super(superClassArguments);
}
```

Named Constructors

You can also define *named* constructors, which are alternative constructors with a different name:

```
class ClassExample {
  ClassExample(parameters);
  ClassExample.constructorName(otherParameters);
}
```

Regular Constructors

Dart also supports regular constructor with their own body, that can optionally also take advantage of automatic property assignment.

Here's an example of a class that has a constructor that takes an integer value and assigns its square to the var1 while assigning var2 and var3 directly:

```dart
class ClassExample {
  ClassExample(this.var1, this.var2, this.var3);
  ClassExample.withSqrtOfVar1(int var1sqrt, this.var2, this.var3) {
    var1 = var1sqrt*var1sqrt;
  }

  int var1;
  String var2;
  Function var3;
}
```

Static Members

Static class members can be accessed without requiring instantiation:

```dart
class ClassExample {
  // (...)

  static num square(num val) =>
    val*val;

  // (...)
}
// Unlike in C++, we can use regular dot notation
var n = ClassExample.square(0.1);

/*
 * Comparing floating-point numbers
 * using == is unreliable in
 * most programming languages,
 * including Dart, so use
 * syntax like this instead
 */
assert(n < 0.011 && n > 0.009);
```

Abstract Classes

An abstract class is a class that you can't instantiate: you can't create objects of that class. They are declared by substituting the class keyword with abstract class. Abstract classes are usually used as mixins (covered in Writing a Class with a Mixin, on page 310) or interfaces (covered in Writing a Class That implements an Interface, on page 310).

An abstract class can contain abstract methods, which are method that don't have an implementation, but it can also contain regular methods:

```
abstract class MyClass {
  void regularMethod() {
    // do something
  }

  void abstractMethod();
}
```

An abstract method may be implemented by either a subclass or a class that implements the MyClass interface, as explained in the following sections.

Subclasses, Interfaces, and Mixins: extends, implements, and with

Classes can interact with each other in three ways: a class can be a subclass of another, inheriting all of its members and optionally overriding some of the methods; it can implement another class's interface; or it can use methods defined in another class (called a mixin).

extends

Especially in Flutter, extending another class is a very common occurrence. By doing that we create a subclass, and the class we extend is called the superclass. We can decide to declare new methods or re-implement (override) existing methods. A subclass can have its own variables and use the super-class's by accessing the superclass itself through the super object.

@override

When creating subclasses, you might want to implement one of the super-class's methods, you can do that by prefixing it with the @override annotation, as we do for the build() method when defining widgets:

```
class MyWidget extends StatelessWidget {
  // (...)

  @override
  Widget build(BuildContext context) {
    // (...)
  }
}
```

the method can also be defined as:

```
@override Widget build(context) {
  // (...)
}
```

Sometimes you might want to call the superclass's corresponding method by adding super.methodName() at the start of the new method's definition so that the new method acts as an addition, not a replacement, like we have to do when we redefine the State class's initState() when writing StatefulWidgets:

```
class _MyWidgetState extends State<StatefulWidget> {
  // (...)

  @override
  void initState() {
    super.initState();
    // our own instructions
  }

  // (...)
}
```

We have to do that for the State class because it has been defined in the Flutter widgets library with the @mustCallSuper annotation, and we can do the same in case we want to define classes for which we think subclasses will be created and a certain overriding method is supposed to call the superclass's overridden method.

Writing a Class with a Mixin

A mixin is a class that contains methods to be used by other classes, without requiring those classes to inherit from the mixin directly by extending it and becoming a subclass of it. A mixin can be defined simply as a class and be used by declaring any class that wants to use it (*applying* the mixing) with the mixin, like in the following example:

```
// the mixin
class MyMixin {
  String myMethod() => "Hi from the mixin";
}

class MyClass with MyMixin {

}

var obj = MyClass();

assert(obj.myMethod() == "Hi from the mixin");
```

Writing a Class That implements an Interface

An interface is a class that only defines the return type and arguments of its methods, requiring other classes to implement those methods. Fittingly, this is done using the implements keyword:

```
abstract class MyInterface {
  abstract void myMethod();
}
```

```
class MyClass implements MyInterface {
  void myMethod() {
    // do something
  }
}
class MyOtherClass implements MyInterface {
  void myMethod() {
    // do something else
  }
}
```

After doing that, you can instantiate and use the MyClass and MyOtherClass, and you can use them knowing that they implement all of the methods described in MyInterface.

Typedef and Callbacks

typedef is what is used to create callback types like VoidCallback, which is a void callback type for functions that don't require arguments. A callback is a kind of *closure* that is provided as an argument to a function to be called when some conditions are met. A closure is a function that is defined a lot like a variable. The VoidCallback type is a special kind of Function that takes no arguments and has a void return type and it can be defined in the following way using typedef:

```
typedef VoidCallback = void Function();
```

If you wanted to define a callback of a different type that takes some sort of arguments, you'd write the following:

```
typedef IntFunctionCallback = int Function(int n);
```

or the following very common mathematical definition of a real function of a real variable:

```
typedef RealFunctionOfARealVariable = double Function(double n);
```

Definitions can be type-independent (this kind of syntax can be used with anything in Dart):

```
typedef OneArgumentCallback<T> = T Function(T a);
```

After defining such a type or just using the generic Function type, we can create functions just like we create variables. For example, if we wanted to recreate in Dart equivalent the $f(x) = e^x$ exponential function (where e is Euler's number, better known in some countries as Napier's number), we would write the following, using pow() and e from dart:math:

```
RealFunctionOfARealVariable f = (x) => pow(e, x);

assert(f(2) == pow(e, 2));
assert(f(1) > 2.71 && f(1) < 2.72);
```

Mastering import

The import directive in Dart, as is the case in many other modern language, doesn't only handle inclusion of external library files in the code like the good old C #include: it can do more than that to make our life easier when dealing with libraries and packages.

The Basics

We'll start with the basics: importing an entire file to the current namespace.

Importing a Local File

You can import another local Dart file by using a relative path to it:

```
import 'filename.dart';
```

Importing a Built-In Dart Library

You can import a built-in Dart library by prefacing the name of the library with dart::

```
import 'dart:async';
```

Importing from a Package

You can import a file from a package by using:

```
import 'package:packagename/filename.dart';
```

Which can be used to import files from the Flutter SDK by using flutter as the package name:

```
import 'package:flutter/services.dart'
```

This syntax can also be used to import files in the app's lib directory by using the app's package name as the package name.

Using as to Import Under a Namespace

You can also import under a namespace, by using the following syntax:

```
import 'customlib.dart' as MyCustomLib;
```

So that, for example, if there is a CustomLibraryClass class defined in that file, you can access it by using MyCustomLib.CustomLibraryClass instead of just CustomLibraryClass.

This allows you to import many libraries without cluttering your main namespace, keeping each library separated, without risking having multiple classes with the same name.

Another great advantage comes when you go back to your code after a while: you will know exactly which library that class is from, without having to figure that out first.

Using show to Only Import Some Parts of a File

import can also be used to only import some classes inside a file.

For example, if you only need the CustomLibraryClass from the customlib.dart file and don't want to import other classes (maybe because they have the same name as other classes in your namespace and you don't want to use as and deal with extra dot notation), which you can do with the following code:

```
import 'customlib.dart' show CustomLibraryClass;
```

Conversion Between Native Java/Apple and Dart Data Types

Type	Dart	Java	Objective-C/Swift
Integer number	int	Integer/Long depending on size	NSNumber NumberWithInt:/NumberWithLong: depending on size
Boolean value	bool	Boolean	NSNumber NumberWithBool:
String of characters	String	String	NSString
Monodimensional and uniform collection of elements	List	ArrayList	NSArray
Key-value pair list	Map	HashMap	NSDictionary

Where You're Going Next

If you have read this appendix before reading the book itself, go back to the beginning and get started! All of the stuff in this appendix will be really easy to apply to building user interfaces using Flutter's great declarative UI syntax.

If you've already read through the rest of the book, the next appendix will show you how to make your apps look native on iOS and how to use the platform-specific configuration to set a custom app name and app icon to prepare your app for distribution.

Apple-Like Look and Additional App Configuration

There are many things you can't set in standard Flutter Dart code, like custom app names containing spaces and capitalized letters, as well as custom app icons. There also are many things to be learned about the various features of the pubspec.yaml file.

But first, let's talk about how you can make your app look more at home on an iPhone by discovering Cupertino widgets.

Cupertino Widgets

Before we venture out of Flutter Dart code too much, there is one thing you might have noticed in pubspec.yaml: the dependency on cupertino_icons. We have actually never used what is contained in it in the body of the book, because it doesn't really allow you to do anything you couldn't do before in Flutter apps: it contains icons to be used by widgets that look like native Apple widgets and can be used instead of the Material Design widgets.

This means you have the following two choices regarding the look of your app:

- Make your app look the same on Android and iOS by either using the Material widgets or the Cupertino widgets.

- Make your app look like other apps built for each platform by using Material widgets on Android and Cupertino widgets on iOS.

Obviously you could choose to show your iOS users the Material widgets and the Android users the Cupertino widgets, but that's probably not the smartest choice for most people.

The Counter Increase App with Cupertino Widgets

As a way to get an idea of how to use Cupertino widgets, we're going to rewrite the counter app that Flutter itself gives as an example of basic Flutter UI that we saw in the first chapter, this time using Cupertino widgets instead of Material widgets.

What We're Going to Build

It will look like the following screenshots, keeping in mind that floating action buttons aren't part of regular Apple Design:

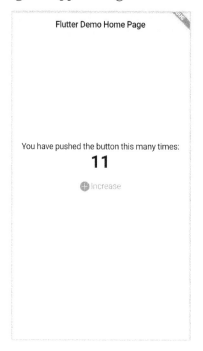

The alternative would have been to add it to the right of the title in the navigation bar (the Apple app bar), but doing it this way allows us to look at more of the Flutter Cupertino widgets.

Importing the Cupertino Library

Let's start by changing the imports, we only need to import the Cupertino Flutter library, given that we won't be using any Material widgets:

cupertino/counter_cupertino/lib/main.dart
```
import 'package:flutter/cupertino.dart';
```

From MaterialApp to CupertinoApp

The MaterialApp is the next thing that needs to change, to become a CupertinoApp. The name isn't the only thing that needs to change: the theme needs to be of class CupertinoThemeData and not just ThemeData. The CupertinoThemeData takes a primaryColor instead of a primarySwatch, and it needs to one of the CupertinoColors, which aren't the regular colors you use with Material apps: Colors.blue will become CupertinoColors.activeBlue, which is the default color.

Material-Based Cupertino Theme Data

Given that you're probably going to build apps for both Android and iOS using both Material and Cupertino widgets, you might want to create one ThemeData for the Material Design app and derive the styling of the Cupertino version from that Material Design theme. This can be done using MaterialBasedCupertinoThemeData(materialTheme: themeData), which takes as a named argument called materialTheme the ThemeData we want to derive the new CupertinoThemeData from.

Our CupertinoApp

Because of that, the theme argument could be skipped entirely unless you want your app to have a dark background that is supposed to be with an activeOrange primary color. We're going to stick with a regular light theme with a blue primary color, providing the same arguments that were used in the original Material example to keep the example as close to the original as possible:

cupertino/counter_cupertino/lib/main.dart
```dart
class MyApp extends StatelessWidget {
  @override
  Widget build(BuildContext context) {
    return CupertinoApp(
      title: 'Flutter Demo',
      theme: CupertinoThemeData(
        primaryColor: CupertinoColors.activeBlue,
      ),
      home: MyHomePage(title: 'Flutter Demo Home Page'),
    );
  }
}
```

Unchanged Widgets

StatefulWidgets, StatelessWidgets and States are all the same as with Material apps, and the same goes for Rows, Column, Containers and Center widgets, as well as simple widgets like Icons (even though the IconData used for them should be taken from the CupertinoIcons instead of taking it from the Icons) and Text.

The Scaffold and App Bar

Before getting to them, though, the Scaffold needs to switch to a CupertinoPageScaffold (there is a CupertinoTabScaffold for scaffolds that have bottom navigation, there's no CupertinoScaffold), which (as I anticipated earlier) takes a CupertinoNavigationBar as the navigationBar argument instead of taking an AppBar as the appBar argument as we did with Material apps. Additionally, the CupertinoNavigationBar takes three peculiarly named arguments: leading, middle and trailing for widgets to place in the navigation bar. Usually the left side is reserved for a back button, the right side for an important action and the middle is where we should put the title of the page:

cupertino/counter_cupertino/lib/main.dart
```
return CupertinoPageScaffold(
  navigationBar: CupertinoNavigationBar(
    middle: Text(widget.title),
  ),
```

The CupertinoButton

The button to increase the counter will be a - *you guessed it* - CupertinoButton. It takes a child widget for which we can use a simple Row:

cupertino/counter_cupertino/lib/main.dart
```
CupertinoButton(
  onPressed: _incrementCounter,
  child: Row(
    mainAxisAlignment: MainAxisAlignment.center,
    children: [
      Icon(CupertinoIcons.add_circled_solid),
      Text("Increase")
    ]
  )
)
```

CupertinoIcons.add is the + icon that should be used when it appears alone, CupertinoIcons.add_circled has a circle around it and CupertinoIcons.circled_solid is what's in the screenshot you saw earlier.

Wrapping Up

The full code, including the things that are the same as the app we saw in the first chapter, is the following:

cupertino/counter_cupertino/lib/main.dart
```
import 'package:flutter/cupertino.dart';

void main() => runApp(MyApp());
```

```dart
class MyApp extends StatelessWidget {
  @override
  Widget build(BuildContext context) {
    return CupertinoApp(
      title: 'Flutter Demo',
      theme: CupertinoThemeData(
        primaryColor: CupertinoColors.activeBlue,
      ),
      home: MyHomePage(title: 'Flutter Demo Home Page'),
    );
  }
}

class MyHomePage extends StatefulWidget {
  MyHomePage({Key key, this.title}) : super(key: key);

  final String title;

  @override
  _MyHomePageState createState() => _MyHomePageState();
}

class _MyHomePageState extends State<MyHomePage> {
  int _counter = 0;

  void _incrementCounter() {
    setState(() {
      _counter++;
    });
  }

  @override
  Widget build(BuildContext context) {
    return CupertinoPageScaffold(
      navigationBar: CupertinoNavigationBar(
        middle: Text(widget.title),
      ),
      child: Center(
        child: Column(
          crossAxisAlignment: CrossAxisAlignment.center,
          mainAxisAlignment: MainAxisAlignment.center,
          children: [
            Text(
              'You have pushed the button this many times:',
            ),
            Text(
              '$_counter',
              style: CupertinoTheme.of(context).textTheme.navLargeTitleTextStyle,
            ),
```

```
        CupertinoButton(
          onPressed: _incrementCounter,
          child: Row(
            mainAxisAlignment: MainAxisAlignment.center,
            children: [
              Icon(CupertinoIcons.add_circled_solid),
              Text("Increase")
            ]
          )
        )
      ],
    ),
  ),
);
  }
}
```

Other Cupertino Widgets

This is meant to be just a quick introduction to how to build iOS-style UIs and is meant as a starting platform, not as a comprehensive guide, so we will only be talking about the most important Cupertino widgets. You can find more of them in detail in a dedicated section of Flutter's official website.[1]

Cupertino Navigation

Before talking about some of the UI elements that need to be converted to Cupertino widgets, we'll see how to implement navigation using Cupertino widgets. There are a few differences between Material Design and iOS layouts that need to be clarified: the drawer side navigation menu is a typical Material Design element, so it doesn't have a Cupertino equivalent and navigation is handled using either a bottom tab bar or simple push/pop navigation.

Tab-Based Navigation Using the CupertinoTabScaffold

Let's talk about something we briefly mentioned in the previous section: the CupertinoTabScaffold. This widget isn't actually necessary to have tab-based navigation (since theCupertinoTabBar can be used to call setState() and render different data based on the selected tab), but it makes it very easy.

It takes two arguments:

- The tabBar, which has to be set to a CupertinoTabBar with the needed items list of BottomNavigationBarItems.

---

1. https://flutter.dev/docs/development/ui/widgets/cupertino

- The tabBuilder which, given the context and the int index, has to return the content of the tab corresponding to that index, usually returning a CupertinoTabView that gives each tab its own navigation history and state, containing a CupertinoPageScaffold for the content of the tab.

An example of how to do that is the following:

```
class HomePage extends StatelessWidget {

  final data = [
    {
      "Train",
      CupertinoIcons.train_style_one
    },
    {
      "Search",
      CupertinoIcons.search
    },
    {
      "Share",
      CupertinoIcons.share
    }
  ];

  @override
  Widget build(context) =>
    CupertinoTabScaffold(
      tabBar: CupertinoTabBar(
        items: data.map(
          (el) =>
            BottomNavigationBarItem(
              title: Text(el.first),
              icon: Icon(el.last)
            )
        ).toList(),
      ),
      tabBuilder: (context, i) =>
        CupertinoTabView(
          builder: (context) =>
            CupertinoPageScaffold(
              navigationBar: CupertinoNavigationBar(
                middle: Text(data[i].first),
              ),
              child: Center(
                child: Icon(data[i].last, size: 80.0)
              ),
            )
        )
    );
}
```

which produces the following view when opened:

and it gives us a chance to notice the iOS Share icon, which is very different from the Material Share icon, when tapping on the third tab:

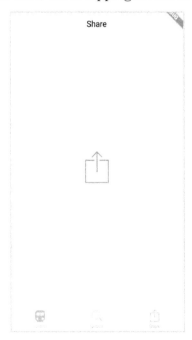

Push/Pop Navigation with the CupertinoPageRoute

The Navigator itself works just like in Material apps, but we need to replace the MaterialPageRoute with the CupertinoPageRoute, but not necessarily. The MaterialPageRoute actually adapts to the native animations typically used for transitioning between pages (vertical on Android, horizontal on iOS), but it is contained in material.dart. In case you want to use the iOS animation (CupertinoPageTransition) on Android or you don't want to use widgets from material.dart because the current file only imports cupertino.dart, you can use the CupertinoPageRoute just like you use the MaterialPageRoute, by passing it to Navigator.push() or similar methods, passing to the CupertinoPageRoute constructor the usual context and a builder callback.

After pushing a page, the leading widget of the navigation bar (if present) will be a button that allows the user to go back to the previous page.

Replacement for Some UI Elements

There are a few UI elements that are worthy or being discussed as replacements for Material widgets we've seen during the course of this book.

CupertinoTextField

One of the widgets that needs to be changed is the TextField, and it doesn't only require a name change, unlike some other Cupertino widgets: the CupertinoTextField's decoration is of type BoxDecoration (the same we used with the Container) and not InputDecoration. The InputDecoration is what we used to provide a labelText, which now is an argument of the CupertinoTextField itself called placeholder:

```
TextField(
  controller: _controller,
  decoration: InputDecoration(
    labelText: "Description"
  ),
  onSubmitted: (val) {
    // do something with value
  }
)
```

will become:

```
CupertinoTextField(
  controller: _controller,
  placeholder: "Description"
  onSubmitted: (val) {
    // do something with value
  }
)
```

CupertinoActivityIndicator

The replacement for the CircularProgressIndicator is the CupertinoActivityIndicator, which looks like this:

CupertinoAlertDialog

The Cupertino library provides the CupertinoAlertDialog to be launched with showCupertinoDialog() as a replacement for the Material AlertDialog that is launched using showDialog().

The CupertinoAlertDialog takes three arguments: the title widget (presumably some Text, the content widget and a list of widgets (presumably buttons) called actions to show at the bottom of the dialog:

```
CupertinoAlertDialog(
  title: Text("Dialog title"),
  content: Text("Content of the dialog, usually longer than the title"),
  actions: <Widget>[
    CupertinoButton(
      child: Text("Action 1"),
      onPressed: () {}
    ),
    CupertinoButton(
      child: Text("Action 2"),
      onPressed: () {}
    )
  ],
)
```

It will look like this when launched with showCupertinoDialog(context: context, builder: (_) => CupertinoAlertDialog(...)):

Automatically Switching Between Cupertino and Material

If we want our app to be able to change what it displays based on what OS it runs on, we need to be able to know what platform we're running on from the Dart code. This is possible thanks to the Platform class in the dart:io library, which can be used in the following way:

```
if(Platform.isIOS) {
  // render Cupertino widgets
} else {
  // render Material widgets
}
```

It also provides Platform.isAndroid, Platform.isFuchsia, Platform.isMacOS, Platform.isWindows and Platform.isLinux, but you probably won't need the latter three given that at the time of writing Flutter on the desktop won't work for most apps.

The easiest way to take advantage of that is to have different UI trees for different platforms, but it isn't really the most elegant solution. That's why many Flutter developers choose to implement generic classes that have factory methods to render different widgets for different platforms.

The Flutter Platform Widgets Package

The implementation of that, though, can be repetitive and it is suited to the creation of a library, which does indeed exist: the flutter_platform_widgets package. This package provides classes like PlatformApp, PlatformScaffold, PlatformAppBar, PlatformButton and PlatformPageRoute (full list and usage available on the package's API reference[2]) that will automatically use the Material or Cupertino equivalents on each platform.

---

2. https://pub.dev/documentation/flutter_platform_widgets/latest/

It also provides a generic PlatformWidget that takes an ios and an android argument that you can use for widgets not provided by the library with a dedicated class or if the choice of widgets made by the authors of the library isn't what you want or need for your app.

pubspec.yaml

pubspec.yaml is the file that defines all of the information that Dart needs to build the app.

Basic Package Data

The most basic data contained in pubspec.yaml is the name and the description. The description can contain upper and lower case characters as well as spaces and punctuation, whereas the name must only contain lower case letters and underscores.

Given that the name you set when creating the app project is also the default app name, the user experience isn't helped by having to select an app that only has lowercase letters and spaces in it, which isn't really the style that is favored in the mobile industry at the moment (there aren't many spaces being used, but names are usually capitalized). We'll be solving this problem at Platform-Specific Setup, on page 327. In that section we'll also be seeing how to change the app icon from the default Flutter logo.

Setting the Version

One of the things that can be set in pubspec.yaml is the version. If you're building a package to be released on Pub, it's obviously going to be used by your users when they are installing the package. In the case of apps, it is automatically added to the platform-specific configuration of each app so that you don't need to change the app version in multiple files every time.

Dependency Versions, Caret Syntax, and Semantic Versioning

Versions of Dart dependencies can either be specified by providing just one version number, which will force the installation of that version of the package, as a range using comparison operators (for example, >=1.0.0 < 1.7.3) or by prefixing a version with the ^ character (for example, ^1.2.0), which will allow all versions that are backwards compatible with calls that worked in that version of a library. This is called caret syntax. It was introduced in Dart 1.8.3, which is the reason why the environment section in pubspec.yaml is specified using traditional syntax: we need to make sure we can use it before we use it, and we make sure we can use it by depending on newer versions of Dart.

That environment section should be kept in mind when changing the app using features that were only recently introduced to Dart.

This means the version can't just be a number you make up: it should follow semantic versioning, which is a standard followed by most package managers and explained in detail in its own website.[3] In case you're not aware, it is based on the idea that the version should follow the *MAJOR.MINOR.PATCH* template, meaning that the first number should be changed when making breaking changes, the second should be changed when adding new features without breaking compatibility, and the third should be changed when fixing bugs.

Dart versions are made of the version specified according to semantic versioning and, optionally, a plus sign and a number called the *build number*, which is usually used when a new version only introduces documentation or configuration changes.

Platform-Specific Setup

In this section we'll see how to change the app name and launcher icon of a Flutter app by editing the platform-specific configuration.

Setting a Custom App Name

The Dart package name (which is also the default app name) has to be composed of just lowercase letters and underscore, which isn't really much. That's why we are going to set our own app name by digging into the platform-specific configuration.

Setting the Android App Name

The app name displayed on Android can be changed by changing the android:label attribute of the application tag in the AndroidManifest.xml file found in appdir/android/app/src/main. This is what it would look like if we were configuring the *Chat on Fire* app we built in the last chapter of the book:

```
firebase/chatonfire2/android/app/src/main/AndroidManifest.xml
<application
    android:name="io.flutter.app.FlutterApplication"
    android:label="Chat on Fire"
    android:icon="@mipmap/ic_launcher">
```

Setting the iOS App Name

The app name displayed on iOS is usually changed by opening the Runner.xcworkspace Xcode project in the ios directory in Xcode and changing the

---

3.   https://semver.org/

Display name project-level setting. Alternatively, add a key called *CFBundleDis-playName* followed by a string to the Info.plist file in the appdir/ios/Runner directory, like in the following example:

```
firebase/chatonfire2/ios/Runner/Info.plist
<key>CFBundleDisplayName</key>
<string>Chat on Fire</string>
```

Setting the Launcher Icon

Any decent app needs a custom icon, and Flutter apps certainly don't make for an exception to that. There is a CLI tool on Pub called flutter_launcher_icons that simplifies this, but you may choose to do that manually. This section will cover both cases.

Using Flutter Launcher Icons to Change the Launcher Icon

The Flutter Launcher Icons package is the typical example of a package that should be added to the dev_dependencies section in pubspec.yaml:

```
firebase/chatonfire2/pubspec.yaml
dev_dependencies:
  flutter_launcher_icons:
  flutter_test:
    sdk: flutter
```

After doing that and running:

```
$ flutter packages get
```

it's time to configure the package.

A Quick and Simple Example

This can be done either in pubspec.yaml or in a new file by adding a flutter_icons section:

```
firebase/chatonfire2/pubspec.yaml
flutter_icons:
  image_path: "icons/launcher_icon.png"
  android: true
  ios: true
```

This is what you'll use most of the time: the image_path will be the path to the image that will be used to overwrite the default launcher image for both Android and iOS when you run:

```
$ flutter packages run flutter_launcher_icons:main
```

Choosing a Different Path for the Configuration File

That command will work if the configuration is either in pubspec.yaml or in a file you create called flutter_launcher_icons.yaml. If you want to use a custom file with a different name you can use the -f option in the following way:

```
$ flutter packages run flutter_launcher_icons:main -f filename.yaml
```

Using Different Files for Android and iOS

Instead of providing one image_path for both Android and iOS, you might choose to set an image_path_android for Android and an image_path_ios for iOS. You might want to do that because, unlike Android, iOS will replace any transparency with black, meaning that iOS app icons have to fill the entire image and not have transparent borders, unlike Android icons.

Changing the Launcher Icon Manually

Instead of using the flutter_launcher_icons package, you might want to change the launcher icon yourself. This is very time-consuming to do 100% manually: for Android, you can change the app icon by providing different resolutions of the launcher icon for devices with different pixel density values in the appdir/android/app/src/main/res/mipmap-*dpi (following the official Android Developer guidelines[4]). A similar process is required for iOS icons to replace the ones in the appdir/ios/Runner/Assets.xcassets/Appicon.appiconset.

A way to bypass some of that is by using Android Studio's *Image Asset* creation tool that will automatically generate different resolutions of the icon, and by opening Assets.xcassets in appdir/ios/Runner with Xcode and using that to replace the default icons.

With that, your app should be ready for distribution to your users, whatever operating system their phone runs on.

---

4.   https://developer.android.com/guide/topics/resources/providing-resources

Index

Thank you!

How did you enjoy this book? Please let us know. Take a moment and email us at support@pragprog.com with your feedback. Tell us your story and you could win free ebooks. Please use the subject line "Book Feedback."

Ready for your next great Pragmatic Bookshelf book? Come on over to https://pragprog.com and use the coupon code BUYANOTHER2020 to save 30% on your next ebook.

Void where prohibited, restricted, or otherwise unwelcome. Do not use ebooks near water. If rash persists, see a doctor. Doesn't apply to *The Pragmatic Programmer* ebook because it's older than the Pragmatic Bookshelf itself. Side effects may include increased knowledge and skill, increased marketability, and deep satisfaction. Increase dosage regularly.

And thank you for your continued support,

Andy Hunt, Publisher

Agile Web Development with Rails 6

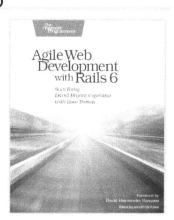

Learn Rails the way the Rails core team recommends it, along with the tens of thousands of developers who have used this broad, far-reaching tutorial and reference. If you're new to Rails, you'll get step-by-step guidance. If you're an experienced developer, get the comprehensive, insider information you need for the latest version of Ruby on Rails. The new edition of this award-winning classic is completely updated for Rails 6 and Ruby 2.6, with information on processing email with Action Mailbox and managing rich text with Action Text.

Sam Ruby and David Bryant Copeland
(494 pages) ISBN: 9781680506709. $57.95
https://pragprog.com/book/rails6

Modern Systems Programming with Scala Native

Access the power of bare-metal systems programming with Scala Native, an ahead-of-time Scala compiler. Without the baggage of legacy frameworks and virtual machines, Scala Native lets you re-imagine how your programs interact with your operating system. Compile Scala code down to native machine instructions; seamlessly invoke operating system APIs for low-level networking and IO; control pointers, arrays, and other memory management techniques for extreme performance; and enjoy instant start-up times. Skip the JVM and improve your code performance by getting close to the metal.

Richard Whaling
(260 pages) ISBN: 9781680506228. $45.95
https://pragprog.com/book/rwscala

Fixing Your Scrum

Broken Scrum practices limit your organization's ability to take full advantage of the agility Scrum should bring: The development team isn't cross-functional or self-organizing, the product owner doesn't get value for their investment, and stakeholders and customers are left wondering when something—anything—will get delivered. Learn how experienced Scrum masters balance the demands of these three levels of servant leadership, while removing organizational impediments and helping Scrum teams deliver real-world value. Discover how to visualize your work, resolve impediments, and empower your teams to self-organize and deliver using advanced coaching and facilitation techniques that honor and support the Scrum values and agile principles.

Ryan Ripley and Todd Miller
(240 pages) ISBN: 9781680506976. $45.95
https://pragprog.com/book/rrscrum

Software Estimation Without Guessing

Developers hate estimation, and most managers fear disappointment with the results, but there is hope for both. You'll have to give up some widely held misconceptions: let go of the notion that "an estimate is an estimate," and estimate for your particular need. Realize that estimates have a limited shelf-life, and re-estimate frequently as needed. When reality differs from your estimate, don't lament; mine that disappointment for the gold that can be the longer-term jackpot. We'll show you how.

George Dinwiddie
(246 pages) ISBN: 9781680506983. $29.95
https://pragprog.com/book/gdestimate

Test-Driven React

You work in a loop: write code, get feedback, iterate. The faster you get feedback, the faster you can learn and become a more effective developer. Test-Driven React helps you refine your React workflow to give you the feedback you need as quickly as possible. Write strong tests and run them continuously as you work, split complex code up into manageable pieces, and stay focused on what's important by automating away mundane, trivial tasks. Adopt these techniques and you'll be able to avoid productivity traps and start building React components at a stunning pace!

Trevor Burnham
(190 pages) ISBN: 9781680506464. $45.95
https://pragprog.com/book/tbreact

Seven Mobile Apps in Seven Weeks

Answer the question "Can we build this for ALL the devices?" with a resounding YES. Learn how to build apps using seven different platforms: Mobile Web, iOS, Android, Windows, RubyMotion, React Native, and Xamarin. Find out which cross-platform solution makes the most sense for your needs, whether you're new to mobile or an experienced developer expanding your options. Start covering all of the mobile world today.

Tony Hillerson
(370 pages) ISBN: 9781680501483. $40
https://pragprog.com/book/7apps

Designing Elixir Systems with OTP

You know how to code in Elixir; now learn to think in it. Learn to design libraries with intelligent layers that shape the right data structures, flow from one function into the next, and present the right APIs. Embrace the same OTP that's kept our telephone systems reliable and fast for over 30 years. Move beyond understanding the OTP functions to knowing what's happening under the hood, and why that matters. Using that knowledge, instinctively know how to design systems that deliver fast and resilient services to your users, all with an Elixir focus.

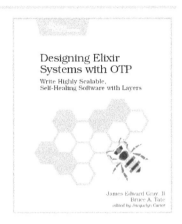

James Edward Gray, II and Bruce A. Tate
(246 pages) ISBN: 9781680506617. $41.95
https://pragprog.com/book/jgotp

Programming Phoenix 1.4

Don't accept the compromise between fast and beautiful: you can have it all. Phoenix creator Chris McCord, Elixir creator José Valim, and award-winning author Bruce Tate walk you through building an application that's fast and reliable. At every step, you'll learn from the Phoenix creators not just what to do, but why. Packed with insider insights and completely updated for Phoenix 1.4, this definitive guide will be your constant companion in your journey from Phoenix novice to expert as you build the next generation of web applications.

Chris McCord, Bruce Tate and José Valim
(356 pages) ISBN: 9781680502268. $45.95
https://pragprog.com/book/phoenix14

Programming Kotlin

Programmers don't just use Kotlin, they love it. Even Google has adopted it as a first-class language for Android development. With Kotlin, you can intermix imperative, functional, and object-oriented styles of programming and benefit from the approach that's most suitable for the problem at hand. Learn to use the many features of this highly concise, fluent, elegant, and expressive statically typed language with easy-to-understand examples. Learn to write maintainable, high-performing JVM and Android applications, create DSLs, program asynchronously, and much more.

Venkat Subramaniam
(460 pages) ISBN: 9781680506358. $51.95
https://pragprog.com/book/vskotlin

Programming Elm

Elm brings the safety and stability of functional programing to front-end development, making it one of the most popular new languages. Elm's functional nature and static typing means that runtime errors are nearly impossible, and it compiles to JavaScript for easy web deployment. This book helps you take advantage of this new language in your web site development. Learn how the Elm Architecture will help you create fast applications. Discover how to integrate Elm with JavaScript so you can update legacy applications. See how Elm tooling makes deployment quicker and easier.

Jeremy Fairbank
(308 pages) ISBN: 9781680502855. $40.95
https://pragprog.com/book/jfelm

The Pragmatic Bookshelf

The Pragmatic Bookshelf features books written by professional developers for professional developers. The titles continue the well-known Pragmatic Programmer style and continue to garner awards and rave reviews. As development gets more and more difficult, the Pragmatic Programmers will be there with more titles and products to help you stay on top of your game.

Visit Us Online

This Book's Home Page
https://pragprog.com/book/czflutr
Source code from this book, errata, and other resources. Come give us feedback, too!

Keep Up to Date
https://pragprog.com
Join our announcement mailing list (low volume) or follow us on twitter @pragprog for new titles, sales, coupons, hot tips, and more.

New and Noteworthy
https://pragprog.com/news
Check out the latest pragmatic developments, new titles and other offerings.

Save on the ebook

Save on the ebook versions of this title. Owning the paper version of this book entitles you to purchase the electronic versions at a terrific discount.

PDFs are great for carrying around on your laptop—they are hyperlinked, have color, and are fully searchable. Most titles are also available for the iPhone and iPod touch, Amazon Kindle, and other popular e-book readers.

Buy now at *https://pragprog.com/coupon*

Contact Us

Online Orders:	*https://pragprog.com/catalog*
Customer Service:	*support@pragprog.com*
International Rights:	*translations@pragprog.com*
Academic Use:	*academic@pragprog.com*
Write for Us:	*http://write-for-us.pragprog.com*
Or Call:	+1 800-699-7764

Milton Keynes UK
Ingram Content Group UK Ltd.
UKHW031833020124
435363UK00013B/1068